THE LIBER LEGIS SCANIAE

The Latin Text with Introduction, Translation and Commentaries

Edited by Ditlev Tamm

Routledge
Taylor & Francis Group

LONDON AND NEW YORK

First published 2018
by Routledge
2 Park Square, Milton Park, Abingdon, Oxon OX14 4RN

and by Routledge
711 Third Avenue, New York, NY 10017

Routledge is an imprint of the Taylor & Francis Group, an informa business

British Library Cataloguing-in-Publication Data
A catalogue record for this book is available from the British Library

Library of Congress Cataloging-in-Publication Data
A catalog record for this book has been requested

ISBN: 978-1-138-68084-5 (hbk)
ISBN: 978-1-315-11472-9 (ebk)

Typeset in Times New Roman
by Apex CoVantage, LLC

CONTENTS

A general introduction to the Medieval Nordic Laws translation   vii
Foreword   ix
List of abbreviations   x

PART I
Introduction   1

The author   3
The text   8
  Household and family 8
  Land 8
  Offences against life, body or property 9
  Contracts 9
The *Liber legis Scaniae* in Danish legal historiography   14
The manuscripts   16
Bibliography: introduction   18

PART II
The text   21

The Latin text with English translation   23
  Antique leges Scaniae 24
  I Liber legis Scaniae 25
**Correspondence between *Liber legis Scaniae* and the
Law of Scania**   150
  Liber legis Scaniae – the Law of Scania 150
  The Law of Scania – Liber legis Scaniae 152
Bibliography: text   155

CONTENTS

PART III
Vocabulary   **157**

Andrew Sunesen's language   **159**
   1. How did Andrew learn his Latin? 159
   2. Pronunciation and spelling 161
   3. The vocabulary, syntax and style of Lex Scaniæ *163*
Bibliography: vocabulary   **174**

Glossary Latin – English   175
Index   189

A GENERAL INTRODUCTION TO THE MEDIEVAL NORDIC LAWS TRANSLATION

The oldest laws of the Nordic countries are written in the vernacular. The earliest manuscripts stem from the thirteenth century and are younger than the texts of the laws, some of which date back to the twelfth century. They are, of course, important in Nordic law and legal history, but they are equally significant for different branches of history, being the oldest written sources we have in the Nordic countries of the society at that time, dealing with the household and social, sometimes administrative, ecclesiastical and agrarian matters and also for philology.

These laws were intensely studied by legal historians as the foundation of national law. During the last decade there has been a revival in the interest in these early laws in the Nordic countries manifested in, for example, an influential conference series in early law at the Carlsberg Academy in Denmark, an initiative of an interdisciplinary network project called *Medieval Nordic Laws (MNL)*, funded by The Leverhulme Trust and based at the University of Aberdeen, and some other local initiatives. In order to open up the floodgates for international interest and research on these laws and to facilitate comparison, it was decided in the *MNL* project to translate the laws into English. Besides the obvious scoop of an international interest in the laws based on new translations, another gain with this initiative was the rethinking of the position of the laws in connection with the redaction of new introductions to the laws. The Nordic medieval laws were previously subjected to thorough analysis from both legal and historical points of view, and they have been translated into modern Nordic languages. This happened mainly in the 1930s and 1940s, but the laws have long played a central role in Nordic legal history. In the second half of the nineteenth century, the Nordic laws were seen in German scholarship as important expressions of the so-called *Germanenrechte*, and intense learning was used in developing and describing a specific Nordic variant of such law. This approach was never fully accepted in the Nordic countries, and a more critical study of the laws based on the idea that they reflected both older and newer layers of law started in the 1920s and continued up to the 1980s in Scandinavia. Today's legal historians in the Nordic countries tend to see the laws in a European context, as new law written down as such. However, most of the Nordic scholarship was only published in Nordic languages. Research into the medieval legal world has continued in later years, and a translation and introductions in English will make the newest research accessible to an international audience. Iceland holds a somewhat different position and has already seen two of the old law codes, the *Grágás* and the *Jónsbók*, given modern translations and introductions recently. The edition of the old Icelandic law has been an inspiration for the present project.

The work has been pursued on a national basis by local teams with occasional meetings to discuss it. The original plan for these new translations was either to establish a team of scholars working with the laws, as in Denmark, or individual experts already acquainted with the law in question, as in Norway and Sweden, to do the work. To assist these translators, reference groups were assembled with some of the most prominent scholars in the fields of law, legal history, canon law, history and philology. A crucial issue when dealing with translations of this kind is to find a 'normative' text to base the translation on, chosen from the many (sometimes diverging) manuscripts which some laws can display. It has been up to each team or translator to make this decision; it would have been desirable but technically very complicated to use the original text. To make the volumes accessible to a broader readership, we have decided not to have the Old Nordic texts included; in most cases these can be found online.

Stefan Brink,
Professor of Scandinavian Studies,
University of Aberdeen

Ditlev Tamm,
Professor of Law,
University of Copenhagen

FOREWORD

This second volume of the edition of *The Danish Medieval Laws* is dedicated to a text in Latin based on the Law of Scania. The text is ascribed to Archbishop Anders (Andrew) Sunesen, and it stems, like most of the Danish medieval law texts, from the first part of the thirteenth century. The Latin text with a Danish translation as it was edited in 1933 in a scholarly critical edition formed the basis for the present edition, however, with changes in the orthography to make it more readable and without the apparatus of the Danish edition. This text belongs traditionally to the corpus of Danish medieval laws in which it may, as will be explained, play a more important role than hitherto acknowledged. The editors therefore have considered the publication of this text as a necessary supplement to the texts in Danish. However, in order to make it possible to bring both the original text in Latin and an English translation, the choice has been to bring this text in its own volume.

This present edition is the first attempt of translating this text into English. The translator and editor received invaluable support from a series of persons who dedicated their time and knowledge to this project. First of all Kate Gilbert should be thanked for her dedication over a long period to the making of a draft translation of most of the text. Important suggestions and contributions have at later stages been made by Tue Søvsø and Ken Pennington. The editor wants to express his sincere gratitude for this help to Merike Ristikivi, who prepared the Latin text for this volume, and together with Tue Søvsø redacted the Latin glossary. Sten Ebbesen contributed with a brilliant chapter on the Latin language of the text. Helle Vogt generously offered valuable practical help and her competent advice during the entire work on the translation.

Ditlev Tamm
Copenhagen, July 2016

ABBREVIATIONS

A&O: (*Arvebog og Orbodemål*) Book of Succession and Crime

ASun: (*Anders Sunesens Parafrase af Skånske Lov*) Anders Sunesen's Paraphrase of The Law of Scania/*Liber legis Scaniae*

Cod: *Justinian's Code*

DD: (*Diplomatarium Danicum*) Danish Diplomatics

Decr. *Grat: Decretum Gratiani*

DgL: (*Danmarks gamle Landskabslove med Kirkelovene*) The Old Provincial Laws of Denmark, including The Church Laws

Dig: The Digest

EsL: (*Eriks sjællandske Lov*) Erik's Law of Zealand

Inst: Justinian's Institutes

JL: (*Jyske Lov*) The Law of Jutland

SkKl: (*Skånske Kirkelov*) The Church Law of Scania

SkL: (*Skånske Lov*) The Law of Scania

VsL: (*Valdemars sjællandske Lov*) Valdemar's Law of Zealand

X: Liber Extra

Part I

INTRODUCTION

THE AUTHOR

The original title in Latin, if there has ever been one, of the work presented here is unknown. It is named in one of the four extant manuscripts[1] as the *Liber legis Scaniae* and in another as the "Old laws of Scania," the *Antique leges Scaniae*. It is not a direct translation or a Latin version of the Danish text. Most of what is found in the Danish text is found in this Latin text in another order and is also supplemented by articles not found in the Danish text or explained and commented upon in a way not presented in the Danish text. It thus seems based on the Danish text of the Law of Scania, which is quite faithfully rendered as to its contents, although in a somewhat different order and in a language much more elaborate than the Danish version. This Latin version of the Law of Scania has no official title. In one later manuscript it is called the *Liber legis Scaniae*, whose title is being used for this edition, albeit with some hesitancy as it is hardly original. All in all it is a different work with presumably a different scope from the Danish text. The *Liber legis Scaniae* was earlier often known just as a "paraphrase"[2] of the Law of Scania due to its reliable rendering of the Old Danish text. It is a thesis underlying the present translation that this denomination underestimates the importance of the Latin text and its author. The Latin text should – according to this editor – be seen as a work interacting with the Danish text and as a decisive part of what was the earliest writing down of the Danish provincial laws. It might thus even be that the preparation of such a book in Latin was the inspiration for collecting and writing down the norms of Scanian law in Danish, which was later followed up by the other laws.

A long tradition, which will not be questioned here, ascribes this treatise of the Law of Scania to Anders Sunesen,[3] Archbishop of Lund, in the first two decades of the thirteenth century from 1201–1223. Whether he personally wrote or dictated it and how much he may have been helped is unknown. The exact time of the redaction is similarly unknown. Its authorship has never seriously been challenged. It seems also that at that time in Scania only a few persons, if indeed there were any, would have been in possession of the necessary legal and general knowledge, not to speak of the language skills, to compose such a book. As will be explained by Sten Ebbesen in a chapter on the language of Anders Sunesen, his Latin language is learned and adorned and thus that of a highly educated person.

3

As is often the case regarding the Middle Ages we have only a little exact knowledge of personal lives, and so little is known of Anders Sunesen's earlier years before he became archbishop. We do not even know his exact year of birth, but we suppose that he had reached the canonical age of 30 when he was appointed archbishop in 1201. He belonged to an immensely rich Zealand-based family of landowners. Together with his brother Peder he was prepared to take over the central Danish bishopric of Roskilde and the archbishopric of Lund. In the foreword to his *Res Gesta Danorum*, the contemporary historian Saxo mentions that Anders studied for years in France – as did his brother Peder – and additionally in Italy and England. However, we have no details of when, where and with which teachers he studied in Paris and, probably, Bologna, nor do we know anything of a supposed stay in England. In Paris he would have concentrated on studies of theology, whereas in Bologna he might have studied canon law and Roman law. The second half of the twelfth century was the time when a professional legal profession was in its making, and Anders would have come to a university of Bologna in which legal studies were carried out at a high level. Both Roman law and canon law were well-developed subjects, and we may suppose that when Anders studied law he achieved both the necessary legal background in Roman law and carried out more profound studies of canon law based on the *Decretum Gratiani*. Canon law was in its making, and the collections of papal decretals which formed a new and modern canon law were not edited yet. It is quite clear from the text presented here that the author knew some Roman law on a basis corresponding to at least the elementary textbook and the *Institutes* of Justinian (the didactic style of which is somewhat recognizable in the text), but most probably he had also studied or at least known some parts of the *Digests* and the later legislation in the *Codex* and *Novellae*. However, his project of translating and putting the Danish Law of Scania into an order different from the Danish text had a more limited range and did not pose legal questions of such a depth as to reveal whether he was a real learned lawyer. We know from his will that his library had included legal works by Stephen of Tournai, Huguccio and the *Decretum Gratiani*, which means that he might have undertaken more profound studies and have had a more-than-ordinary knowledge of the legal thinking of his time. We suppose that in Bologna he personally met the later Pope Innocent III, as in his later correspondence with the pope when he was archbishop we also find legal questions discussed.[4] The treatise of Anders Sunesen is a product of its time. It belongs in a legal climate influenced by the university studies of law in Bologna in the late twelfth century and to a time during which more practical guidelines to the handling of the law were produced in England and elsewhere (as with Glanville, mentioned later).

Anders is presumed to have come back to Denmark in the 1190s when he was offered the position of chancellor to the king, which thus made him responsible for royal charters. In 1201, as had been prepared for a long time, he succeeded his great-uncle Absalon as Archbishop of Lund. As archbishop Anders did not only take care of the internal administration of the diocese. He also played an active political role in the defence of the Nordic church, and especially in the expansion of Danish power towards the eastern Baltic regions. He took an active part in the Danish mission known as the crusades in Estonia, and for extended periods he was away from Scania until he resigned from his office in 1224 for health reasons and eventually died in 1228.

In 1200, a year before his nomination as archbishop, a royal ordinance in Latin of homicide had been issued in Scania.[5] That such an ordinance, with its detailed regulation of payment of compensation and fines, needed a Danish translation to be known among Scanians to whom it was directed was obvious. A translation into Danish of that ordinance – which Anders Sunesen may have authored himself while chancellor – may therefore have appeared as priorities for the new learned archbishop when he took over this position after Absalon. That may further have led to his translation and systematization of the Scanian law. The dating of the text has been disputed, but for the reasons mentioned earlier, it most likely stems from the time immediately after his appointment, and thus from the first decade of the thirteenth century. Together with the redaction of the Danish text it can be seen as an endeavour to establish a new written framework for legal life in the diocese, which was strongly needed due to the many new questions of law stemming from changes in society to which one found no answers in a rather rudimentary older law. An overview, systematization and new legal concepts were needed to accomplish this task. Following this line of thought, we may see the project of the archbishop in a wider perspective as the writing down of the local customary law with additions and in a form based on knowledge of the learned law.

We still find the ordeal by hot iron mentioned in the text. We therefore suppose that it could not be written later than 1215, the year in which the Church at the Fourth Lateran Council officially distanced itself from this means of proof. It seems unlikely that the archbishop would explain in as much detail as he does the functionings of this ordeal without commenting upon its contrariety to canon law if the text were written down with knowledge of the decisions of the Lateran Council. A royal ordinance[6] issued by King Valdemar II, the text (but not the date) of which we know in the version written for the province of Scania, abolished the use of ordeal by hot iron in Scania, substituting this with men nominated to investigate those cases that were formerly decided using the ordeal. If we take into account the strong position of both the archbishop and the king in Scania, there is substantial reason to believe that Anders Sunesen would not have left it uncommented if at that time this proof was used (contrary to the decrees of the Church and the king).

We can establish a possible date of the text by considering Anders Sunesen's reference to a new statute on homicide,[7] which he says was issued most recently (*novissima*) by King Valdemar II and wise men of the province. Valdemar became king in 1202, and as this ordinance is mentioned in direct connection with the ordinance on homicide of 1200, this reference can be seen as further evidence that the text of Anders Sunesen must have been written in the first part of his period as archbishop. This ordinance apparently had not been issued (or had not been accepted generally) at the time when the Old Danish version of the law was finished and is not part of the Danish text, but only found as an *additamentum* to the

Danish text of the Law of Scania. It is incorporated in the text of Anders Sunesen, who most probably had been a strong supporter – or even the author – of this new regulation.

The incorporation of the new regulation of homicide into the Latin text is one of only a few more substantial material differences between the Danish and Latin texts of the Law of Scania. It may therefore be presumed that they were written down at approximately the same time, probably with the scope of having a fixed written base upon which to judge the many legal questions that were due to arise in a changing world. In a few other cases reference is made to divergences between the king and the local conception of the law, and in some other cases Anders Sunesen even seems to take pleasure in mentioning and discussing different local opinions as to what the law is in specific situations. An example of such a discrepancy between locals and the king is that the king wanted (ch. 50) compensation for damage done by a slave to a free man to not exceed three marks unless the free man was killed, whereas the Scanians wanted greater compensation.

Readers of this Latin version of the Law of Scania may have been found among students at the cathedral school and among those who in their daily life were confronted with questions of law. For anybody knowing Latin, reading the text of Anders Sunesen would be a shortcut to an understanding of Scanian law even if the Danish text is written in a comprehensible and rather clear Danish. This could have included the ecclesiastical courts in Lund or local priests, including clerics of foreign origin who could not read Danish. The number of people who might be interested in local law would have increased drastically in the last decades of the twelfth century. The half-century preceding the time of the redaction of the Law of Scania and the present *Liber legis Scaniae* was also the period of the foundation of important monasteries in Scania by Benedictines, Cistercians and Premonstratensians. A book like *Liber legis Scaniae* would thus find interested readers among abbots and other ecclesiastical persons eager to protect or add to the property of their institution. As people with responsibility for church property, they would have had to defend their monasteries or churches in the many property conflicts that could arise; or in the conflicts stemming from damage caused by water mills; or from protection of woods, or streams or other church property. Therefore such important details – in matters involving disputes, as terms to be fixed and legitimate excuses to be made by him who is summoned but does not appear, and the exact proof that should be carried out and when – are repeated and explained for each kind of conflict or offence. Such persons could also be expected to give advice in local legal matters, and they definitely had to know such rules, which could conflict with canon law. For someone acquainted with Latin and Latin terms, the more logical system and the more exact way in which the law was explained in the text by Anders Sunesen must have been a help when such questions of law were at issue.

The purpose of the *Liber legis Scaniae* thus seems to have been both didactic and practical. In some manuscripts the *Liber legis Scaniae* ends with the words "*composuit ad utilitatem totius terre*", thus indicating "that the work was done for the benefit of the whole province". If it was so, we may understand that the purpose of explaining the law and guiding those who might be in a position to be leader of an assembly or give advice to parties for Anders Sunesen must have been an issue on par with his basic idea that knowing Latin (specifically legal Latin) and being good at it was in itself useful and necessary knowledge.

Notes

1 A list of these can be found in the section on the manuscripts.
2 See e.g. Kroman and Iuul 1945.
3 Here the Danish version of his name is used, which in English is rendered as Andrew, see; Sten Ebbesen: *Andrew Sunesen's Language*.
4 Correspondence with Innocens III see DD. 1:4, no. 36, 38, 85, 87, 88, 94–97, 107–112, 125, 126, 145, 161; DD. 1:5, no. 2, 13, 28, 31, 37, 38, 41, 76, 79.
5 For an English version of the ordinance see vol. 1, *Knud VI's Ordinance on Homicide*.
6 For an English version of the ordinance see vol. 1, *The Ordinance on Ordeal by Hot Iron*.
7 For an English version of the ordinance see vol. 1, *The Ordinance on Compensation*.

THE TEXT

Neither the Law of Scania itself nor the *Liber legis Scaniae* are divided into books or more systematic chapters. However, in the *Liber legis Scaniae* great attention is paid by the author to the way the several articles belong together, and on this basis the chapters are placed in a somewhat altered structure. The order is basically the same, starting out with family law and succession followed by the village rules and chapters on crime and torts, with homicide, violence, theft and sexual crimes at the centre of attention. The 241 articles or chapters found in the Danish version of the Law of Scania have been systematized into 150 chapters in the *Liber legis Scaniae*. In this way the text only follows the main structure of the Old Danish text with considerable systematic changes.[1]

At the end of both the Danish and the Latin version we find some chapters on specific contracts. A total of twelve chapters (chapters 23, 36, 38, 43, 44, 47, 61, 64, 80, 81, 84 and 140 in the *Liber legis Scaniae*) are without correspondence in the Danish version of the law, and must be seen as a supplement to the local law in the Danish text. Additions to the Danish text are also the several explanations and more general observations that Anders Sunesen makes on why the law is as it is. The style of the text in such cases comes close to what could be found in Justinian's *Institutes*. Here the style is also didactic, some historical development is explained and more general statements are given as to the law.

The division of the chapters is as follows:

Household and family

Inheritance, division of the household, right of disposition as to land, house-
leading for maintenance (1–20)
Guardianship (21–24)
Children born out of wedlock (24)
Answering for someone else (25)

Land

Division of land, roads, borders in the village (26–37)
Prescription and conveyance of land (36–42)

Offences against life, body or property

Homicide and compensation (43–59)
Violence, loss of peace, wicked advice (60–63)
Beating and wounding by free men (65–70), by slaves (71) and by animals (72)
The law of slaves (73–84)
Theft (85–98)
Ordeal by hot iron (99)
The right to what is found on the foreshore (100–101)
Fencing of fields (102–106)
Seizure of animals (107–113)
Protection of woods (114–121)
Water and streams (122–125)
Protection of the marriage and the woman: rape, adultery and other sexual
    crimes (126–130)
Fire and arson (131–32)

Contracts

Contracts of service as farm manager, payment, loan, hire, deposit and tenancy
(133–150)

The Danish text of the Law of Scania is commented upon in the first volume
of this edition, and basic information as to the Law of Scania may be found there. In
this introduction some remarks on the specific composition and characteristics
of the Latin text shall be added. The *Liber legis Scaniae*, however, is not primar-
ily a theoretical reflection on the law, but a highly plain-spoken description of
how to proceed in different cases. The main scope seems to be guiding through
the procedure at the assembly when a conflict arose. This explains the relative
importance of rendering the exact procedure to be followed when someone is
summoned.

Anders Sunesen often gives explanations and makes definitions in his text which
are not found in the plain text of the law. Additionally as mentioned earlier, the rendering and discussion of different opinions is another characteristic of his style. In
ch. 25, for example, he mentions that a person who has promised to answer for others
can be forced even to ordeal by hot iron and thus must take the "consequences of
his stupid temerity, that he was willing to defend an ungrateful person." Chapter 37
explains that an oath must stand and says of the oath givers that "as it is not to be
believed that they should be so unmindful of their salvation that they will prefer
something of this world to it". On the term of three years for prescription ch. 37
says, using an argumentation that reminds one of Justinian's *Institutes* (Inst. 2,6), that

not without reason was such brevity of prescription introduced, because it is
not advantageous for the ownership of property to be in uncertainty for long,

and a timely decision appears to cut down the root of evils before it happens that harm sprouts from it.

In ch. 43 Anders Sunesen marks a transition to homicide and other crimes by introducing the Devil, the enemy of mankind, as the instigator of homicide. The following chapters on homicide and payment of compensation provide information as to the more specific procedure to be followed which is not found in the Danish text. We are thus told of the oaths to be given by the kinsmen of the killer and the kinsmen of the victim in order to mitigate the shame of receiving compensation instead of taking revenge and in order to prevent revenge (ch. 46). These oaths are rendered in their Old Danish version. Furthermore, we also find a detailed and instructive description of the procedure to be followed at the assembly, when this compensation is to be paid.

Anders Sunesen sometimes reflects on human nature, as when the *pietas* of the mother is mentioned as a reason to grant her custody of small children, or how people are more inclined to behave badly than do good (ch. 48). He also explains why a person who is injured should be compensated in the case of accident, regardless of his personal fault (ch. 67), even if this local rule was not in accordance with the basic canon law view that only intentional and negligent damage should be compensated. Obviously Anders Sunesen saw it as his task to inform about the local law and, apart from a few cases, he does not comment on whether the law was just or not.

Whereas the Danish text basically is a plain writing down of rules, the Latin text thus moves in different spheres. As will be explained later, the whole setup and language are accordingly much more sophisticated.[2] The language of the text is characterized by several special features, such as metaphors, poetic figures, non-translated Old Danish words, Latin neologisms based on Old Danish words and vocabulary from both Roman law and the ecclesiastical world. Examples of these features and an elaboration on their function are to be found in the later chapter on Anders Sunesen's language by Sten Ebbesen.

By introducing baptism as a general condition for accepting an inheritance, as also in the Danish text, the law refers to the reincarnation of man through the holy sacrament. Several references are given to natural equity, and thus the law of man is placed in a setting governed by God and norms higher than the written law itself. The Devil, as mentioned earlier, suddenly appearing in ch. 43 gives the text a transcendental dimension, which is also found in ch. 102. Here the fruits of the fields are mentioned as given by God. In ch. 127 the marriage is mentioned as a matter to be decided upon by heavenly judgement and not by earthly courts. Ch. 143 on hire of land is introduced by a general statement on the problems that can arise between landlord and tenant, and in this and the following chapters the danger of oppression of one of the parties is mentioned, as is "generosity" as a principle underlying the handling of property rights (ch. 115). In ch. 127 the relation between canon law and local law is even compared to that between a mistress and a maid. It is clear that apart from a comment in this article, which actually stemmed from the Church Law of Scania,[3] the archbishop did not see his task as that of criticizing the local law, but as finding ways to reconcile it with canon law if any difference could be ascertained. On the other hand, the duty to pay what is due to the archbishop is often stated. The law of marriage is only rarely touched upon, which may be seen as evidence that the archbishop considered marriage to be well inside the competence of the Church. Only in the case of taking to the ordeal by hot iron as a means for a husband to achieve a separation from his adulterous wife did he feel the necessity of stressing that he was describing a procedure which manifestly was against what was demanded by canon law. Also noteworthy are references to ordinances or opinions of the king. His explanation of what is the old law and what is new regarding homicide is a precise but subtle way to express his dissatisfaction with the local procedure in homicide cases. The law clearly is not only what the *prudentes* of the provincial assembly in Lund decide. The king, although a player whose consent adds to the authority of the law, however, can also still be considered a mere player, who could not change the law without local consent. A question treated with utmost care and developed in detail by Anders Sunesen is the summoning before the assembly, known in the text simply as *jus*, just as you would expect to find in a work meant for those who in practice are to handle cases or be asked for their advice at the assembly. As to what we would conceive as criminal pleas, Anders Sunesen seems to base his system on a rather simple division into protection, respectively, of life and body, freedom and property. Concerning property, a basic distinction exists as to the crime of theft and other kinds of disrespect for ownership, such as not respecting the fields, other people's woods, their right not to be flooded or to reserve the water for their own fishing devices. The bridge between the serious accusation of theft, which was heavily punished and normally directed against someone of a lower social status who might have difficulty in defending himself or finding others to do so, and other more trifling offences to someone's property, is marked by an extensive explanation of the different ways of performing the ordeal by hot iron. This could still be an issue in cases of adultery and arson, treatment of which in the *Liber legis Scaniae* follows after protection of fields, woods and waters. Adultery is clearly seen as an offence committed against either the husband, or in case of the illicit intercourse of unmarried women, the family, whose marriage strategy was hampered through rape or illicit intercourse. The *Liber legis Scaniae* ends in the same way as the Old Danish text with some chapters on the law of contract. The author is evidently influenced by the concepts of Roman law, especially as to consensual contracts, even stressing that the important contract of service, which in his system is called by the Roman law term *locatio-conductio*, is valid by mere consent. These chapters seem even in their Danish version to be the work of someone learned in the law. They may have been conceived by Anders Sunesen himself and added to the Danish text. Chapter 143 stresses that hire may be contracted by consent, mentioning that local custom accepts that it can be waived as long as it is not confirmed by shaking hands. Behind these neutral words may lie a concealed critical commentary against this custom.

The Latin version of the Law of Scania is the result of an encounter between two different approaches to the law, namely learned law as taught and studied at the universities and local law as practiced by laymen in local courts and assemblies. In some cases Anders Sunesen did not try to find a Latin term for a local legal expression and chose to keep local words with a specific legal meaning.[4]

The text by Anders Sunesen on the Scanian law has no parallel in the other Nordic countries. As already mentioned, the style of Justinian's *Institutes* may have been a source of inspiration, and it seems to be a fair overall assessment of the text that, like the *Institutes* for Roman law, this text was meant to serve as an introduction to the Law of Scania. Even if the Danish language of the law is quite plain, for someone educated in Latin, it would be easier to grasp the rules when they were read in this language. It should also be stressed that the Latin text is more detailed as to the practical handling of cases before the assembly or among parties outside the assembly. Anders Sunesen may have known *The Treatise on the Laws and Customs of the Kingdom of England*[5] attributed to the chief justiciar of England, Ranulph de Glanville, which appeared in England between 1187 and 1189. If Anders Sunesen in fact visited England around 1190 he may have met Glanville and his successor as justiciar, William Longchamps, who also wrote a treatise on the law, known as *Practica legum et decretorum* (1183–89). Whether he actually was in England and whomever Anders Sunesen may have met in England, however, and whether this Latin text of the Law of Scania can be seen as a fruit of such a visit is mostly conjecture. Glanville's work in many ways differs from the work of Anders, and only similarities (rather than any direct influence) can be shown. Remarkable parallels, however, can be found between the procedural system explained by Glanville and by Anders Sunesen's *Liber legis Scaniae*. The two treatises, even if independent of each other, both correspond to the need for a practical guide to the way the law functioned in practice. In Glanville's treatise on English law, how to execute the summons correctly is also a central issue, and a first chapter is dedicated to an explanation of how to proceed in this matter. The basic rule, both in England and in Scania, as well as in canon law, is that a defendant should be summoned three times (ASun chs. 41, 57, 90, 91). If he then appears, he has the right to excuse himself by alleging that he was not summoned or that the summons was invalid as he was on pilgrimage, in search of his animals or had fallen ill (chs. 41, 72, 91,132, also ch. 88 on terms when a person accused of theft refers to people living afar or separated by the sea). Likewise in Glanville we find mentioned, corresponding to ASun ch. 91, the sending of so-called "essoiners", also known in the Law of Normandy, to prove that the defendant is lawfully excused from attendance either because he is sick, or because he has not been in the neighbourhood or has been travelling far away. Other parallels to Glanville are found in Anders Sunesen's treatment of situations in which a free person is claimed to be a slave or a slave is claimed to be free. Thus remarkable parallels exist between the two texts, although these may be casual or due to other influences or to similarities between the legal systems of Denmark and England. The way the *Liber legis Scaniae* is written, not least if compared to the contemporary work of

Glanville, indicates that the two works both aimed at giving information to those who needed legal guidance on how to resolve conflicts. Additionally it could have been used as introductory teaching material at the cathedral school, which we assume was attached to the cathedral, in order to provide practical knowledge of handling cases in Scania and to prepare those who needed knowledge of the law when consulted about the local law.

The *Liber legis Scaniae* basically concerns itself with the handling of civil and criminal cases before district assemblies. Crimes handled by local courts are not treated in any detail by Glanville, who concentrates on the procedure before the royal courts. Such courts did not exist in Denmark at the time. Whatever was the inspiration for Anders Sunesen to write his *Liber legis Scaniae* on the Law of Scania, it is evident that he had the necessary training and grasp of legal terminology as a scholar to systematize and understand the local law and render it into a learned language. The *Liber legis Scaniae* is the only extant piece of Danish legal scholarship from before the mid-fifteenth century, when a glossed edition of the Law of Jutland was made by a bishop of Viborg. Not only does it give us invaluable information on how justice was handled at that time, but its particular charm is due to its mixing knowledge of local law with reflections derived from a mind formed by university studies, and hence demonstrating great intelligence and learning.

Notes

1 See part II for a list of correspondences between chapters in ASun and SkL.
2 See Sten Ebbesen: *Andrew Sunesen's Language*.
3 See vol. I, part II.
4 He thus chose not to translate such concepts as the local divison of land in *bool* (ch. 26), certain land apart as *hornome* (33), oath givers who should be *hotolbonder* (33), harvest that could take place as *thrænnæ halma* (37), division of compensation for killing into *sal* (44), specific oaths as *thryg* (46), *jafhnethe eth* (46) and *asswerueth* (57, 87, 90, 99, 110, 113), robbing from corpses, *walruf* (48), damage as *lindabot* (52), specific forms of hot iron, *scuz iærn* (57,90, 99,127) and *truxiærn* (92, 99), popular weapons which are *folcwapn* (60), upper-class people who are *hetwarthreman* (63) and different kinds of wounds not found in Roman law as *athwasar* (65) and *holsar*, specific sanctions as *matban* (90) and being *frithlos* (90), damage known as *gornithings werk* (110), slaves who were *sætis ambut* (130), a measure as *tolfmynning* (131) and deposit in the form of *halzfæ* (142).
5 For an English and Latin version see G. D. G. Hall, *The Treatise on the Laws and Customs of the Realm of England Commonly Called Glanvill, Tractatus De Legibus Et Consuetudinibus Regni Anglie Qui Glanvilla Vocatur* (London: Nelson in Association with the Selden Society, 1965).

THE LIBER LEGIS SCANIAE
IN DANISH LEGAL
HISTORIOGRAPHY

Much scholarly speculation has focused on the question of the relation between this *Liber legis Scaniae* and the Old Danish text of the Law of Scania and as to the purpose of the *Liber legis Scaniae*.[1] There are those who see a strong connection between the Danish and the Latin texts and a contemporaneity in the writing of the Law of Scania and the *Liber legis Scaniae*, respectively. Others assume that the Danish text of the Law of Scania was redacted first as an independent enterprise and that the *Liber legis Scaniae* was written later as a Latin version of the Danish text. The latter theory, that the Old Danish text was the older, was that of the founder of Danish legal history, Peder Kofod Ancher, in 1769,[2] whereas in 1827[3] J.F.W. Schlegel launched the opposite view, namely that the *Liber legis Scaniae* was completed at the same time as the Old Danish text and that the Old Danish text was built on material collected by Anders Sunesen. J.L.A. Kolderup-Rosenvinge[4] returned to the standpoint that the *Liber legis Scaniae* was based on a text of the Old Danish text and not the opposite. This opinion was dominant until, due to differences between the texts, the Swedish legal historian and editor of legal texts, C. J. Schlyter (1862)[5] proposed that Anders Sunesen had based his work on an older text of the Law of Scania, now lost. The existence of a lost text was also supposed by Poul Johs. Jørgensen (1922),[6] who, however, would attribute both the Old Danish and the Latin text to the initiative of Anders Sunesen.[7] The present edition is also based on the supposition that Anders Sunesen played a key role in the redaction of the Law of Scania and that a connection exists between the Danish and the Latin version. Establishing the exact relation is hindered by the fact that the Danish texts of the Law of Scania all stem from a later time (the earliest from around 1280) and may have been submitted to changes.

Notes

1 For an updated and useful survey see Dieter Strauss, *Mittelalterliches nordisches Recht bis 1500* (Berlin/New York: De Gruyter, 2011), 301–318.
2 Peder Kofod Ancher, *En dansk Lov-Historie: Fra Kong Harald Blaatands Tid til Kong Christians V's*, vol. 1 (Copenhagen, A. H. Godiche, 1769–1771), 15–16.
3 J. F. W. Schlegel, *Om de gamle Danskes Retssædvaner og Autonomie* (Copenhagen: Det Kgl. Danske Videnskabers Selskabs Skrifter, 1827), 115–127.

4 J. L. A. Kolderup-Rosenvinge, *Grundrids af den Danske Retshistorie*, vols. 1–2 (Copenhagen: Gyldendal, 1832), 13–33.
5 Carl Johan Schlyter and Hans Samuel Collin,, eds., *Samling af Sveriges gamla Lagar: Corpus juris Sueo-Gotorum antique*, vol. 9 (1862) (Stockholm, 1827–1877), I–CLXXX.
6 Poul Johs. Jørgensen, *Manddrabsforbrydelsen i den Skaanske Ret fra Valdemarstiden* (Copenhagen: Universitetsbogtrykkeriet, 1922), 14–25.
7 It has also been suggested that the purpose of the present text was to provide a survey of the law for a papal representative, Gregorius de Crescentia, whose visit to Denmark in 1222 had been announced by the pope. According to these conjectures, which have no foundation in the existing source material, the *Liber legis Scaniae* was built upon a redaction of the Law of Scania made by a commission around 1220 in order to establish the law after the Fourth Lateran Council. That such redaction should have been made and survived in several manuscripts seems implausible. Michael H. Gelting, "Skånske Lov og Jyske Lov. Danmarks første kommissionsbetænkning og Danmarks første Retsplejelov," in *Jura og Historie: Festskrift til Inger Dübeck som forsker*, eds. Finn Taksøe-Jensen, Henrik Dam & Lise Dybdahl. (Copenhagen: DJØF, 2003), 43–80. See also Stig Iuul, "Anders Sunesen som Lovgiver og forfatter," *Svensk Juristtidning* (1948), 6–21.

THE MANUSCRIPTS

The number of manuscripts of the *Liber legis Scaniae* is remarkably smaller than the number of extant manuscripts of the Old Danish text. The text probably did not circulate in as many copies; moreover, also with time, the usefulness of the Latin text may have proven less obvious as procedures changed, whereas possession of just the Old Danish text may also have satisfied the need for a text of the law. It may be that the text had its heyday at the time of Anders Sunesen and later lost its importance when his personal authority was not present.

The text of Anders Sunesen's *Liber legis Scaniae* is preserved in four medieval manuscripts, known as A, B, C and D,[1] and was edited in a printed version by Arild Huitfeld in 1590 (E). The present edition is based on the Ledreborg 13 kvart manuscript (A) from the first part of the fifteenth century, originally belonging to the library of the Ledreborg mansion, and therefore known as the Ledreborg Manuscript (now at the Royal Library, Copenhagen), which is considered to render the text most correctly. The manuscript is divided into 142 chapters without numbers, which in this edition are added from other manuscripts. This manuscript was the one edited in *Danmarks gamle Landskabslove* I.2 (1933),[2] and in the same manuscript we find a Latin version of the *Ordinance on Ordeal by Hot Iron* by King Valdemar. The manuscript, however, has no headline.

The oldest version of the text is in a manuscript from the second half of the thirteenth century[3] containing the Church Law of Scania (AM 37, 4to), to which a later hand has added *Leges antique Scaniae*. The scribe seems quite unfamiliar with Latin, and many errors are present.[4] A later hand has further added some explanations. This manuscript, known as C corrected from the former A, is the basis of the edition by C. J. Schlyter (1859).[5]

Also from the beginning of the fourteenth century is the text contained in a manuscript known as B, now in the University Library of Uppsala (de la Gardie 44 4to), likewise without title, starting after a Danish chronicle leading up to 1340. The same manuscript also contains the Church Law of Scania, the *statute Synodalia* of Anders Sunesen, the previously mentioned *Ordinance on Ordeal by Hot Iron*, some excerpts of Valdemar's Law of Zealand and a few other legal texts from the thirteenth century.

The fourth manuscript, known as D, was written in the middle of the sixteenth century with the headline *Lex Scaniensis* (Gks 3125 4to), created by two different hands. The text is divided into seventeen books corresponding to the division in the printed Danish edition of the Law of Scania. Many errors in the text are found similar to those in C, but to some extent corrected. This manuscript probably had C as its model and perhaps the manuscript edited as E. This manuscript is bound together with an Old Danish text of the Law of Scania and the *Book of Succession and Crime* and an Old Danish version of the *Ordinance on Ordeal by Hot Iron* and some other texts. One additional manuscript is known to have perished in London by fire in 1727.

Notes

1 A: Ledreborg 13 kvart, The Royal Library, Copenhagen. B: De la Gardie 44 4to, The University Library of Uppsala. C: AM 37, 4to, The Arnamagnaean Institute, Copenhagen. D: Gks 3125 4to, the Royal Library, Copenhagen.
2 *Danmarks gamle Landskabslove med Kirkelovene*, vol. 1.2, ed. Johs. Brøndum-Nielsen and Poul Johs. Jørgensen (Copenhagen: Det Danske Sprog- og Litteraturselskab, Gyldendal, 1933–1961).
3 AM 37, 4 to is a composite of two manuscripts, respectively, dated to the second half of the thirteenth century and the first half of the sixteenth century. This manuscript mentions Anders Sunesen as author of the text.
4 See Sten Ebbesen: *Andrew Sunesen's Language*.
5 C. J. Schlyter and D.H.S. Collin, eds., *Samling af Sveriges gamla Lagar: Corpus juris Sueo-Gotorum antique*, vol. 9 (1862) (Stockholm, 1827–1877).

BIBLIOGRAPHY
Introduction

Bergerow, Jürgen. *Die Paraphrase zum Schonenrecht von Andreas Suneson: Insbe. Das Ungefährwerk*. Kiel: Universität Kiel, 1962.

Brøndum-Nielsen, Johs., Poul Johs. Jørgensen, Svend Aakjær, Anders Sunesen, Erik Kroman, Peter Skautrup, Stig Iuul, Peter Jørgensen, Knud Mikkelsen, Erik Buus and Mogens Lebech, ed., *Danmarks Gamle Landskabslove med Kirkelovene*, vols. 1–8. Publ. by Det Danske Sprog- og Litteraturselskab. Copenhagen: Gyldendalske Boghandel/Nordisk Forlag, 1933–1961.

Dinkova-Bruun, Greti. "Why Versify the Bible in the Later Middle Ages and for Whom? The Story of Creation in Verse." In *Dichten als Stoff-Vermittlung: Formen, Ziele, Wirkungen. Beiträge zur Praxis der Versifikation lateinischer Texte im Mittelalter. Beiträge der Studientagung 8./9. Juni 2007 am Mittellateinischen Seminar der Universität Zürich*. Edited by Peter Stotz and Philipp Roelli. Zürich: Chronos, 2008. 41–55.

Diplomatarium Danicum. Publ. by Det Danske Sprog- og Litteraturselskab. Copenhagen: Ejnar Munksgaard, 1938–2000.

Dübeck, Inger. "Skånske lov og den europæiske baggrund." *Historie* 18 for 1989–1991 (1991). 396–420.

Ebbesen, Sten. *Anders Sunesen, stormand, Teolog, administrator, digter, femten studier*. Copenhagen: Københavns Universitet, Center for Europæiske Middelalderstudier, Gad, 1985.

———. "Corpus Philosophorum Danicorum Medii Aevi, Archbishop Andrew († 1228), and Twelfth-Century Techniques of Argumentation." In *The Editing of Theological and Philosophical Texts from the Middle Ages: Acts of the Conference Arranged by the Department of Classical Languages, University of Stockholm, 29–31 August, 1984*. Edited by Monika Asztalos. Stockholm: Almqvist and Wiksell International, 1986. 267–280.

———. *Dansk Middelalderfilosofi: Ca. 1170–1536*. Den Danske Filosofis Historie 1. Copenhagen: Gyldendal, 2002.

———. "How Danish Were the Danish Philosophers?" In *The Birth of Identities: Denmark and Europe in the Middle Ages*. Edited by Brian Patrick McGuire. Copenhagen: Reitzel, 1996. 213–224.

———. "The Semantics of the Trinity According to Stephen Langton and Andrew Sunesen." In *Topics in Latin Philosophy from the 12th–14th Centuries: Collected Essays of Sten Ebbesen*. Farnham: Ashgate Studies in Medieval Philosophy, 2009. 43–67.

——— and Lars Boje Mortensen. "A Partial Edition of Stephen Langton's *Summa and Quaestiones* with Parallels from Andrew Sunesen's Hexaemeron." *Cahiers de l'Institut du Moyen-Age grec et latin* 49 (1985). 25–224.

Gelting, Michael H. "Skånske Lov og Jyske Lov. Danmarks første kommissionsbetænkning og Danmarks første Retsplejelov." In *Jura og Historie: Festskrift til Inger Dübeck som forsker*. Edited by Henrik Damm et al. Copenhagen: DJØF, 2003. 43–80.

Hägglund, Bengt. "Frågen om nåd och natur i Andreas Sunesons Hexaëmeron." In *Nordisk Teologi, idéer och män. Till Ragnar Bring Den 10 Juli 1955*. Lund, 1955. 218–234.

Hall, George Derek Gordon. *The Treatise on the Laws and Customs of the Realm of England Commonly Called Glanvill, Tractatus De Legibus Et Consuetudinibus Regni Anglie Qui Glanvilla Vocatur*. London: Nelson in Association with the Selden Society, 1965.

Hammerich, Frederik Adolph. *En Skolastiker og en Bibeltheolog fra Norden*. Copenhagen: Selskabet for Danmarks Kirkehistorie, 1865.

Hermanson, Lars. *Släkt, vänner och makt: En studie av elitens politiska kultur i 1100-talets Danmark: Afhandlingar från Historiska Institutionen i Göteborg 24*. Gothenburg: Historiska institutionen, Göteborgs universitet, 2000.

Iuul, Stig. "Anders Sunesen som lovgiver og juridisk forfatter." *Svensk Juristtidning* 48 (1948). 6–21.

Jørgensen, Poul Johs. *Manddrabsforbrydelsen i den Skaanske Ret fra Valdemarstiden*. Copenhagen: Universitetsbogtrykkeriet, 1922.

Kabell, Aage. *Über die dem Dänischen Erzbischof Anders Sunesen Zugeschriebenen Sequenzen*. Bruxelles: Union Académique Internationale, 1958.

Kofod Ancher, Peder. *En dansk Lov-Historie: Fra Kong Harald Blaatands Tid til Kong Christians V's*, vols. 1–2. Copenhagen: Universitetsbogtrykkeriet, 1769–1771.

Kolderup-Rosenvinge, Janus Lauritz Andreas. *Grundrids af den Danske Retshistorie, III*. Copenhagen: Gyldendal, 1832.

Kolderup-Rosenvinge, Janus Lauritz Andreas, Anders Sunesen, and Thord Degn. *Samling Af Gamle Danske Love*. Copenhagen: J. Deichmann, 1821.

Kroman, Erik and Stig Iuul. *Danmarks gamle Love paa Nutidsdansk*, vols. 1–3. Copenhagen: Det Danske Sprog- og Litteraturselskab, 1945–1948.

McGuire, Brian Patrick. *Da himmelen kom nærmere, fortællinger om Danmarks kristning 700–1300*. Frederiksberg: Alfa, 2008.

Mortensen, Lars Boje. "The Nordic Archbishoprics as Literary Centres around 1200." In *Archbishop Absalon of Lund and His World*. Edited by Karsten Friis-Jensen and Inge Skovgaard-Petersen. Roskilde: Roskilde Museum, 2000. 132–158.

———. "The Sources of Andrew Sunesen's Hexaemeron." *Cahiers de l'Institut du Moyen-Age grec et latin* 50 (1985). 111–216.

Müller, Peter Erasmus. *Vita Andreae Sunonis, Archiepiscopi Lundensis, Programma, Qvo Inaugurationem*. Copenhagen, 1830.

Murray, Alan V. *Crusade and Conversion on the Baltic Frontier, 1150–1500*. Aldershot: Ashgate, 2001.

Nielsen, Torben K. *Anders Sunesen, Danmark og verden i 1200-tallet*. Mindre Skrifter/ Laboratorium for Folkesproglige Middelalderstudier, Odense Universitet, vol. 18. Odense: Odense Universitet, 1998.

———. "Archbishop Anders Sunesen and Pope Innocent III: Papal Privileges and Episcopal Virtues." In *Archbishop Absalon of Lund and His World*. Edited by Karsten Friis-Jensen and Inge Skovgaard-Petersen. Roskilde: Roskilde Museum, 2000. 113–132.

———. *Cølibat og Kirketugt: Studier i forholdet mellem ærkebisp Anders Sunesen og Pave Innocens III. Afhandlinger fra Aarhus Universitet*. Aarhus: Aarhus Universitetsforlag, 1993.

————. "Vicarius Christi, Plentitudo Potestatis og Causae Maiores: Teologi og jura hos Pave Innocens III. (1198–1216) og ærkebiskop Anders Sunesen (1201–1223)." *Historisk Tidsskrift* 16, no. 3 (1994). 1–29.

Nilson, Alfred B. *Anders Suneson och hans ö: Et Blad ur Skånes Historia.* Malmö, 1911.

Olsen, Birger. "Trois étudiants danois á Paris au XIIe siècle." In *Hugur: Mélanges d'histoire, de littérature et de mythologie offerts à Régis Boyer pour son 65e anniversaire.* Edited by Claude Lecouteux and Olivier Gouchet. Paris: Paris-Sorbonne University Press, 1997. 87–96.

Perron, Anthony. "Metropolitan Might and Papal Power on the Latin-Christian Frontier: Transforming the Danish Church around the Time of the Fourth Lateran Council." *The Catholic Historical Review* 89, no. 2 (2003). 182–212.

Rydbeck, Otto, Carl M. Fürst and Agnes Branting. *Ärkebiskop Andreas Sunessons Grav i Lunds Domkyrka: En Undersökning.* Lund: Gleerup, 1926.

Schlegel, Johan Frederik Wilhelm. *Om de gamle Danskes Retssædvaner og Autonomie.* Copenhagen: Det Kgl. Danske Videnskabers Selskabs Skrifter, 1827.

Schlyter, Carl Johan and Hans Samuel Collin , eds., *Samling af Sveriges gamla Lagar: Corpus juris Sueo-Gotorum antique,* vol. 9 (1862). Stockholm, 1827–1877.

Skov, Sigvard. "Anders Sunesøn og Guterloven." In *Festskrift Til Erik Arup Den 22. November 1946.* Edited by Erik Arup, Astrid Friis and Albert Olsen. Copenhagen: Gyldendal, 1946. 107–117.

————. "Anders Sunesøns Parafrase af Skånske Lov." *Scandia* 13, no. 2 (1940). 171–195.

————. *Dansk Videnskab af Verdensry.* Vi Og Vor Fortid 12. Copenhagen: Schultz, 1944.

Spreckelsen, Henrik. *En Gengivelse paa danske af de 950 Første Vers Af Anders Sunesøns latinske Læredigt Hexaëmeron.* Ringkjøbing, 1927.

Strauss, Dieter. *Mittelalterliches nordisches Recht bis 1500.* Berlin/New York: De Gruyter, 2011.

Sunesen, Anders. *Andreae Sunonis filii archiepiscopi Lundensis Hexaëmeron libri duodecim.* Edited by Martin Cl. Gertz. Copenhagen: Libraria Gyldendaliana, 1892.

————. *Andreae Sunonis Filii Hexaemeron, Post M. Cl. Gertz.* Edited by Sten Ebbesen and Laurentius Boethius Mortensen. Corpus Philosophorum Danicorum Medii Aevi, vols. 1–2, 11–11.2. Copenhagen: Det Danske Sprog- og Litteratur Selskab, Gad, 1985–1988.

————. *Hexäemeron.* Translated by Henrik Ditlev Schepelern. Copenhagen: G.E.C. Gad, 1985.

————. *Incipit Prooemium Primi Libri in Exameron.* Edited by Arne Magnussen. 1701.

————. *Konkordans Til Anders Sunesens Hexäemeron, (M. Cl. Gertz's Udgave).* Odense: Odense Universitet, 1984.

————. *Leges Provinciales Terræ Scaniæ Ante Annos 400 Latinæ Redditæ.* Edited by Arrild Huitfeldt. Copenhagen: Impr. Laurentius Benedictus, 1590.

Thorsen, Peder G. *Skånske Lov og Eskils Skånske Kirkelov, Tilligemed Andreæ Sunonis Lex Scania Prouincialis, Skånske Arvebog og det Tilbageværende af Knud den 6.'s og Valdemar den 2.'s Lovgivning Vedkommende Skånske Lov.* Publ. by Det Nordiske Litteratursamfund. Copenhagen: Det Berlingske Bogtrykkeri, 1853.

Part II

THE TEXT

THE LATIN TEXT WITH ENGLISH TRANSLATION

Antique leges Scaniae[1]

1. De uentre in possessionem mittendo, et que porcio uxorem superstitem contingat, et cuius sit defensio, si questio oriatur de partu, an sit procreatus an baptizatus, an parenti superuixerit.

Marito defuncto sine liberis, si se uxor ipsius asserat impregnatam, ob spem future sobolis indiuise debet hereditati cum suo legittimo defensore xx[ti] septimanarum spacio preuidere. Quo transacto tempore, si ueracium matronarum intuencium uentrem ipsius testimonio spem future prolis constiterit inanem fuisse, omnia, que in hereditate sunt mobilia uel se mouencia uel immobilia precio tempore matrimonii comparata, equis sunt partibus diuidenda, mediate heredes defuncti proximos cum prediis, que propria ipsius fuerant, et uxorem altera cum suis prediis contingente; probacione, per duorum testimonium et duodenum ab aduersario nominatorum xii[cim] de probantis progenie iuramentum, affirmanti, non neganti partum post uiri obitum procreatum seu adeptum baptismatis sacramentum seu parenti superuixisse, si super aliquo istorum casuum oriatur questio, incumbente, non uxore, sed ipsius defensore iurisiurandi religionem exhibente.

2. Quod non regeneratus baptismatis sacramento hereditatem consequi non possit.

Numquam regeneratus baptismatis sacramento, ac si numquam fuerit generatus, nullum potest hereditatis commodum obtinere.

3. De bonis auitis que porcio contingat nepotes post obitum filii familias.

Filii familias in sacris paternis cum uxore constituti, si sine diffinicione certe quantitatis bonis patris addiderit bona, que ipse habuit cum uxore, quotcumque fuerint filii, de communi substancia, etiam prediorum post contractas nupcias comparatorum, cum auo et aliis consortibus post obitum patris uiriles et equales accipient porciones, per priorem gradum ab aliis prediis excludendi. Si uero in mansione patris bona, que habuit cum uxore, fuerint diffinita, illa sola, si iuente auo pater obierit, filii quotcumque fuerint obtinebunt.

I *Liber legis Scaniae*

Ch. 1 On how to give possession to offspring in the womb, and what portion corresponds to the surviving wife, and who has a right of defence, if a question arises concerning the birth, whether the child is born or baptized or whether it has survived its parent.

When a man dies childless and his wife asserts that she is pregnant, she shall due to the expectation of future offspring be in charge of the undivided estate together with her lawful guardian for a period of twenty weeks. When this time has elapsed and it is established by the testimony of trustworthy women, who have examined her womb, that the expectation of future offspring was vain, then the whole estate, whether movable or animate or immovable acquired during the time of the marriage, shall be divided into equal parts, a half to the nearest heirs of the deceased along with the lands that were his own, and the other to the wife along with her lands. It shall be up to the party who affirms and not that which denies to prove by the testimony of two witnesses and the oath of twelve kinsmen of the swearing party, chosen by the opposing party, that the child was born after its father's death, or was baptized or that it survived its parent, if a question should arise as to any of these matters, and it is not the wife but her guardian who shall offer the oath.[2]

Ch. 2 That he cannot inherit who has not been reborn through the sacrament of baptism.

He who has never been reborn through the sacrament of baptism, just as if he had never been born, cannot obtain the benefit of inheritance.

Ch. 3 On the portion of the grandfather's property that corresponds to the grandchildren after the death of a son of the house.

When a son of the house has lived together with his wife in their father's household and the property which he had with his wife has been added to his father's property without determining the quantity of it, then, after their father's death, regardless of how many sons there are, they shall take equal capital lots from the common property together with the grandfather and the other partners,[3] even from lands acquired after the marriage was contracted, and be excluded from other lands by the heirs of the first degree.[4] If, however, the property that he had with his wife in the father's house has been ascertained, and the father should die while the grandfather was still alive, then the sons, however many there may be, will acquire this alone.

4. Que porcio contingat preuignum uel preuignam post obitum nouerce, et qualiter facienda sit diuisio, et qualiter hereditates compensande.

Patrifamilias, non habenti filios uel habenti, si mulier nupserit et ad eum cum liberis uel sine liberis cum bonis suis transierit, si non fuerit determinatum, que porcio quemque contingat, quantumcumque dispar fuerit bonorum collacio, pares tamen partes omnes, cum a communione recesserint, obtinebunt, salua sexus prerogatiua, ut masculus duplo maius femina consequatur, nisi uxor fuerit uel mater, que marito uel filiis adequatur et tantum, consorcii masculini gratia filiabus prefertur. Huic diuisioni eciam immobilia subiacent a tempore nupciarum precio comparata. Alia predia nouaque hereditas, que post contractas nupcias alteri accessit coniugum, suos semper dominos comitantur, nisi patrem ad bonorum omnium tam mobilium quam immobilium uocet consorcium superstes procreata soboles maternorum, matre tamen ad paternorum bonorum participium nullatenus aspirante, sed solo patre, propter laboriose prouisionis onera, istud sibi priuilegium uendicante, et nisi hereditatem, licet uberiorem, uel hereditates, exceptis immobilibus, primo obiecta hereditas haut tribus marcis exilior ad particionis protrahat rationem. Eodem modo quotcumque de nouo sibi delate occurrerint hereditates, numero pares, licet censu sunt impares, compensantur. Si qua tamen super parem numerum concurrencium hereditatum excreuerit, absque diuisionis diminucione, nisi quid ex ea eciam ad communes usus consumptum fuerit, permanebit.

5. Quid iuris sit, si bona uxoris alienata fuerint a marito.

Nulla prole suscitata uel superstite, alienare non debet predium uxoris maritus. Si tamen alienauerit, stabit alienatio, per uxorem, cui non conuenit de uiro suo con-queri, nullatenus infirmanda; sed ab eo, si iure diuino, uel ab eius herede quamuis communi filio, si dire mortis imperio soluta fuerit, ipsa uel eius heres terre sue, quam constat alienatam esse, in terra uel, si terra defuerit, in rebus quibuslibet iuste estimatis, recipiet compensacionem, marito uel eius herede probante quantitatem distracte terre, si super ea fuerit orta dissensio, negacionem eciam, si negauerit alienacionem, duodeno sui et bondonum xi, qui suo nomine terras possident, iura-mento. E contra marito, cui pro libito suis est uti licitum, si quid in quoscumque usus distraxerit, non recompensabitur ab uxore uel eius heredi ab illius herede. Si quid tamen de precio mariti remanere constiterit inconsumptum, ipsi uel eius heredi relinquitur indiuisum.

Ch. 4 On the portion that corresponds to a stepson or stepdaughter after the death of the stepmother, on how division is to be made and how inheritances are to be set off against each other.

When a woman marries a householder and moves in with him, with or without children, together with her property and it is not determined what portion belongs to each, then, when the partnership is dissolved, regardless of whether he has children or not and of how disproportionate the amount of property brought in may have been, they will nevertheless all take equal parts, except for the privilege of sex that twice as much is due to a male than to a female, unless she is a wife or mother as she is then even with husband or sons and has a better position than daughters due to her having a male consort. Immovable goods acquired during the marriage also fall within this division. Other lands and later inheritance which come to one of the spouses after marriage shall always follow their owners unless either surviving offspring summons the father to take part in all maternal property, both movable and immovable – and the mother shall never aspire to share in paternal goods, as it is only for the father to enjoy this privilege due to the burdensome task of maintenance – or unless an inheritance, even if it is more abundant, or more inheritances, except for immovable property, draws an earlier heritance of not less than three marks to be included in the division. In the same way, later inheritances of whatever kind that might occur and come to them will be set off against each other when they are of the same number, even if they are different in worth. If, however, there is one inheritance more than the equal number of concurring inheritances, then it shall remain free from diminishing by division, unless some of it has been consumed for common use.

Ch. 5 How to proceed when a wife's property is alienated by her husband.

When no surviving offspring has been produced, a husband must not alienate his wife's land. If, however, he does alienate it, the alienation will stand, and it cannot be invalidated by the wife for whom it is not suitable to complain about her husband; but from him she or her heir will, if she is freed by the law of God, or from his heir, even if he is their common son, if she is freed by the command of frightful death, receive compensation from land or, if no land is there, from any other goods justly valued; and the husband or his heir may, if dissent arises over it, prove which quantity of land was sold, or, if he denies the alienation, the denial, by an oath of twelve, himself and eleven householders who possess land in their own name. On the other hand, the husband, who may do with his own property whatever he will, if he has sold something for any purpose whatsoever, he will not be compensated by his wife, nor his heir by her heir. If, however, something of what the husband received from the sale remains unconsumed, it can be kept undivided by him or his heir.

6. Quod aurum uice predii fungitur in diuisione.

Aurum patrimoniale, licet sit mobile, patrimonalis tamen predii uice fungitur in diuisione; sed si que predia eciam auro fuerint comparata, quantum ad diuisionem, condicionem mobilium imitantur; quidquid tamen de auro consumptum fuerit, ex parte neutra restauratur.

7. De trina citacione.

Si quis ad ius citatus uenire contempserit, in duabus horis erit aduersario pro citacione qualibet et in tribus marcis regi tandem pro citacione tercia condempnandus. Post hoc si se presentauerit, et se non noluisse, sed non potuisse uenire, uel minus legittime uel minime citatum fuisse duodeno docuerit iuramento, omnem euacuare poterit condempnacionem, principalem litem iterum subiturus.

8. Quoto iuramento fidem facere debeat, qui negat totalem hereditatem uel partem.

Siquis delatam alteri hereditatem ad se negauerit peruenisse, licet tribus marcis nihil amplius continentem, ut fidem et robur obtineat sua negacio, xxxvi bondonum requiritur iuramentum. At si quid se confessus fuerit accepisse ad ipsius solucionem, dum tamen minus non fuerit una hora nummorum, cum duodeno bondonum iuramento, quod nil amplius ad eum peruenerit, a peticione se poterit liberare.

9. De communis consorcii lucro uel dampno.

Uniuersos contingit de communi consorcio, quidquid uel culpa amittitur uel industria conquiritur singulorum.

10. Qualiter emancipacio fieri debeat uel quid iuris, si fiat.

Uolens emancipare filium suum in iure coram omnibus protestetur, quod eum a sua liberet potestate, et quod nolit de factis suis de cetero respondere, nulli de cetero responsurus de suis excessibus preter reatum homicidii, interdum eciam a cognatis emendandum, probaturus eciam emancipacionem, si super ea oriatur questio, duobus testibus testificantibus, quod interfuerunt in communi iure ipsius legitime promulgacioni. Et e contra, si pater emancipacionem uoluerit diffiteri, audietur, negacionem suam duodeno corroborans iuramento ut semper aduersus filium patri defensio deferatur. Nec cogendus est pater emancipato aliquid de suis bonis supra sue uoluntatis beneplacitum assignare, nec de bonis maternis quidquam filium post mortem matris contingentibus contra uoluntatem filii retenturus.

28

Ch. 6 That gold is to be treated just as land in division.

Patrimonial gold, even though it is movable, is nevertheless treated as patrimonial land with regard to division; but if lands are bought with gold, they are treated as movable property when it comes to division; what was used up of such gold, however, shall be compensated from neither side.

Ch. 7 On a summons repeated three times.

If a person summoned to the assembly disdains to come, he shall be sentenced to pay two ounces to the opposing party for each time he is summoned and finally three marks to the king for being summoned thrice. If he presents himself thereafter and he proves by an oath of twelve that he had not been unwilling but unable to come, or that he was not summoned legally or was not summoned at all, he can be freed from all sentences and again undergo the principal case.

Ch. 8 How big an oath he must swear who denies an entire or a part of an inheritance.

If someone denies that an inheritance meant for someone else has come to him, even if it is of not more than three marks, an oath of thirty-six[5] householders is required for his denial to be trustworthy and firm. If he admits that he has accepted it as payment to himself, and as long as it is not less than an ounce of money, he can free himself from the claim by an oath of twelve householders that nothing more has come to him.

Ch. 9 On the profit or loss in partnership.

When something is lost through the fault or gained through the diligence of individual members of a common partnership, it concerns all members.[6]

Ch. 10 How emancipation shall be done and how to proceed when it is done.[7]

He who wishes to emancipate his son shall affirm publicly at the assembly that he is freeing him from his power and that from now on he will not answer for his acts or his misdeeds except the crime of homicide, which in some instances must be compensated for by kinsmen. If a question arises about the emancipation, he shall confirm the emancipation by two witnesses who testify that they were present in the common assembly at the making of this lawful statement. On the other side, the father shall be heard if he wishes to deny the emancipation and corroborates his denial by an oath of twelve, because a father is always granted defence against a son. Nor is the father forced to convey to his emancipated son any of his property beyond his own free will,[8] nor should he against the son's will after the mother's death keep anything whatsoever of the maternal property that belongs to the son.

29

11. Quid iuris sit, defuncto uel filio familias uel emancipato uel uitrico uel nouerca, quantum ad successionem.

Patre superstite defunctus filius familias nullum habet, ac si fuisset numquam genitus, successorem. Emancipato sine posteritate defuncto solus pater succedit, exclusis fratribus tam emancipatis quam in potestate patria constitutis quam ex matre tantum coniunctis, licet ipsi ad bona uitrici non debeant aspirare. Partem facit defuncto uitrico uel nouerce relictus preuignus uel preuigna, in communione cum filiis et filiabus persone mortue, ipsis tantummodo relinquendam. Post patris obitum cuicumque sine posteris decedenti filio cum matre succedunt fratres pariter et sorores; emancipati tamen ad communia bona eum fratribus parciendum nullatenus admittuntur, nisi reportauerint quecumque prius eis a patre fuerant assignata. Regi quoque in tribus marcis iidem sunt condempnandi, nisi statuto die in communi iure quidquid acceperant parati fuerint reportare, facienda fide duodeno iuramento, si super quantitate referendorum fuerit dubitatum.

12. De iniqua differencia tollenda anteriorum et posteriorum in successione matris.

Iniqua differentia anteriorum et posteriorum sublata, ad defuncte matris hereditatem in omnibus tam mobilibus quam immobilibus diuidendam eque admittuntur filii priores ex maritis prioribus ut posteriores ex marito nouissimo suscitati.

13. Quod illi heredes pociores habeantur in defensione, qui commune aliquid dicunt, quam qui proprium allegant.

Illis uocatorum ad ea, que post mortem alicuius relicta sunt, diuidenda, qui terram aliquam allegant precio comparatam et sic ad omnes consortes pariter peruenire, cum duodeno deferri debet defensio sacramento, non illis, qui, patrimonialem dicentes, eam sibi solis cupiunt uendicare. Idem obseruatur inter heredes tantum ex altero parente coniunctos, ut illis tantum defensio deferatur, qui ad omnes ex quacumque causa contendunt aliquid pertinere; uel utraque pars ex uno tantum parente coniunctorum sibi dissidencium de communi sex uiros nominet parentela, ut illi xii^{cim} nominati, sacramento prius prestito, quod a iusticie non uelint tramite deuiare, determinando, que terre patris fuerant et que matris et que precio comparate, omnem eis amputent super diuisione facienda materiam litigandi. Pari modo inter fratres ex utroque parente coniunctos super particione bonorum est omnis controuersia sopienda.

Ch. 11 How to proceed with regard to succession after the death of either a son of the house or an emancipated son or a stepfather or a stepmother.

A son of the house who dies while his father is still alive has no successor, just as if he had never been born. If an emancipated son dies without posterity, only the father succeeds, to the exclusion of brothers, whether emancipated or in paternal power or solely connected through the mother, although these shall not hope for their stepfather's property. The surviving stepson or stepdaughter in a partnership with the sons and daughters of the deceased will, when their stepfather or stepmother dies, take a lot, which shall only go to them.[9] After the father's death, brothers and sisters succeed equally with the mother to any son who dies without posterity; emancipated sons, however, will in no way be admitted to division of the common property with their brothers unless they bring back whatever was previously given to them by their father.[10] They shall also be sentenced to pay three marks to the king, unless they are ready on the appointed day to bring back at the common assembly whatever they have accepted, swearing an oath of twelve if there is doubt about the quantity which has to be given back.

Ch. 12 On the abolishment of the unjust difference between former and later siblings with regard to succession after their mother.

After the unjust difference between former and later children has been abolished, former children with former husbands, as well as later children born with the most recent husband, are equally admitted to division of the estate of the deceased mother both movables and immovables.

Ch. 13 That those heirs shall be nearer to prove it who say that something is common than those who assert that it is individual property.

Of those invited to divide what has been left after someone's death, the right of proof by an oath of twelve should be granted to those who assert that some land has been bought and thus belongs to all members of the partnership equally and not to those who wish to claim it for themselves alone by saying that it is paternal land. The same is observed between heirs who are half-siblings – the right of proof is thus granted to those who contend that for whatever reason something belongs to everyone; otherwise, each of the parties, when they disagree about the partnership and they are such who are conjoined by one parent, shall nominate six men from their side so that the twelve men who have been nominated, after having sworn an oath that they will not deviate from the course of justice[11] when they decide which of the lands were paternal and which were maternal and which were acquired, shall bereave them of any reason to further litigate as to the division. In the same way, all controversy shall be decided over the partition of property among brothers who have both parents in common.

14. Qui quibus in successione preferuntur.

Naturali statutum est equitate, ut, exclusis ascendentibus et transuersalibus, primo hereditas solis descendentibus deferatur, salua graduum prerogatiua, ut priores in gradu semper posterioribus preferantur. Succedentes ergo in primo gradu filii et filie uiriles accipiunt porciones, seruato tamen sexus priuilegio, ut semper filio duplo maior quam filie pars hereditaria relinquatur. Deficientibus primi gradus liberis, admittuntur neptes et nepotes, non uiriliter, sed in stirpes, ut ex illis quique nihil amplius obtineant, quam parentes eorum, si uiuerent, obtinerent. Puta unica neptis, ex filio defuncto relicta, duplo maiorem recipiet porcionem quam nepotes et neptes, quotcumque fuerint, ex defuncta filia procreati, inter illos tamen, qui ex uno parente prodeunt, sexus differentia custodita. Cessantibus duobus primis gradibus, pronepotes et proneptes absque sexus differentia omnes equaliter admittuntur, eodem iure in cunctis ulterioribus gradibus obseruato. Cessante linea descendenti et deficientibus patre et matre in linea ascendenti et fratribus et sororibus in linea transuersali, auus paternus et auia paterna, auus maternus et auia materna, patruus et amita, auunculus et matertera, fratris et sororis filii et filie, omnes equales partes, exclusa sexus differentia, consequentur.

15. Quid seculo renunciancium monasterio conferri possit a sano uel egro, a transeunte ad religionem uel non transeunte.

Cui licet et libet mundum relinquere, licet quoque cum bonis omnibus ipsum contingentibus, si sanus est et incolumis, religionis causa monasterium introire. Si uero propter grauis morbi periculum de rebus suis disponere urgeatur, medietatem tantum porcionis ipsum contingentis conferendi habet monasteriis siue extraneis, quibus uoluerit, facultatem, medietate reliqua non ad uxorem, sed tantum ad filios et filias pertinente. Ipsum uero contingens porcio nominatur, que, diuisione facta inter ipsum et filios et filias et alios, si qui fuerint communium bonorum consortes, sibi soli competere comprobatur. Si uero solus sit et absque liberis, cuncta, que possidet, ipsum sunt contingencia, ui de illis, sicut determinatum est, ordinandi habeat potestatem. Ad religionem conuersus uelud mundo mortuus ad nullum habet de cetero successionis commodum aspirare, nisi quid ei religionis uel alterius fauoris intuitu conferatur.

Ch. 14 Who takes precedence over whom in succession.

By natural equity[12] it is established that inheritance is granted in the first instance to descendants only, with the exclusion of ascendants and collaterals, thus respecting the prerogative of degree, so that those of the first degree always take precedence over those more distant. Therefore, sons and daughters who are successors of the first degree take their own lots, with respect, however, to the privilege of sex, so that a son is always left with a hereditary portion which is double that of a daughter. When there are no children of the first degree, the granddaughters and grandsons will be admitted, not so that each takes his own lot, but according to lineage, so that none of them will get more than their parents would have received if they were alive. For example, a granddaughter, the sole survivor of a deceased son, will receive twice the lot of grandsons and granddaughters, however many there are, who are born of a deceased daughter; also among those who stem from the same parent, the difference of sex is regarded. When the first two degrees are lacking, then great-grandsons and great-granddaughters are all admitted equally without difference of sex, the same law being observed in all more distant degrees. When there are no more descendants and neither father nor mother in ascending lineage, nor brothers and sisters in collateral lineage, then the paternal grandfather and grandmother, maternal grandfather and grandmother, the paternal uncle and aunt, maternal uncle and aunt and the sons and daughters of a brother and sister will all take equal lots without regard to the difference of sex.

Ch. 15 On that which can be given to a monastery by those renouncing the world, healthy or sick, entering religious life or not.

He who wants and is permitted to leave the worldly sphere is also permitted to enter a monastery for the sake of religion with all his property if he is healthy and unimpaired. If, however, due to the danger of grave illness, he must dispose of his property, he can only give half of the lot corresponding to him to the monasteries or strangers whom he wishes; the remaining half shall fall not to his wife but only to his sons and daughters. His lot is that which after a division has been made between himself and his sons and daughters and others, if there are partners of the common property, is considered as belonging to him alone. If, however, he is unmarried and without children, all that he possesses is his so that he can dispose of it as has been said. A man who has entered religious life is as if he was dead to the world[13] and thereafter can expect no benefit of succession, unless this has been given to him for the sake of religion or for some other favour.

16. Quantum liceat patri nepotibus conferre, uiuentibus filiis et eorundem nepotum patruis.

Licet cuique post mortem filii quantum ipsi deberetur, si uiueret, eius filio nepoti conferre; cui, si super collatis possessionibus impetatur, defertur defensio possidenti duodeni iuramenti et duorum assistencium per scotacionem ab auo facte legitime dacioni, probacione tantum duodeni iuramenti, si nepos non possideat, heredi proximo concedenda, quod ab auo terre, de quibus agitur, nullatenus scotate fuissent.

17. De transeuntibus pro alimonia in alterius potestatem.

Siquis propter rerum penuriam uel propter corporis debilitatem, ex torpore senii uel languoris angustia procedentem, uel ob alia miserabilia fortune grauamina sibi non sufficiat uite necessaria procurare, cum heredibus suis conueniat, ut inter eos bona, que possidet, parciatur, ab eis, per uices circumeunde singulos, uite necessaria recepturus, in communi iure facta coram omnibus protestacione, ne sic legitime facta conuencio uel ualeat immutari uel in dubium reuocari. Si uero singulos ita noluerit circuire, in diuisione bonorum unam sibi retineat porcionem, et cum ea ad quem uoluerit heredum accedat, illo, ad quem accesserit, partem illam, si tantum tres marcas uel minus ualeat, obtinente. Si quid uero super tres marcas excreuerit, diuidendum uniuersis heredibus attinebit. Si uero nullus cognatorum ei uoluerit necessaria ministrare, in iure dies prefigatur, in quo, si cognati cum eo noluerint conuenire, libertatem habeat cum bonis suis ad extraneum, quem uoluerit, transeundi. Transeuntem pro alimonia in alterius potestatem quidquid lucri uel dampni pro suorum excessuum satisfactione, si sui iuris esset, respiceret, hoc ad suscipientem eum similiter pertinebit. Unde suscepto uel occiso uel alium occidente, qui suscepit uel partem terciam satisfactionis recipiet uel prestabit, duabus terciis remanentibus ad suscepti cognatos tam paternos pertinentibus quam maternos. Nouo tamen iure prestabit totam solus suscipiens satisfaccionem. In ius alterius pro alimentis susceptus si conqueratur, quod exilem tolerare non ualeat procuracionem, qui promisit alimoniam duobus testibus et duodeno fidem faciat iuramento, quod, sufficientem prebens alimoniam, nihil minus, unde querimonia iure moueri posset, exsoluerit, quam promisit; uel in iure uiri probi de prouincia nominati mittantur ad inuestigandum, si necessaria ministrentur, et iniusta querimonia deprehensa, si non potuerint iratum placare, sed a suo recedat contra sanum consilium prouisore, si bona, que attulit secum, non deferat, sciat non detinenti iuste, sed fatuitati sue pocius ascribendum.

Ch. 16 How much a father is allowed to give to his grandsons when his sons, who are paternal uncles of the grandsons, are alive.

After the death of a son, it is permitted to everybody to give his son, their grandson, as much as would have been due to him if he had lived; if the grandson is sued as to the property given in his possession, he shall defend himself by an oath of twelve and two witnesses who were present when the gift was lawfully conveyed by the grandfather; if the grandson is not in possession, it is granted to the nearest heir by the oath of twelve only to prove that the lands in question have never been conveyed by the grandfather.

Ch. 17 On those who pass into someone else's power for support.

If someone is unable to procure sufficiently what is necessary for life because of poverty or bodily weakness caused by the burden of old age or the distress of sickness or due to other pitiable troubles of fortune, he can agree with his heirs that the property which he owns is to be shared among them and that he shall have from them what is necessary for life by moving around to each of them in turn, but first he has to make a declaration before everyone in the common assembly in order that such a lawful agreement cannot be altered or called into doubt. If he does not wish to move around to each of them in this manner, he can, when the property is divided, retain for himself one portion, and with that he may go to whom he wishes of the heirs; that portion – if it is worth only three marks or less – shall be taken by the one whom he chooses to go to. If it exceeds three marks, the rest is to be divided by all heirs. If none of his kin wishes to supply him with his necessities, then a day is to be fixed at the assembly on which, if his kin does not wish to make an agreement with him, he will be free to pass with his property to any person he may choose outside the kin. What gain or loss from compensation for offences would have been his, if he was on his own, will likewise be taken over by him who receives him. Therefore, if a man who has been received is killed or kills another person, then he who received him will either get or pay a third part of the compensation, and the remaining two-thirds will fall upon or to the kin, paternal as well as maternal. According to the new law, however, he who received him shall pay the entire compensation alone. If someone who at the assembly has accepted the support of another says that his meagre sustenance is not sufficient to sustain him, he who has promised support shall with two witnesses and an oath of twelve swear that he has supplied him with sufficient living and has fulfilled what he promised and not less, so that there is no reason for complaint; or else worthy men of the district nominated at the assembly shall investigate whether what is necessary is being provided; and when an unjust complaint is discovered, and they are unable to placate the aggrieved party and he leaves his provider against sound advice, and if he does not take away the property that he brought with him, he shall know that this cannot justly be blamed upon him who keeps it, but rather on his own foolishness.

18. Quibus prohibitum sit alienare predia sua usque ad certum tempus.

Bona maris impuberis, donec quartum decimum annum compleuerit, et femine, quam diu innupta permanserit, alienacioni iuris censura prohibet subiacere, nisi forte propter famis urgentis necessitatem, que legem non habet, in iure, ne fraus in occulto fiat, iudicentur propter alimoniam distrahenda, uel nisi forte per patrem ad utilitatem filie terra sua in alteram commutetur. Que uero secus, quam dictum est, lege alienata fuerint prohibente, refuso precio et, si super eius quantitate moueatur questio, duodeno addito iuramento, quod nihil remaneat de suscepto precio, reuocantur. Tribus annis post transcursum tempus, quo alienatio prohibetur, si super alienatis nulla questio moueatur, uel eius, qui detinet, possessio nullo modo fuerit interrupta, omnis excluditur reuocandi facultas. Orta probabili dubitacione super alienacione, utrum in pupillari uel legitima etate fuerit celebrata, est prestanda defensio etatem legitimam alleganti. Matrona quelibet seu uidua, circumspecto freta legitimi prouisoris consilio, de bonis suis alienare que uoluerit non uetatur.

19. Utrum licet alicui predium auitum alienare proximis inconsultis.

Ob hoc solum non est uendicio dissoluenda, quod cum extraneo fuerit celebrata, et tamen uenditor in tribus marcis satisfacere suo tenetur proximo, quod eum excluserit per emptorem extraneum a predii, quod progenitorum suorum fuerat, empcione, uel peticionem satisfaccionis elidat excipiendo, quod oblatum sibi ante predium pro iusto precio idem suus proximus recusauerit comparare, excepcione sacramento duodecimo roborata. Quorundam tamen iudicio sic emptum predium emptor non potest aliter retinere, nisi uenditor duodeno fidem fecerit iuramento, quod idem suus proximus, qui empcionem accusat, oblatum sibi predium renuerit pro iusto precio comparare. Sed prior sentencia rationabilior a prudentibus estimatur. Quin autem predium possit pro predio, inuitis consanguineis, commutari, dum modo non maius tribus marcis nummorum precium adiungatur, non oportet in dubium reuocari.

Ch. 18 Who may not dispose of their land until a certain time.

The property of a male child cannot lawfully be disposed of until he completes his fourteenth year[14] nor of a female for as long as she remains unmarried, unless, for example, it is necessary due to imminent hunger, which has no law,[15] and to avoid fraud being secretly committed, the assembly allows it to be sold for sustenance, or unless some of the daughter's land is exchanged for another by the father for her benefit. That which, however, has been disposed of not so as has been said but against the prohibition of the law shall be revoked, and if when the price has been paid back the quantity is questioned after an oath of twelve has been given that nothing remains of what was received. If no claim is raised within three years after the period within which disposal was prohibited, and the possession of he who holds it has in no way been interrupted, all possibility of revocation is excluded. If credible doubt arises as to whether a disposal occurred during the guardianship or whether legal age had been reached, he who claims legal age shall prove it. A wife or a widow shall not, when she is guided by the prudent advice of the legitimate guardian, be excluded from disposing of what property of hers she wishes to.

Ch. 19 Whether someone is permitted to dispose of his paternal land without consulting the next kinsmen.

A sale shall not be declared void for the sole reason that it has been contracted with a person outside the kin, but still the seller must satisfy his next of kin with three marks because he excluded him through an outside buyer from buying land that had been of his ancestors, or he can avoid the claim of satisfaction by relying on the exception[16] that this same next of kin refused to buy the land that had been offered to him for a just price[17] and confirm the exception by an oath of twelve. However, according to the opinion of some people, the buyer cannot retain land thus bought unless the seller swears by an oath of twelve that this same next of kin who is making a complaint against the sale refused to buy the land when it was offered to him for a just price. The first opinion, however, is considered by prudent men to be the most reasonable. On the other hand, it should not be doubted that land can be exchanged for land without the next of kin consenting, provided that not more than three marks of money was paid.

20. Qualiter diuisio sit inter fratres facienda.

Fratres, inter quos facta est hereditatis diuisio, assignatas sibi sortis iudicio porciones et legitimo possessas tempore manu duodecima defendentes, easdem, quam diu uixerint, adequare, si ab eorum aliquo inequalitatis moueatur querimonia, tenebuntur, rationem equalitatis nullatenus obtinere ualente, qui prius suam alienauerit porcionem, et ad eandem fratrum defunctorum filiis non cogendis, qui, quecumque patres eorum quiete et pacifice mortis tempore possedisse noscuntur, duodeno sacramento titulo pro herede sibi defendere permittuntur. Siquis uero fratrum in deterioris partis compensacionem se dicat additamentum aliquod recepisse, contradicens ei, equalitatis funiculum offerendo, falsum esse quod asseritur duodeno probare permittitur iuramento. Sortes uero mittende sunt pro numero personarum, non pro numero porcionum, ne, si forte sibi unus plures comparet porciones, pro pluralitate sortium in locis pluribus eas possit, ad uexacionem aliorum, eorundem porcionibus inmiscere.

21. De tutelis.

Ad tutelam inpuberis tutor legitimus inuitatur in coniunctione sanguinis ei quicumque proximus reperitur, si se ipsum tamen et alium possit defendere et prouisor esse uelit, non dissipans deuastator, ut onus senciat in defensione, quem emolumentum respiceret post mortem inpuberis in successione. Inter plures uero eque coniunctos, et ex una parte tantum, in subeunda tutela semper prefertur antiquior iuniori; inter eque coniunctos, sed ex utraque parte, agnatus, licet sit iunior, cognato preponitur, quamuis eciam seniori, ut auus paternus auo materno et patruus auunculo. Auus tamen maternus, quia maiorem affectum habere creditur ad nepotem, licet agnatum, patruum antecedit. Tutor de bonis inpuberis pro delictis ipsius tenetur satisfacere hiis, qui uel in rebus ab eo dampnum uel in corpore perpessi sunt lesionem; nequaquam enim multum eorum interest ab infante pocius quam adulto dampnorum molestiis aggrauari. Regi uero uel pontifici pro illius etatis excessibus, que causam inuestigare non sufficit castigacionis, equitatis ratio non permittit aliquid emendari.

Ch. 20 On how to make division between siblings.

When an inheritance was divided between siblings, the portions assigned to them by the casting of lots and which they by an oath of twelve can prove to have held in possession for the time prescribed by the law, those same portions they shall as long as they live be obliged to even out if one of them raises a claim that it was unequal; however, he who has previously disposed of his portion cannot have a valid reason for equalizing the division, neither can it be forced upon the children of deceased siblings who are allowed by an oath of twelve to defend their title as heirs to whatever their parents are known to have possessed quietly and peacefully at the time of their death. But if any of the siblings says that he got something additional as compensation for a meaner portion, he who contradicts him and offers the equalizing rope may prove by an oath of twelve that what is being asserted is false. Lots are to be thrown according to the number of people, not according to the number of portions, so that it does not happen that someone who may perchance have bought for himself several portions having several lots in distinct locations to the vexation of the others can have them intermingled with their portions.

Ch. 21 On guardianship.[18]

He shall be called to guardianship as lawful guardian of someone under age who is found to be the closest relative if he is able to protect himself and others and is supposed to be a provider and not a squandering devastator, so that he feels the burden of protection who receives the benefit of succession after the death of a child under age.[19] Among several kinsmen equally related on only one side the older always takes precedence over the younger in undertaking guardianship, and among those who are equally related on both sides the one who is related on the father's side, even if he is younger, is put before the one who is related on the mother's side, even if he is his senior, so that a paternal grandfather comes before a maternal grandfather and a paternal uncle before a maternal uncle. However, a maternal grandfather takes precedence over a paternal uncle, even though the latter is related on the father's side, because the former is supposed to have greater affection for his grandson. The guardian of the property of a child under age is obliged to compensate those who have suffered damage to their property or harm to their body from him since for them it is of no importance that it was due to a child and not to an adult that they are burdened with damage and difficulty. But equity does not permit the payment of anything to the king or archbishop for excesses committed at this age, where the ability to understand the reason for punishment is not sufficiently developed.

22. De tutela materna.

Iuris permittit equitas et suadet ratio pietatis matenrum affectum, mortis imperio mariti consorcio uiduatum, iusto solacio filiorum cum bonis eorum omnibus materne custodie mancipandorum, quam diu nouos amplexus aspernata fuerit, recreari, coniunctorum filiis proximorum consilio prouisionis feminee defectum supplente. Matre uero ad secundas nupcias conuolante, bona statim reseruanda tutoris fidei committuntur. Infans uero, donec septimum annum compleuerit, prouisioni relinquitur pietatis materne, et quoniam usque ad illud tempus a matre pro morte filii mater ecclesia requirit penitencie satisfactionem, et ab ea doctius infancie tractari crepundia et necessaria solent affectuosius exhiberi; a tutore custode bonorum singulis annis ualens dimidiam marcam nutricium receptura, nisi forte propter uberiorem rerum copiam uel generis claritatem plus gratis fuerit erogatum.

23. Qualiter tutor ualeat deprehendi suspectus.

Ad inique fraudis et sinistre suspicionis omnem materiam submouendam uel ad communionem redigenda sunt omnia sapienter consilio propinquorum, ut habeantur pro indiuiso quecumque tutoris et inpuberis bona fuerint in rebus mobilibus constituta, ut in illis et lucrum et dampnum, quodcumque contigerit, non unius proprium, sed pro rata partis cuiusque commune sit utriusque, uel tutor inpuberis bona tali condicione recipiat estimata, ut in restitucione bonorum nihil diminuere ualeat de quantitate estimacionis. Tutor uero, qui de rebus pupillaribus hanc negauerit prestare cautelam, a tutela uelud suspectus poterit amoueri, locum eius secundum leges proximo subeunte.

Ch. 22 On guardianship by the mother.

The equity of the law permits and regard to familial devotion suggests that the affection of a mother who has been bereaved of her husband's company by the command of death is re-created by the just comfort of her children, who are to be entrusted to their mother's custody with all their property, as long as she rejects new embraces, with the counsel of the kinsmen closest to the children compensating for the weakness of feminine care.[20] If the mother does not hesitate to enter[21] into a second marriage, the property shall be put immediately under the protection of a guardian for the sake of preservation. A small child who has not yet completed its seventh year shall assuredly be left to the providence of maternal devotion because until that time mother church requires penitence for the death of a child and because the playthings of early childhood are customarily more skilfully managed and its necessities provided with more affection by her; every year she shall have a half-mark as food allowance from the guardian who oversees the property, unless more happens to be supplied freely due to abundance of property or the distinction of the family.

Ch. 23 How a guardian can be detected as suspect.[22]

In order to avoid any grounds for unfair deception or improper suspicion all property shall be taken into a partnership with the prudent counsel of the nearest kin, so that whatever of the ward's and guardian's property is in movable property will be held in common, and whatever happens to them, be it gain or loss, will fall not to one of them alone but to both in common in proportion to each one's share, or the guardian shall receive the ward's property under such a condition that upon restoring the property he cannot diminish any of its quantity as it was estimated. A guardian who refuses to provide this security for a ward's property can be removed from the guardianship as suspect and his place be taken by the nearest kin according to the laws.

24. De filiis concubinarum.

Diuersis temporibus a diuersis regibus diuersa sunt iura prodita super concubinarum filiis, quibus ad incerti patris hereditatem condicionibus uocarentur. Exegit quandoque iuris censura, ut talis filius patrem sibi per candentis ferri iudicium declararet. Sed iniquum uisum est processu temporis, ut talis filii pater inuitus quisquam constitueretur. Unde constitutum est, ut naturalis filii pater non nisi uoluntarius haberetur, qui se patrem quoque in iure coram communi audiencia fateretur, et ibidem scotaret que uellet immobilia uel, non habens immobillia, que conferre uellet de mobilibus aperiret; nec prodesset omnis ista solemnitas, nisi reperiretur in morte patris aliquid de paterna munificencia possidere, illud totum et solum de paterna substancia retenturus et per illud, licet modicum, in futuris successionibus fratris uel sororis uel alterius coniuncte persone cuiuslibet, tamquam legitimus, porcionem integram habiturus, solemnitate paterne professionis, scotacionis uel alterius donacionis per ipsum patrem et non per aliquam personam suppositam adimplenda. Hoc ius, suis temporibus obseruatum, nouo iure in multis est articulis inmutatum. Nouum quippe ius, quod nunc obtinet, hoc solum exigit, ut in iure tantum per patrem professionis, scotacionis uel alterius donacionis solempnitas celebretur. Et quamuis nihil possideat de paterna largitate mortis tempore, in ius succedet naturalis filius, si solus in gradu fuerit, uniuersum. Si uero filii legitimi secum in gradu fuerint, illud solum, quod mortis tempore de paterna collacione possidet, obtinebit. Si uero filius naturalis diffiteatur se collacionem patriam recepisse, in sacris patris et familia usque ad patris obitum constitutus, ne a maiori hereditaria porcione per collacionem modicam excludatur, duobus testibus probans suam negacionem et xii^{cim} iuramentalibus audiatur. At si nihil possideat, quamuis pater, quando legitimorum spem non habuerit filiorum, ei scotauerit uniuersa, suscitatis postea legitimis, duplo minorem partem quam legitimus uel, si talis persona filia naturalis fuerit, duplo minus quam filia legitima obtinebit.

Ch. 24 On the children of concubines.

At various times various laws were given by various kings concerning the terms upon which the children of concubines are invited to the succession of an uncertain father. At one time the law stated that such a child should prove who his father was by means of the ordeal by hot iron. With the passage of time, however, it has been considered unjust that one could be recognized as the father of such a child against his will. Therefore, it was determined that a natural child should have no father if there was no volunteer who would also declare in the common assembly before the general public that he was the father and in the same place convey what immovable property he wished, or, if he had no immovable property, would declare what movable property he wished to confer; but this whole solemn procedure would be of no use if he was not found upon the father's death to possess some of that which stemmed from paternal generosity, and this he should keep solely and fully from the father's belongings, and through this, even if it was modest, he should take a full portion in the same way as a legitimate child in future successions of a brother or sister or any other relative, when the solemn declaration of the father or the conveyance of another gift was performed by the father himself and not by any other person in his place. This law, observed in its day, has been changed in many of its parts by new law. This new law, which is now in force, requires this alone, namely, that the declaration of the father, the conveyance or other gift is carried out at the assembly. And even if he possesses nothing from his father's liberality at the time of his death, a natural son succeeds to all of the inheritance, if he is the only one in his degree. If there are legitimate sons in the same degree as he, he obtains only what was conveyed to him and was possessed by him at the time of death. If a natural son denies that he received anything from his father and he stayed in his father's house and family until the father's death, his negation will be heard with two witnesses and an oath of twelve so that he is not excluded from a greater hereditary portion by the conveyance of a small amount. But if he possesses nothing, then, even if the father conveyed everything to him at a time when he did not have hope of legitimate offspring, and afterwards legitimate children were born, he will obtain half as much as the part of a legitimate son, or, if such a person is a natural daughter, half as much as a legitimate daughter.

43

Post recepcionem uero quamuis partis exigue de bonis paternis naturalis in successione fratris uel sororis uice fungetur heredis legitimi, porcionem integram consequendo, a matris uel fratrum uel sororum ex matre coniunctorum hereditate nullatenus excludendus, quamuis se patrem nullus uoluerit confiteri. Patrem uero ut se quispiam fateatur, naturalis potest persuadere racio pietatis et spes in bonis filii succedendi, nature turbato ordine, si fortassis patrem preueniat moriendo, ad hereditatem ipsius nullatenus admittendum, nisi legitime se prius patrem fuerit protestatus. Non prodesse hoc potest filio naturali sine memorate solemnitatis interuentu, quod ipsius pater putatiuus matrem suam duxerit in uxorem. Non idcirco minus post mortem mariti bonorum omnium tam mobilium quam immobilium, que funguntur uice mobilium, uxori sine liberis derelicte medietas attinebit, quod maritus tandem post cohabitacionem habitam cum uxore legitima confessus fuerit se habere filios naturales, qui tamen, si duobus testibus et duodeno bondonum iuramento probare uoluerint professionem patriam contractas nupcias precessisse, audiendi sunt, ut inter nouercam et ipsos hereditas pro uirilibus porcionibus diuidatur. Maiorem pro filio naturali et seruo proprio, ex ancilla propria procreato, quam pro alio seruo quolibet non prestabit pater et dominus satisfactionem.

25. Quid iuris sit, si aliquis pro alio ceperit respondere.
Pro absente in iudicio quicumque ceperit respondere, non absenciam excusando, sed, ne condempnetur absens, iusticiam offerendo, si promissam iusticiam reus non exhibuerit principalis, responsalis eam debet, quamuis in candentis ferri consistat iudicio, exhibere, temeritatis sue inputaturus stulticie, quod pro ingrato uoluerit respondere.

26. De distribucione per funiculum facienda.
Communis uniuersorum et priuata deposcit utilitas singulorum, ut sint in uilla qualibet quedam communia, uie uidelicet et platee, et quedam propria, seruiencia pro dominio quarumlibet personarum usibus earundem, in quibus omnem iniustam occupacionem debet equitatis funiculus emendare, cuius dimensione tota uilla in equales redigitur porciones, quas materna lingua uulgariter *bool* appellant, et nos in latino sermone mansos possumus appellare, earum fundis inter se prediisque inter se, fundis ipsis adiacentibus, adequandis.

A natural child who has received but a small part of the paternal property will be entitled in the succession of a brother or sister just as a legitimate heir to an undiminished portion and shall in no way be excluded from the inheritance from his mother or the brothers or sisters connected to him through the mother, even if no one has declared himself the father. The reason that someone declares himself father can be that regard to familial devotion persuades him or the hope of inheritance after the death of the child, if the order of nature is disturbed and the child should die before the father, who in no way has access to the inheritance from the child unless he lawfully beforehand has declared himself father. When the formalities mentioned are not carried out, it will not benefit the natural child that his presumed father has taken his mother as wife. After the death of the husband half of all his property, movable and the immovable that is treated as movable, goes to the wife when there are no children; but when the husband after having had intercourse with his legitimate wife confesses that he has natural children, they shall, however, be heard if they can prove with two witnesses and an oath of twelve householders that the declaration of the father was made before the marriage, so that the inheritance shall be divided in capital lots between their stepmother and themselves. The father and master shall not pay higher compensation for a natural son being his own slave born by his own servant than for any other slave.

Ch. 25 How to proceed if someone takes upon himself to answer for someone else.

If someone takes upon himself to answer for someone who is absent in a lawsuit, not excusing his absence but offering to fulfil the law[23] in order to prevent that he is sentenced in absence, then he is responsible for carrying it out if the principal defendant does not fulfil the law, even if it is the ordeal by hot iron, thus taking the consequences of his stupid temerity that he was willing to defend an ungrateful person.

Ch. 26 On distribution made by the rope.

The utility of both the common general interest and of the private singular interest requires that a village should include both certain common areas such as roads and squares, and something singular to serve their own needs according to the size of their property, and within which all unlawful occupation must be corrected with the rope of equalization, by the measuring of which the whole village is divided into lots that in the maternal vulgar language are called *bool*, and which we can call *mansus* in the Latin tongue, by which their land and the curtilages with the land adjacent to it are evened out among them.

45

27. Qualiter uniuersitas, quod in loco publico factum fuerit, poterit demoliri.
Ad demoliendum edificium uel opus aliquod, quod iniuste quis in publico loco posuerit, uniuersitati duorum testimonium cum duodeno sufficit iuramento. Sed auctor operis, si de fundi sui angustiis conqueratur et debito minorem alleget, per funiculi beneficium pro sue partis exigencia obtinebit debitam quantitatem, illo in tribus marcis regi condempnando, qui statuto tempore metiendi iusti funiculi contradixerit equitati.

28. Qualiter uniuersitas possit impeditum tramitem ad uiam publicam restaurare.
Uille cuiuslibet incolarum transitus ad stratam publicam impeditus per eosdem est cum duodecim iuramentalibus et duobus testibus statuendus.

29. Qualiter transitus constitui debeat prouincialibus ad ciuitatem uel ad nemora uel ad mare.
Ad constituendum transitum prouincialibus ad ciuitatem uel ad nemora uel ad mare coram rege uel antistite uel in iure sunt xii bondones de prudentibus tocius prouincie nominandi, quorum in tribus marcis regi sunt singuli condempnandi, nisi statuto die cum duobus testibus uiam publicam sacramento suo parati fuerint declarare.

30. De transitu parochianorum ad ecclesiam.
Ad expediendum iter ecclesie de parrochianis xii coram antistite nominati si, quod iussi sunt, statuto die noluerint adimplere, multa trium marcarum de singulis ad episcopum pertinebit.

31. De pena publicam uiam inutilem facientis.
Qui ad transeundum inutilem uiam fecit publicam, uel sepe posita uel fossato facto uel alia quouis opere fabricato, ad trium marcarum regi tenetur satisfaccionem.

32. Qualiter cogendi sunt consortes bonorum communium ad diuisionem faciendam.
Si quid pro indiuiso ab incolis uille cuiuslibet habeatur commune, uolentibus ad agriculturam redigere partes suas si diuisionis ratio denegetur, in iure diuisionis faciende dies cunctis consortibus prefigatur, quo contumaciter pretermisso, qui diuisionis iudicium expetebant pro parte sua nichilominus bonis communibus, quibus modis uoluerint excolendis, utendi liberam habeant facultatem, non cogendi de cetero ab aduersariis ad particionem aliquam faciendam, donec ipsi partes suas conuerterint in culturam.

Ch. 27 How the community can demolish what is put up in a public place.

In order to demolish a building or work of any sort that someone has illegally placed in a public place, the community needs only the testimony of two and an oath of twelve. But the builder can, when he complains of the narrowness of his curtilage and alleges that it is smaller than it ought to be, get what is due to him according to his lot through the benefit of the rope and he who at the fixed time opposed the equal measuring by lawful roping shall be sentenced to pay three marks to the king.

Ch. 28 How the community can restore a blocked footpath to the public road.

If a passageway to the public road has been blocked for the inhabitants of any village, this must be stated by them with the oath of twelve and two witnesses.

Ch. 29 How a passage shall be established for men of the district to a city or to the woods or to the sea.

In order to establish a passage for the district men to the city or to the woods or to the sea, twelve householders shall be nominated from prudent men of the entire district before the king or bishop or in the assembly, each of whom shall be sentenced to pay three marks to the king if on the appointed day they are not prepared to declare a road to be public by their oath.

Ch. 30 On the passageway for parishioners to church.

If twelve parishioners nominated before the bishop with the purpose of opening up a road to church are not willing to fulfil what they are asked to do on the appointed day, a fine of three marks from each of them shall be paid to the bishop.

Ch. 31 On the penalty for those making a public road unusable.

He who makes a public road unusable for passage, whether by a fence placed or a ditch made or by any other work done, must pay three marks to the king.

Ch. 32 How partners in common property can be forced to make division.

If anything is held in common and undivided by the inhabitants of a village and those who wish to prepare their parts for cultivation are barred from making a division, then a day for the division shall be appointed at the assembly for all the partners together, and if it is obstinately neglected, then those who want a decision by division shall in any case for their part be free to use the common property and cultivate it in whatever way they want, and they shall not be forced thereafter by the others to make any partition until they have themselves included their own parts for cultivation.

33. Qualiter sopiri debeat controuersia super limitibus duarum uillarum uel super terra, que *hornome* uulgariter appellatur.

Ad sopiendam controuersiam exortam super limitibus duarum uillarum, quamuis unam ex alia constet originem habuisse, uel super terra, que *hornome* uulgariter appellatur, quam quasi precipuam ad diuisionem uenire cum aliis non permittit priuilegium dignitatis, eligendi sunt in iure xii de prudencioribus tocius prouincie, quos *aldungebønder* natale nominat ydioma, ut ipsi terminos demonstrent, et super terra, que priuilegiata dicitur, an ita sit, seu quanta sit, omnem aperiant ueritatem, per iurisiurandi religionem affirmantes, quod nec alicuius odii causa nec fauoris gracia confingant aliquam super expediendis negociis falsitatem, et quod credunt esse uerum quod asserunt, et quod idem ex relatu suorum antecessorum et prudentium didicerunt antiquorum. Si qui uero ad empcionis uel alterius adquisicionis se conuertunt allegacionem, ne bonis careant, que aliorum uille sic ostensum est adiacere, illis, qui tali remedio possessionis commodum sunt adepti, sacramentum defensionis per se ipsos singulos primo permittitur inchoare, deinde semel tantum per xi, quos *hotolbønder* lingua materna nominat, adimplere. Si quis uero iurare noluerit, ipsius partis restitucio nulli uolenti iurare preiudicium generabit. At si quis absens fuerit prestandi tempore sacramenti, per duos testes ipsius absencia approbata, cum reuersus fuerit, admittitur iterum ad iurandum.

34. De tempore distribucionis per funiculum faciende et de pena funiculum denegantis.

Si super inequalitate mansorum querimonia moueatur, antequam semen solo fuerit commendatum, de sua stulticia conqueratur, si sementem amittat, qui ante funiculi mensuracionem et post factam sibi prohibicionem presumpserit seminare. Si uero, postquam seminatum fuerit, querimonia suscitetur, metiendi iudicium, donec seges collecta fuerit, differatur. Ad metiendum uero unius tantummodo mansi partes non refert, quando querimonia moueatur, nec est, ad commodum seminantis incaute, mensurandi ratio prohibenda. Qui uero non admiserit mensuracionem uocatus ad ius, si se contempserit presentare, tam pro prima quam pro 2ª citacione in duabus horis aduersario, pro tercia uero tam regi quam aduersario in tribus marcis erit secundum iusticiam condempnandus.

Ch. 33 How to settle a controversy over the boundaries between two villages or over land which is commonly called *hornome.*

For the purpose of settling a controversy over the boundaries between two villages, even when one of them is known to have had its origin from the other, or over land that is commonly called *hornome,* which as a kind of exception due to the privilege of dignity shall not be divided with others, twelve of the most prudent men of the entire district, such whom the native language calls *aldungebønder,* shall be chosen at the assembly to indicate where the boundaries are; and with regard to the land that is said to be privileged, they shall uncover the truth as to whether it is so or how much it is, and they shall swear that neither because of any hatred nor as a favour will they invent any falsehood in these affairs, and that they believe to be true that which they assert, and that they learned the same from what their predecessors and prudent men of the past have said. If someone takes resort to the allegation that they have bought or acquired land by other means in order that they shall not give up property which is proven to be part of another village, then those who in such a way have acquired the benefit of possession are allowed first to swear on their own and then to supplement their oath by one of eleven men whom the mother tongue calls *hotolbønder.* But if someone refuses to swear, the restitution of his part shall be prejudicial to nobody wishing to swear. But if any-one is absent at the time of giving the oath and his absence has been corroborated by two witnesses, then he will be permitted to swear again when he comes back.

Ch. 34 On the time for distribution through the rope, and on the penalty for refusing the rope.

If a complaint is made about the inequality of lots and it is before seed has been sown in the soil, he who dares to sow before the measurement by the rope and after a prohibition has been made against him must blame himself for his foolishness if he loses what he has sown. If there is a complaint after it has been sown, the deci-sion by measuring will be deferred until the crops have been gathered. In measur-ing parts of a single unit, it is of no importance when the complaint is made, and the measuring shall not be prohibited just for the benefit of an imprudent sower. When someone who did not permit measurement is called to the assembly but disdains to present himself, he shall be sentenced to pay the opposing party two ounces for the first and second summons; but after the third he shall be sentenced according to the law to pay the king as well as the opposing party three marks.

35. Utrum quis possit per fundum, caput uidelicet, predia, membra uidelicet, reuocare, non obstante prescripcione; an se tueri in prediis possit quis per prescripcionem, non inscripta fundi dignitate.

Racione fundorum ueluti digniorum, non adiacencium prediorum, que fundis uelud membra capitibus obsequuntur, pensiones redduntur, et que debentur procuracioni regie persoluuntur, et in quibusdam locis que requirit expedicionis necessitas assignantur. Unde quibusdam prudentibus et iuris peritis uisum est esse consentaneum equitati, ut fundi dominus et possessor de prediis adiacentibus alienatos agros, quantocumque tempore dinoscuntur eos alii possedisse, interuentu duodeni iuramenti ualeat reuocare, si tamen cum fundo anno quolibet saltem unus ager retentus fuerit ad culturam. Alioquin per membra, si cuncta pariter alienata fuerint, posset caput ipsum, fundus uidelicet, tamquam sine membris inutile reuocari. Ita quoque membra possunt per caput repeti, si non alia demonstrentur predia, que pro membris fuerint commutata. Indirecta quoque sic astruunt ratiocinacione, ut, si trium annorum prescripcio uel diuturnior reuocacionem ualeat impedire, nil uel parum utilitatis uideatur habere funiculus distribucionis, cum possit quilibet quantumcumque deprehenditur possidere per prescripcionis beneficium retinere. Econtra probare nituntur alii, quod semper sit duodeni iuramenti defensio deferenda quecumque predia, quoscumque agros legitime possidenti. Alioquin predia, que auferri sibi per iusticiam posse cognosceret, nullus de facili compararet, et sic rebus suis uti libere ad suum commodum, ad uitam miseram sustentandam, ad necessaria conquirenda, per inique legis prohibicionem tacitam uideretur dominis adempta facultas; nec oportet, ut asserunt, equitatem funiculi propter prescripcionis commodum exspirare, cum ibi debeat sibi locum funiculus uendicare, ubi quisque super sextantem uel trientem uel quadrantem uel semissem uel dodrantem uel aliam partem huiusmodi, quam scitur ab aliis et se fatetur solam habere, existimatur aliquid usurpasse. Huic autem posteriori sentencie, tamquam magis fauorabili, communis consensus promeruit confirmacionem.

36. De prescripcione.

Appellari potest prescripcio secundum has leges diffiniti lege temporis in possessione continuatio, propter quam per prestacionem duodeni sacramenti deferri debet defensio possidenti.

Ch. 35 Whether someone by the curtilage, which is the head, can revoke land, which are the limbs, without regard to prescription; whether someone can protect his lands by prescription when they are not included in the dignity of the curtilage.

In relation to curtilages as the more dignified and not to the surrounding lands, which obey the curtilage as the limbs the head, tolls are paid and what is due for the king's maintenance is paid, and in some places what is needed for warfare is assigned. Certain prudent men who knew the law, therefore, found it in accordance with equity that the owner and possessor of the curtilage, if only one acre in any year had been kept for cultivation with the curtilage, should be entitled to revoke by an oath of twelve those acres that have been alienated from the land adjacent without regard to the time others may have had them in possession. Otherwise, the head itself, namely the curtilage, could be revoked by the limbs when they had all been alienated as if it was useless without the limbs. Thus limbs can be called back by the head when no other land is indicated that has been exchanged for the limbs. As an indirect argument they add that if prescription of three years or longer could impede the revocation, division by roping seems to be of little use when anybody can keep whatever he has in his possession due to the benefit of prescription. On the other hand, others try to prove that defence by an oath of twelve shall always be granted to the lawful possessor of whatever land or whatever acres. Otherwise, nobody would that easily acquire land when they knew that it could legally be taken from them, and thus the possibility to use their property freely for their own commodity, to sustain their miserable life or to acquire their necessities would seem to be taken away from owners by the tacit prohibition of an unjust law; and the force of the rope need not expire through the benefit of prescription, as they maintain, because the rope will take place where someone is considered to have taken for themselves something more than a sixth or a third or a fourth or half or three-quarters or another share of that sort which is known by others and which he himself acknowledges to be the only share he has. This last solution has been confirmed by common opinion as the most acceptable.

Ch. 36 On prescription.

Prescription according to these articles[24] is defined as the continued possession for a time determined by the law so that the defence by an oath of twelve is granted to the possessor.[25]

37. Quid sit tempus diffinitum.

Diffinitum tempus trinas agriculturas complectitur, que tribus annis exercentur, unde solet trium annorum prescripcio nominari, licet minus tempus sufficiat, cum tres agriculture duobus annis uel paulo maiori spacio concludantur. In agricultura debet quoque fructuum segetisque collectio comprehendi, sicut ex uulgari nostro, quod *thrænnæ halma* dicimus, euidenter apparet. Alioquin cum agricultura exerceatur semel in ieme, bis in uere, unus annus uel paulo prolixius tempus sufficeret ad prescripcionis huiusmodi consumacionem. Nec prodesse poterit ista prescripcio, nisi in pace continuata fuerit et quiete, non turbata querimoniis, non quouis alio modo ciuili uel naturali ex parte illius, qui terras illas, que possidentur, uendicare nititur, interrupta. Nam qui non metuit uiolenter et iniuste rem quamlibet occupare, uerisimile est, ut in defensione non magis timeat peierare. Cum prescripcione semper requiritur sacramentum; nam cum nullus tractus temporis, nullus annorum numerus possit quemquam sine facto uel delicto uel consensu proprio rerum suarum dominio spoliare, et incertum sit, utrum actor sit dominus uel possessor, hoc in se commodum habet prescripcio, ut ipsius intuitu non actor, sed possessor permittatur suo et xi bondonum sacramento se dominum declarare, cui standum est sacramento, cum credendum non sit, quod salutis sue sic debeant esse immemores, ut preferre uelint ei quamlibet rem temporalem. Non sine racione prescripcionis tanta breuitas est inducta, quia dominia rerum esse diu non expedit in incerto, et consultum uidetur tempestiue radicem malorum, ante quam ex ea contingat pullulare noxia, resecari. Quandocumque affirmat actor eum, qui ad defensionem prescripcionis conuolat, nullomodo uel minus legitime possedisse, eligendi sunt de uicinis xii prudentes bondones, de quibus presumi possit, ut non uelint eciam in causa propria peierare, ut exortam super possessione questionem suo dirimant sacramento, illi defensione, cui possessionem adiurauerint, concedenda. Propter paternam tamen possessionem, quantumlibet breuem, pacificam et quietam et ad patris obitum continuatam, filio iure conceditur duodeni defensio iuramenti, in hac forma exhibendi, quod pater rem, de qua agitur, iuste possederit, et ad filium sic iure hereditario sit deuoluta, ui sibi cum proprietate possessio debeatur; nec cogendus est adquisicionis paterne titulum indicare, qui sibi nititur pro herede rem quamlibet uendicare, nisi querimoniam in uita patris super ea re fuisse constiterit suscitatam.

Ch. 37 What the determined time is.

The determined time covers three periods of farming, which are exercised for three years, whence it is usually called the prescription of three years, although less time will suffice when three farming periods are concluded within two years or a little more. Gathering of fruits and crops must also be included in the farming period, as it evidently appears from our common language because we say *thrœnnœ halma.* Otherwise, one year or a little longer would suffice for the completion of a prescription of this kind because a period of farming can take place once in winter and twice in summer. Nor can this prescription be of use unless it is continued in peace and quietly, not troubled by complaints, not interrupted in any other way whatsoever, legally or materially on the part of the man who strives to claim back those lands that were taken into possession. That is because it is most likely that he who does not fear to seize property of any kind violently and unjustly will not be more afraid of using perjury in his defence. In addition to prescription, an oath is always required, as no span of time or any number of years can deprive anyone of the ownership of his property except for his own action, crime or consent, and when it is uncertain whether the plaintiff is the owner or the possessor, prescription brings this benefit, that not the plaintiff but the possessor is permitted by his own oath and that of eleven householders to declare himself the owner; and this oath shall stand for him, as it is not to be believed that they should be so unmindful of their salvation that they will prefer something of this world to it. Not without reason was such brevity of prescription introduced because it is not advantageous for the ownership of property to be in uncertainty for a long[26] time, and a timely decision appears to cut down the root of evil before harm sprouts from it.[27] When a plaintiff declares that the man who uses the defence of prescription in no way did possess it or possessed it illegally, then twelve prudent householders shall be chosen among the neighbours, of whom it can be presumed that they do not wish to perjure themselves even in their own interest, and they shall decide the question that has been raised about the possession, and he to whom they grant the possession by their oath shall be granted the right of defence. As a consequence of a father's possession and regardless of how brief it may have been, as long as it was peaceful and quiet and continued after the death of the father, the son is by law allowed the defence of an oath of twelve issued to the effect that the father rightly possessed the property concerned and that it has come to the son by the law of succession so that he has possession together with ownership: he who tries to claim something as heir shall not be forced to indicate the title of the father, unless the claim was raised while the father was living.

Dubitari solet, utrum in tali iuramento debeat quoque scotatio, que ad translacionem dominii preterquam in hereditaria successione ubique requiritur, comprehendi. Sed cum ex hereditaria successione nulli alicuius rei dominium adquiratur,
nisi et ille, cui quis succedit, pariter dominium habuisset, uel hereditario iure uel
scotacionis beneficio, predicti uidetur formam sufficere iuramenti, licet nullam
super scotacione uel hereditaria successione faciat mencionem, cum earum neutra
intercedente periurium incurratur, quamuis earum neutra nominetur. Ubi uero pater
negatur in obitu possedisse, nominandorum bondonum xii, sicut iam dictum est,
super hoc exigitur sacramentum. Reperitur et alius casus, in quo sufficit quantumlibet breuis possessio ad defensionem huiusmodi obtinendam, qua munitur
emptor contra proprium uenditorem, quibusdam pro iure uolentibus obseruare,
quod statim dimisso pallio post factam scotacionem non possit uenditor, conuictus duobus legitimis testibus, qui presentes fuerunt, quod factum fuerat diffiteri,
sed cogatur pocius adimplere; ex aduerso aliis asserentibus, quod habere locum
semper possit negatio uenditoris, donec excepcione prescripcionis legitime repelli
ualeat ab emptore; est communi consensu plurium, quodammodo mediam uiam
eligencium, approbatum, ui munitus duobus testibus, qui scotacionis solemnitatibus affuerunt, propter breuem quantumlibet possessionem, iustam tamen, pacificam et quietam, se tueri possit emptor contra proprium uenditorem, licet prefinito
prescripcionis tempore semper indigeat contra quemuis extraneum petitorem; nam
ante prescriptum prescripcionis terminum nulla facultas emptori permittitur se
tuendi, sed incumbit, ut eam defendat, necessitas uenditori. Alioquin, si res euicta
fuerit, refundet precium uel terram restituet, si commutatio celebrata fuerit, satisfaccione trium marcarum insuper adiungenda. Completa uero prescripcione legitima, non habet emptor necesse ad auctoris sui patrocinium conuolare, ne, si per
maliciam uenditoris defensio denegetur, emptor re sibi uendita defraudetur, sed,
adhibitis sibi duobus scotacionis testibus, duodeno bondonum doceat iuramento,
quod a iusto domino comparauerit terram illam, et quod eam tempore legittimo
ad prescribendum possederit, et idcirco eam ipse solus et non alius teneatur iusto
dominio retinere. Si tamen de sua causa diffidat, petat auxilium uenditoris, ut ad
ipsum regressum habere ualeat, si forte ceciderit a defensione, ab eo cum emendacione trium marcarum uel precium, si confessus fuerit, uel duodenum iuramentum,
si negauerit uendicionem, recepturus. Quando uero cadit a defensione qui possidet,
petitori ad uendicandum sibi duodenum bondonum sufficit iuramentum.

There is usually doubt whether conveyance, which is always required for the transfer of ownership outside hereditary succession, should also be included in such an oath. However, as nobody else acquires ownership of a thing by hereditary succession, unless he whom someone succeeds also had the ownership, be it by the law of succession or the benefit of conveyance, the aforementioned form of oath seems to suffice, even if no mention is made of conveyance or succession, as it will be perjury if none of them have taken place, even if none of them is mentioned. When it is denied that the father was in possession at the time of his death, then the oath of twelve nominated householders is required, as has been said. There is also another case in which possession, regardless of how short it may have been, is sufficient to obtain the defence of this kind, namely when the buyer is protected against his own seller, because some will hold it to be just that as soon as the cloak is released after the conveyance is made the seller cannot, when he is convinced by two lawful witnesses who were present, disavow what has happened but rather is forced to comply; on the other hand, there are others who maintain that the vendor can always deny until the buyer can legally contradict him with the exception of prescription; it is approved by the common opinion of a majority as a kind of middle way that when he has two witnesses who were present at the ceremony of conveyance, the buyer can defend himself against his seller even after whatever short time of possession as long as it has been lawful, peaceful and quiet, but he is always restricted by the mentioned time of prescription against anyone from the outside who raises a claim; because before the term prescribed for prescription, nothing permits the buyer to defend himself, but necessity forces the vendor to defend him. On the other hand, if the property was evicted,[28] he shall refund the price or give back the land if lands have been exchanged and in addition pay compensation of three marks. When the time of prescription is lawfully completed, then the buyer does not need to seek the protection of his originator, so that the buyer shall not be defrauded if defence is denied out of the seller's malice, but with two witnesses to the conveyance and with the oath of twelve householders he can prove that he bought the land from its rightful owner and that he has possessed it for the lawful time of prescription and therefore he himself and nobody else shall keep it in lawful ownership. If, however, he is doubtful as to his case, he shall ask the seller for help so that he can hold him responsible if he misses the defence, and from him he shall receive three marks and either his price paid back, if it was admitted, or an oath of twelve if the sale is denied. But when the possessor misses the defence, the claimant needs only twelve householders in order to vindicate.[29]

38. Quid sit scotacio.

In uendicione terrarum ad translacionem dominii est necesse, ut interueniat quedam solemnitas, in qua terre modicum emptoris pallio, extento manibus assistencium, qui, si factum reuocetur in dubium, perhibere possunt testimonium ueritati, apponit uenditor, qui, designans terram, quam distrahit, in emptorem ipsius se transferre dominium profitetur. Hec autem solemnitas ex uulgari nostro producto uocabulo competenter satis potest scotacio nominari.

39. Quid iuris sit, si quis promissionem super uendicione terre noluerit adimplere, uel si quis uoluerit a uendicione resilire.

Qui promissionem super uendicione alicuius terre noluerit adimplere, duas horas secundum quosdam, si nudam et simplicem promissionem fecerit, et ui horas communi iudicio, si contactu manuum roborata fuerit, aut tres marcas, si scotacionis solemnitate interueniente aliena terra uendita, quod promisit, effectui mancipare non potuerit, emendabit. Sin autem propria terra uendita, quam prestare poterit, resilire uoluerit, nullatenus audiendus est ualens factum proprium irritare et propriam inconstanciam allegare, licet trium marcarum offerat satisfactionem.

40. Quid iuris sit, si duorum uterque eandem terram ab eodem domino comparauerit.

Si duorum uterque ab eodem se contendat idem predium comparasse, ille debet omnimodis obtinere, cui coram rege uel antistite uel in iure irreuocabilis suffragatur confessio uenditoris; uerum in alio quouis loco, licet in conuentu incolarum uel parrochianorum, facta professio non preiudicat, quin possit denuo, si uelit, uenditor uendicionem factam alii protestari, priorem confessionem duodeno negaturus, si super ea conuentus fuerit, sacramento.

Ch. 38 What is conveyance.

With regard to sale of lands, it is necessary in order to transfer ownership that certain solemnities are observed by which the seller places a bit of earth in the buyer's cloak, which is held out by the hands of the people present, and who, if the action is called into doubt, can give testimony that it has taken place; and while the seller designates the land which he is selling, he declares that he is transferring his own ownership to the buyer. This solemnity can conveniently be called *scotatio*[30] by using an appellation from our ordinary language.[31]

Ch. 39 How to proceed when someone does not want to fulfil a promise concerning sale of land or if someone wants to withdraw from a sale.

A person who does not want to fulfil a promise concerning the sale of some land will, according to some, have to pay two ounces if he has made a bare and simple promise, and according to common opinion six ounces if it has been strengthened by the contact of hands, or three marks if it was someone else's land that was sold and the solemnity of conveyance has occurred. But if he wishes to withdraw after having sold his own land, which he can provide,[32] he shall under no circumstances be heard when he wishes to make void his own act and refers to his own inconstancy, even if he offers compensation of three marks.

Ch. 40 How to proceed when two people have bought the same land from the same owner.

If two people both claim that they have bought the same land from the same person, the one who is supported by the seller's irrevocable acknowledgment before the king or the bishop or at the assembly shall in all ways prevail; but a public acknowledgment spoken in any other location – for instance, at a gathering of the village people or parishioners, does not stand, and therefore a seller, if he is summoned, can affirm in turn, if he wishes, that the sale was made to the other party and deny his prior acknowledgment by an oath of twelve.

41. Qualiter quis possit uel debeat terram suam, possessam ab alio, reuocare.
Qui super possessione terre impetitur aliene, si nolit adquiescere petitori, uocetur
in ius, et ibi dies prefigatur, in quo uel in suo nomine rem defendat uel actori
deferat ius defensionis. Quociens autem citatus uenire contempserit, in duabus
horis aduersario, regi tandem in tribus marcis in citacione tercia, condempnetur.
Deinde diem iuridici prefigant actori, in quo cum duodecim terram suo nomine
possidentibus ad terram, de qua agitur, accedens, una cum eis duodeno declaret
sacramento et mutuis intricatarum contactibus manuum sibi dominium attinere.
Deinde 4ª uice hoc fecisse se testetur in iure, et tunc illius terre defensor legitimus
iudicetur. Ubi si adhuc reus comparuerit, et duobus testibus et duodeno docuerit
iuramento se minime uel minus legitime citatum fuisse, propter iustam absenciam
peregrinacionis uel inuestigacionis suorum animalium amissorum uel egritudinis
impedimentum, a cunctis prius in eum latis sentenciis absoluatur. Et sic de nouo
uel terram defendat, ut dictum est, uel defendere permittat actorem.

**42. Quod illi pocius sit defensio deferenda, qui scotacionem dicit iure perpetuo
factam, quam ei, qui ypotece nomine factam asserit temporalem.**
Qui scotacionis solemnia confitetur, non auditur, si se tantum ypotece nomine
scotasse asserit, donec debitum solueretur, si possessor legitimus duobus testibus
et duodeno bondonum docuerit iuramento scotacionis alienacionem iure perpetuo
celebratam fuisse.

**43. De homicidio et homicidii emendacione et emendacionis diuisione, com-
posicione, distribucione et temporibus faciende satisfaccionis.**
Instigante humani generis inimico, quia proni semper fuerunt homines in nostris
partibus ad homicidium perpetrandum, pacem angelicam deserentes et sedicionem
diabolicam amplexantes, diuersis temporibus diuersa sunt iura prodita super tanti
reatus per multam pecuniariam castigacionem, quatenus et tantus excessus aliquatenus refrenari et amissionis dampnum quoquo modo posset satisfaccionis pecuniarie tristi solacio compensari; hec autem multa non excedit summam xv marcarum
argenti. Sed occurrunt multa consideranda super ipsius pecunie diuisione, com-
posicione, distribucione, in quibus temporibus et a quo cui debeat assignari.

Ch. 41 How you can or shall recover your land that is in the possession of someone else.

Someone who is sued concerning possession of someone else's land shall be summoned to the assembly if he does not wish to accede to the plaintiff, and there a day shall be fixed upon which he must either claim the property in his own name or grant the right of claim to the plaintiff. As often as the person summoned disdains to come, he will be sentenced to pay two ounces to the opposing party, and at last, upon the third summons, three marks to the king. Then the men of the assembly shall set a day for the plaintiff upon which he shall go to the land in question with twelve men, who possess land in their own name, and together with these twelve he shall declare with his oath and the mutual contacts of their entangled hands that he is the owner. Then, on a fourth occasion in the assembly, he shall swear that he has done this and then he will be considered the legitimate claimant of that land. But if the defendant still appears and with two witnesses and an oath of twelve shows that he was not summoned at all or not legally summoned because of a legitimate absence due to pilgrimage or a search for his missing animals or the impediment of illness, he will be freed from all sentences previously passed on him. And thus he may claim his land anew, as has been said, or allow the plaintiff the defence.

Ch. 42 That defence is to be granted to one who says that a conveyance has been made in perpetual right rather than to one who maintains that as a pledge it was a temporary act.

Someone who admits the solemnity of conveyance is not heard if he maintains that he carried out the conveyance only as a pledge until a debt is paid, if the possessor with two legitimate witnesses and twelve householders proves that disposal by conveyance took place as a perpetual right.

Ch. 43 On homicide and on compensation for homicide, and on the division of compensation, its composition, distribution and the terms for paying compensation.

By instigation of the Enemy of mankind,[33] men in our region are always prone to commit homicide, forsaking angelic peace and embracing strife; and therefore at various times various laws have been brought forth regarding punishment for this crime by a pecuniary fine, both in order that such an excess can to some extent be curbed and so that the injury caused by the loss may in this way be compensated by the sad consolation of pecuniary compensation; this compensation, however, does not exceed the sum of fifteen marks of silver. But many things are to be considered concerning its division, its composition, its distribution, on what terms and by whom and to whom it must be given.[34]

44. De diuisione.

Satis liquet omnibus diuisionem in tres partes equales, uidelicet in tres tercias, faciendam, quarum quelibet ob frequentem usum speciali nomine in uulgari nostro *sal* meruit appellari.

45. De composicione.

Ante tempus nouissime constitucionis occisori uel eius heredi semper incubuit primam tantum de propriis bonis componere porcionem; deinde licuit ei 2^{am} exigere ab agnatis et tandem terciam partem et ultimam a cognatis. Uerum quia plerumque a plerisque agnatis uel cognatis plus debito petebatur et ab inuitis per uiolenciam diripiebatur, ne maleficium esset cuiquam questus occasio congregandi, et hominem quemquam ad malefaciendum ulterius cupiditas lucrandi prouocaret, sapienter occurrit tante malicie felicis memorie rex Kanutus, instituens, quod pro tali furto uel rapina tamquam uerus fur uel latro posset quispiam conueniri pariter et puniri et in tribus marcis iuri regio condempnari; obligatum autem coniunccione sanguinis et tamen satisfacere renuentem ad satisfaciendum ab agnalis et cognatis per exactorem uel ius regium induci debere, occisori collecta pecunia non tradenda ante diem uel horam, in qua coram agnatis uel cognatis eam emendacionis causa persoluere teneretur. Hec autem, in institucione regia comprehensa, licet aliquantulum fraudibus malignancium obuiarent, ad exstirpandam tamen omnem fraudem et pronitatem occidendi minuendam, presertim cum exigua porcio, tocius uidelicet emendacionis tercia tantum, incumberet occisori, minus sufficiencia sunt inuenta, et idcirco auctoritate regis Waldemari, fratris predicti regis Kanuti, prudenciores Scanie tali lege nouissime decreuerunt tantam maliciam reprimendam, ut solus homicida de bonis propriis teneretur ad totam pecuniam pro reatu homicidii persoluendam, nihil ab inuitis agnatis exigens uel cognatis, ne pro facto nocentis innocens grauaretur, et ut solus delinquens penam suo delicto debitam sustineret, et solus auctor pro suis excessibus puniretur. Statuerunt preterea reum homicidii ad beneficium emendacionis nullatenus admittendum, nisi primis tribus diebus continuis post perpetratum homicidium, quibus ad audiendas querimonias in generali iure per totam dyocesim homines congregantur, instanter offerret pro exeessu suo, per se uel per alium, si uenire non posset in propria persona, satisfaccionem.

Ch. 44 On division

It is sufficiently evident to everyone that division should be made in three equal parts, that is, into three thirds, all of which due to frequent usage should be called by their specific name in our vulgar language, *sal*.

Ch. 45 On composition.

Before the time of the newest statute[35] it was always incumbent on the killer or his heir to compose the first portion from his own property; after that he was permitted to demand the second from his paternal kin and finally, the third and last part from his maternal kin. Because, however, very often more than what was owed was demanded from the paternal or maternal kin – and snatched with violence from the unwilling – King Knud of blessed memory wisely tried to prevent such evils, so that committing a crime should not offer anyone the possibility to accumulate profit and that greed for making money should not provoke any man into committing a further crime, and he instituted that anyone could be judicially summoned for theft or rapine[36] of this kind, just as a real thief or robber, and be punished and be sentenced to pay three marks to the king; and that one who was bound to pay compensation by virtue of kinship and refused to pay compensation should be forced in the end to pay by the king's official or the king and not by his paternal or maternal kin, and that the money gathered together on behalf of the killer should not be handed over before the day and hour on which, in the presence of his paternal and maternal kin, he was bound to pay it in full as compensation. Even though all these things included in the ordinance of the king to some degree prevented the fraud of malign persons, it was, however, found to be insufficient for rooting out all fraud and diminishing the propensity for killing, particularly as such a small portion, that is to say a third of the entire compensation, fell upon the killer; and therefore upon the authority of King Valdemar, the brother of the aforesaid King Knud, the most prudent men of Scania decreed by this most recent law to exterminate such evils so that the killer alone should be held liable to pay all the money in full for the crime of homicide from his own property and demand nothing from unwilling paternal or maternal kin, so that an innocent should not be burdened with the deed of the guilty person, and so that only the offender should bear the penalty owed for his offence, and that only he who actually committed the deed would be punished for his offences. In addition they decided that a man guilty of homicide should never and under no circumstances be permitted the benefit of paying off by compensation, unless he himself or someone on his behalf, if he could not come personally, immediately would offer compensation for his offence within the first three successive days after the homicide was committed, upon which men are gathered from the whole diocese to hear complaints in the general assembly.

Hoc autem si facere recusaret, sic indignus pace et patria et conuersacione hominum censeretur, ut quicumque ei contra iusticiam communicare presumeret, regi trium marcarum debitor redderetur, et haberet quilibet infligendi sibi necem, absque metu emendacionis cuiuspiam potestatem, non patente sibi euadendi tantarum calamitatum pericula facultate, nisi se prius a notis et patria per exilium elongaret, numquam de cetero rediturum, nisi a consanguineis interfecti et rege pariter promereri posset licenciam redeundi. Quicumque, principali reo iusticiam offerente uel contra iusticiam infra dyocesim remanente, de quouis consanguineorum ipsius sumeret ulcionem, pene consimili subiaceret; ipso autem in exilium migrante propter ipsius absenciam una satisfaccionis tercia deperibit, duabus residuis porcionibus tunc primo incumbentibus agnatis et cognatis hoc ordine ad soluendum, ut effugere possint periculum ulcionis. Post recessum occisoris primis tribus diebus continuis, ut ante diximus, ad audiendas querimonias deputatis, ipsius proximus de agnatis et proximus de cognatis uel eorum curatores uel procuratores, si fuerint inpuberes uel minores tanti negocii non capaces, offerant suam emendacionis singuli porcionem lege diffinito tempore persoluendam. Quo facto quicumque de ipsis uindictam sumpserit, penam senciet supradictam. Sin autem hoc exsequi supersederint, et de ipsis fuerit uindicatum, de sua negligencia conquerantur, quia sic uindicantes admitti possunt ad commodum emendacionis. Harum duarum hoc modo fieri debet composicio porcionum: tam agnati quam cognati, suis gradibus computatis, talis estimacionis moderamine imponant semper duplo maiorem partem priori gradui quam posteriori, ut utraque tercia per suos gradus ualeat consumari. Cum autem ad x denariorum summam peruentum fuerit, ultra ipsa computatio non descendit. Frater autem occisoris ex utroque parente coniunctus tam cum agnatis quam cum cognatis ad istam uocabitur rationem, tantum autem ex altero parente coniunctus sue partis onera subleuabit, eodem iudicio in gradibus ulterioribus obseruato. Interdum etiam occisori coniunctus isti non subiacet emendacioni, puta quando coniunctior est occiso; uerum equaliter utrumque consanguinitatis linea contingentes nullatenus excusantur, nisi forte, secundum antiquas leges, dandi recipiendique mensura eadem in eisdem locum habere persuadeat compensacionem. Post perpetratum homicidium quicumque natus fuerit, inuitus minime satisfaccionis grauamini subiacebit.

However, if he refuses to do this, he will be considered so unworthy of peace and country and human intercourse that whoever should presume to communicate with him contrary to the law will be obliged to pay three marks to the king; and anyone will have the power to inflict harm on him without the fear of paying any compensation whatsoever, and there shall be no way open to him to avoid such calamities unless he first went away from those he knew and from his country into exile, never thereafter to return unless he could acquire the right of return from the victim's family and the king. Any person who takes revenge upon any of the kinsmen after the principal perpetrator has either offered justice or remains in the diocese contrary to the law shall be subject to a similar penalty; if he himself is going into exile, one-third of the compensation will by his absence fall away, and the two remaining portions only will have to be paid by the paternal and maternal kin in this order, so that they may avoid the danger of revenge. Within the first three successive days of the assembly held after the killer's departure, which, as we have said before, are assigned to the hearing of complaints, his nearest paternal kinsmen and nearest maternal kinsmen, or their guardians or representatives if they are small children or minors incapable of such business, shall each offer their portion of the compensation, which is to be paid at the time determined by the law. When this has been done, whoever of them takes revenge will suffer the penalty mentioned earlier. If, however, they do not see to it that this is carried out, and vengeance is taken upon them, then they can blame themselves for their negligence, because thus the avengers will have the benefit of compensation. The composition of these two portions shall be made in such a way that the paternal kinsmen, as well as the maternal kinsmen, when their degrees of kinship have been calculated, always distribute the amount so that they impose twice as large a part upon the first degree than upon the next in order, so that both thirds are brought together by the respective degrees. Moreover, when you come down to the sum of ten pennies, the computation shall not be continued any further. The brother of the killer who is related on both sides shall be called to pay together with both paternal and maternal kinsmen, but he who is only related on one side shall only take part in the burden on that side, and the same will be observed in more distant grades. Sometimes it may happen that someone related to the killer does not have to contribute to the compensation, namely, when he is closer to the person killed; but those who belong to both families on the same level are in no way excused unless, according to the old laws, the fact that they will give and receive the same for the same recommends a set-off. He who is born after the homicide took place shall in no way unwillingly be burdened with compensation.

46. De sacramento iuratorie caucionis et iuramento equalitatis.

Statim post exhibitam emendacionis terciam exhiberi debet pariter et tercia iuratorie caucionis, quam lingua patria *thryd* appellat, in qua tantum 4^{or} nominati de consanguineis interfecti iurant de hiis, qui satisfecerint, uindictam de cetero cessaturam; nam plenam et integram caucionem xii constituunt nominati, habituram tunc demum locum, cum postremam emendacionis terciam reus exhibuerit principalis; quam caucionem semper debet precedere sacramentum, quod *jafhnethe eth* in lingua patria nominatur, uirorum xii nominatorum de consanguineis occisoris, qui, non sacris reliquiis, sed sacro coram posito tacto libro, iurant in suas animas, et sic sibi deum futurum propicium deprecantur, quod pro consimili delicto consimilem ad interuentum consanguineorum et amicorum ab aduersariis suis sumerent satisfaccionem; quando uero tantum 4^{or} admittuntur ad iuratoriam caucionem, ad equalitatis quoque iuramentum tantum sunt 4^{or} admittendi. Equalitatis autem tanto diligencius semper exigitur iuramentum, quod per ipsum, lesis ledentibus adequatis, auferri uideatur contemptus, qui perpessis iniuriam ex oppressione solet inferencium suscitari; pluris enim semper prudentes faciunt integritatem fame et honoris debiti restitucionem quam pecuniariam satisfactionem.

47. De distribucione.

Secundum antiqua iura sic est persolute pecunie distribucio facienda, ut, unaquaque tercia principali in tres tercias parciales diuisa, per uices singulas una semper parcialium cedat in commodum heredis occisi, et agnatis 2^{a}, cognatisque tercia debeatur, sic per agnatos omnes et cognatos distribucione pecunie facienda, ut semper prior gradus duplo maiorem partem quam posterior consequatur; si tota cederet heredis dominio satisfaccionis pars tercia principalis, heres ipse minus intenderet duabus aliis adquirendis, et sic contingeret agnatos et cognatos sibi debitis porcionibus defraudari; frequenter enim necligencius aliena negocia quam propria procurantur, nec libenter ibi quispiam fatigatur, ubi uel modicum uel nullum commodum expectatur.

Ch. 46 On the oath of surety and the oath of equality[37]

Immediately after the third payment of compensation has been made, the third oath of surety must also be given, the oath which in the native language is called *thrygd*, in which only four men nominated from the victim's kinsmen will swear that there shall be no revenge on those who have given compensation; and twelve nominated men constitute a full and entire surety, which will first take place when the main defendant pays the final third of the compensation, and this surety must always be preceded by the oath, which in the native language is called *jafhnethe eth*, of twelve men nominated from the kinsmen of the killer, who, not by touching sacred relics but with the holy book placed before them, swear by their souls and pray that God will have mercy on them and that for a similar crime they would accept compensation from their adversaries upon a similar intervention of their kinsmen and friends; but when only four are permitted for the oath of surety, only four are also to be permitted for the oath of equality. But the oath of equality is always very keenly required, because by placing those who have harmed on the same level as those who are harmed, it seems that the contempt is thus taken away which normally will affect those who accept the unlawful acts of oppressors; prudent men are namely always more interested in keeping their esteem and honour untouched than in economic compensation.

Ch. 47 On distribution.

According to the old law, the distribution of money that has been paid out is to be done so that each singular third principal part is divided into three different parts so that in turns one third of it will be given for the benefit of the heirs of the deceased, and the paternal kin will take the second and the maternal the third. Among all paternal and maternal kinsmen the division will happen so that the nearest degree will always receive double as much as the later degree; if the whole of the third principal part of the compensation was given to the heir, the heir might be less keen to acquire the two other parts, and the paternal and maternal kinsmen might thus be cheated of the portions due to them; for it is often so that the affairs of others are more negligently handled than our own, and nobody stresses himself willingly when only little or no benefit can be expected.

48. De temporibus faciende satisfaccionis.

Nunc uidendum, quibus temporibus sit emendacio facienda. Igitur ab illo tempore, quo successor occisi ad consenciendum oblate inducitur satisfaccioni, debet annus in tres equales diuidi prociones, ut, in trium parcium anni terminis tribus satisfaccionis tocius partibus persolutis, simul totus annus et tota satisfaccio consumentur. Nec pretereundum, quod ab abhibiti consensus tempore teneatur occisor summopere precauere, ne se suorum sic ingerat aduersariorum conspectui, ut propter suam presenciam offendantur, sed a domo et ecclesia et a uia, in quibus aduersarios suos esse deprehenderit, non spersedeat cum suis proximis declinare, donec tota fuerit satisfaccio cum suis solemnitatibus adimpleta. Est enim consentaneum rationi, ut, curatis per contraria contrariis, per humilitatem quisque studeat emendare, quod presumpsit per superbiam irrogare. Postremo sciendum, quod occisor ipse cum suis consanguineis uel, si defunctus fuerit, heres ipsius proximus uel tutor aut curator eius, si fuerit impubes aut minor, expetita prius licencia per consanguineos et amicos uel uie socios, ut se possit in iure hominum, quorum uniuersitatem in subtractione partis offendit, conspectui presentare, satisfaccionem teneatur offerre et suis temporibus, ut diximus, exhibere ipsius occisi proximo successori, consanguineorum suorum consorcio communito, ne fraus interueniat in pannorum et animalium estimacione, frequenter in partibus nostris supplencium argenti defectum, et ut plures sint hinc inde testes ad perhibendum testimonium ueritati, si forte fuerit factum in dubium reuocatum, et ne illi, quos tangit negocium, si exclusi fuerint, indignentur et sopitum malum nec ad plenum extinctum suscitare per conceptam in corde suo maliciam moliantur; efficaciores multociens sunt homines ad nocendum quam iuuandum, presertim in malo iam accenso, quod ex leui flatu edacis inuidie magnum frequenter suscipit incrementum. Heres occisi quando ad consenciendum oblacioni prestande satisfaccionis inducitur uel ad diem prefigendum, in quo iuxta consilium consanguineorum suorum super hoc debeat respondere, debet aduersariis suis interim pacem promittere et eandem, in signum indissolubilis firmitatis contingendo manu sua manum alicuius alterius, roborare, et hoc facto ad maiorem securitatem aliquis de prudencioribus debet pacis illius deum custodem et fautorem cum sanctis omnibus, cum apostolico, cum rege, cum pontifice, cum iustis omnibus inuocare, execrari uero quemlibet et anathematizare, qui promisse paci presumpserit obuiare.

Ch. 48 On the time for paying compensation.

Now we shall see at what time compensation shall be paid. From the time when the successor to the person killed is induced to accept the compensation that has been offered, the year shall be divided into three equal parts, so that when all three parts of the compensation have been paid at the three terms of the year, the entire year and the entire compensation are brought to an end at the same time. Nor shall it be omitted that from the time when consent is given, the killer shall take the utmost care not to come into the sight of his adversaries so that they can be offended by his presence, but he shall not omit to stay away from the home and church and road where he is informed that his adversaries can be found until the entire compensation with all its formalities has been completed. It seems to be well in accordance with reason, that as opposites are cured by their opposite,[38] so also every man by showing humility may try to remedy what he has caused by his pride. Finally it must be noted that the killer himself with his kinsmen, or if he is dead, his nearest heir or his guardian or supervisor,[39] if he is under age or a minor,[40] shall ask first by means of kinsmen or friends or fellow travellers for permission to present himself in the sight of those whose community he has offended by bereaving it of a member, and he shall be obliged to pay compensation and to pay it on the terms which we have described to the nearest heir, who shall be accompanied by his kinsmen, both in order that no fraud is made as to the valuation of cloth and cattle, which in our country often have to substitute for silver, and in order that there can be more witnesses on both sides to give reliable testimony if what happened should be cast into doubt, and finally in order that those who are affected by the case shall not be offended by being kept out and, as a consequence of the evil which they are housing in their souls, ponder upon having the mitigated but not entirely extinguished evil blow up in flame. Often indeed men are more active in harming than in doing good, especially when the question is about some evil already glowing, which often can be mightily augmented by a light breath of envy. When the heirs of the deceased are willing to give their consent to the offer of compensation to be paid or to the fixed day on which according to the advice of his kinsmen he shall answer, he shall guarantee his adversaries peace for the time being and confirm it by grasping the hand of one of the others as a token of unbreakable firmness; and when that has happened, for the sake of even more security, one of the leading men of the assembly[41] shall pray that God and all the Saints, the Pope, the King, the Bishop and all just men will protect and guard it and curse and excommunicate all who might dare to disturb in any way the peace promised.

Non est hoc eciam transeundum, quod quotcumque uulnera inflixerit aut quotcumque fustium ictus intulerit qui occisus fuerat occisori, tantum unam marcam argenti tantum unius uulneris ratione, fide prius facta duodeno iuramento, quod inflictum fuerit ei uulnus ab occiso, uel tantum duas marcas argenti propter unum ictum fustium, inde prius fide facta per xxiiii hominum iuramenta, in exhibicione tandem partis ultime satisfaccionis occisor sibi poterit retinere. Hec autem locum habent de uno uulnere uel uno ictu illato tempore interfeccionis; sed si super uulnere uel ictu alia illato tempore uel super pluribus uulneribus aut uulnerum aut uerberum deformitatibus accusare uoluerit interfectum, heres, si noluerit, ut satisfaciat, confiteri, secundum imposti sibi mensuram criminis cum iuramentalibus se defendet, uel ante postreme tercie solucionem, ut inter eos omnes simul querimonie sopiantur, uel post omnem prestitam satisfaccionem. Heres quoque occisi si de satisfaccione conqueratur aliquid remanere, occisor, se totum asserens exsoluisse, semper quamlibet trium marcarum peticionem duodeno elidet uirorum negancium iuramento, donec duodenarius iuramentorum fuerit triplicatus; deinde non augebitur iuramentorum numerus, quantumcumque supra nouem excreuerit marcarum peticio debitarum. Quidam tamen uolunt in odium homicide, ut de cuiuslibet tercie totalis satisfaccionis solucione cum duobus testibus et iuramentorum duodenario triplicato fidem facere teneatur, ut, si heres occisi conqueratur de satisfaccione nihil penitus exsolutum, et occisor econtra se totum asserat exsoluisse, occisor ad faciendam fidem assercioni sue primo die ad hoc a iuridicis constituto producat duos testes et iuramentalium duodenarium triplicatum pro prime tercie solucione, et tam 2° quam tercio die tam testes totidem quam iuramentales tam pro secunde quam pro tercie partis solucione producere non omittat; ut uno autem et eodem die sex testes producat et nouies duodenum exhibeat iuramentum, lex non precipit, ne pocius propter impossibile uel nimis difficile legis preceptum quam propter iniustam causam succumbere compellatur. At in aliis uniuersis casibus sufficit duodenarius triplicatus, licet summa centum marcarum uel plurium requiratur. Propter solum homicidium pro facto nocentis innocentes consanguinei satisfacere compelluntur. Si corpus occisi uestimentis suis uel armis, quod crimen *walruf* in lingua patria nominatur, accusetur aliquis spoliasse, si diffiteatur factum accusatus, confirmet negacionem suam manus duodecime iuramento. Si uero fateatur, res ablatas restituat et tres marcas insuper emendet heredi.

It shall not be omitted that regardless of the number of strokes by a rod the deceased may have given the killer, he can, when the last part of the compensation is paid, keep for himself one mark of silver for one wound, and not more, and only after he has first proved by an oath of twelve that the deceased had given him the wound, or two marks of silver for one stroke after having first proved that by an oath of twenty-four. This is the procedure when one wound or one stroke is given at the time when the killing took place; if, however, he will accuse the deceased of more wounds or disfigurement caused by wounds or strokes, then the heir, if he does not agree that he shall pay compensation for that, must defend himself with oath givers according to the seriousness of the crime which he is accused of, either before the payment of the last third, in order that all claims among them can be settled at once, or after the entire compensation has been paid. If, furthermore, the heir of the deceased complains that some of the compensation has not been paid and the killer claims that he has paid it all, then he shall deny the claim for every three marks by an oath of twelve until the oath of twelve has been three times doubled. After that the number of oaths shall not be augmented any more, no matter how much the amount owed may surpass nine marks. Out of hatred towards the killer, however, some want that he shall be obliged with two witnesses and a triple oath of twelve to prove payment of each third of the collected compensation so that if the heirs should complain that no part of the compensation has been paid and the killer on his side claims that he has paid it all, then the killer shall prove his claim by producing two witnesses and three times the oath of twelve for the payment of the first third on the first day fixed by the men of the assembly for that, and on the second and the third day he shall not omit to bring just as many witnesses and oath givers for the payment of the second and third parts. But it is not prescribed by the law that he should produce six witnesses and give nine times an oath of twelve on one and the same day in order that he shall not give up due to a demand of the law which is impossible or all too difficult to comply with rather than an unjust case. But in all cases an oath of three times twelve is sufficient, even if the sum of a hundred marks or more is demanded. It is only in the case of homicide that the innocent kinsmen are forced to pay for the actions of the guilty person.[42] If someone is accused of having taken from the body of the deceased his clothing or weapon, which crime in our native language is called *walruf*, and he denies having done it, the accused shall confirm his denial by an oath of twelve. But if he confesses, he shall return the things taken and on top of that pay three marks to the heir.

49. De homicida, qui certam non habet habitacionem.

Homicida non habens certam aliquam habitacionem, et presertim incognitus, sic dabit operam emendacioni, ut et amicorum obtineat interuentu ad offerendum satisfaccionem licenciam apparendi, et eorundem fideiussione de satisfaccionis exhibicione mereatur, ut sua peticio sorciatur effectum. Uno uero confesso legitime et in iure super homicidii perpetracione, non debet alius super eodem homicidio conueniri. Accusatus super homicidio si, quod imponitur sibi, confiteatur suum mancipium perpetrasse, tribus iuramentalium duodenis se primo studeat expurgare, deinde pro delicto serui sui condignam exhibeat satisfaccionem. Si tamen in presencia patrisfamilias uel filiifamilias, ad hoc cooperantis uel facto uel precepto, seruus homicidium perpetrauerit, et hoc constiterit per ipsius patrisfamilias confessionem uel alio modo legitimo, ipse paterfamilias, non pro seruo, sed pro suo uel filii sui nomine, ad plenam homicidii tenebitur emendacionem; ipse quidem, qui cooperatur seruo et auctoritatem ad hoc prestat, ut plenarie pro se satisfaciat, fecisse uidetur.

50. De homicidio, quod facit seruus.

Pro serui homicidio semper, cum sex marcis numorum, ad arbitrium et eleccionem domini uel noxe dandus est seruus ipse, uel tribus marcis numorum noxe dedicio redimenda. Secundum quorundam sentenciam, ubicumque liber homo ex facto proprio ad xl marcarum constringitur emendacionem, ibi ad satisfaccionem nouem marcarum uel sex marcarum cum noxe dedicione serui ex facto serui dominus obligatur. Sed rex Waldemarus noluit consentire, ut ultra trium marcarum satisfaccionem, nisi quando perimitur liber homo, pro serui facto in liberum suus dominus obligetur.

51. De satisfaccione pro mancipio interfecto suscipienda.

Tribus marcis numorum pro mancipio interfecto secundum antiqua iura domino persoluendis secundum noua iura tantum debet occisor apponere, ut secure duodeno possit astruere iuramento interfectum mancipium nihil ultra satisfaccionis precium ualuisse. Post exhibitam tamen huiusmodi satisfaccionem nullum caucionis uel equalitatis requiritur iuramentum.

Ch. 49 On a killer who has no certain dwelling.

A killer who has no certain dwelling, and especially a stranger, shall see to it that he pays compensation in such a way that he, by having friends to go between, gets permission to appear and offer compensation and, by his friends who guarantee the payment of compensation, can arrange that his petition is accepted. And when a man in the assembly has confessed in the proper way that he has committed the homicide, then no one else shall be summoned for the same homicide. If someone accused of homicide claims that what is imputed to him was done by his slave, then he shall first try to purge himself by the oath of three times twelve men and then pay the compensation due for an offence by a slave. If, however, the slave has committed the homicide in the presence of the householder or his son so that they have been his companions either by advice or by action, and this is proven by the confession of the householder himself or in another lawful way, then the householder shall pay full compensation for the homicide not on behalf of his slave but on behalf of himself or his son; by collaborating with the slave and giving him the order to do it, he himself indeed seems to have acted in such a way that he must pay the full compensation.[43]

Ch. 50 On homicide committed by a slave.

For homicide committed by a slave at the will and choice of the master, always together with six marks in money, either the slave himself is to be given as noxal[44] surrender or noxal surrender be avoided by three marks in money. According to the opinion of some, in all those cases where a free man is forced to pay compensation of forty marks for his own act, a master is liable by a slave's act to pay compensation of nine marks, or six marks together with the noxal surrender of the slave. But King Valdemar would not agree to the master being obliged to pay for his servant's act towards a free man more than three marks as compensation, unless a free man loses his life.[45]

Ch. 51 On the compensation to be received for the homicide of a slave.

In addition to the three marks in money due to the master for the homicide of a slave according to the old laws, the killer must, according to the new laws, pay such an amount that he can safely prove by an oath of twelve that the slave killed was not worth more than the price of compensation.[46] However, after the payment of such compensation, no oath of surety or equality will be required.

52. Quod duplo minor satisfactio prestatur pro liberto quam pro ingenuo.

Duplo minor pro homicidio liberti, ab eo uel in eo commisso, prestatur satisfaccio quam pro homicidio ingenui, ex uentre libero procreati, ab eo recipienda uel prestanda, qui eum, cum in iure libertate donaretur, suo generi sociauit et se pro factis ipsius annuit responsurum, satisfaccionis tamen illius tantum tercia uel bonis ipsius adicienda uel de bonis prestanda, ipsi liberto reliquis duabus terciis uel ad retinendum attinentibus uel prestandum; a quo si non potest alias satisfacere, tribus annis continuis uniuersa, que possidet, usque ad cingulum auferantur, aut si talem tolerare recusauerit satisfaccionem uite sue consulere per fuge presidium non omittat; et hec emendacio in uulgari nostro *lindabot* apellatur. Ad idem quoque tenebitur, sibi soli toto satisfaccionis onere incumbente, puta cum nec liberum quemquam habet consanguineum, nec ab aliquo, sicut ante diximus, in consanguineum est susceptus. Ubi uero quisquam super hoc conuentus fuerit, quod libertum in cognatum susceperit, negacioni sue duodeno fidem faciat iuramento. At ubi, aliis inficiantibus, hoc de se quispiam confessus fuerit, aut quod sibi attineat ex coniunccione sanguinis satisfaccio pro liberto, assertioni sue debet duobus testibus et duodeno fidem facere iuramento.

53. Si arbor succisa quempiam occiderit.

Arbor cesa si quempiam ad mortem oppresserit, incisores heredi proximo tribus marcis numorum huiusmodi euentus infortunium emendabunt. At si casu fortuito lignum lapsum de manu cuiuspiam quemquam ad mortem percusserit, qui tenebat ad integram homicidii tenebitur emendacionem.

54. Quid iuris sit, si quis in puteum specialem alicuius uel in communem omnibus lapsus fuerit.

Siquis in puteum lapsus uitam finiuerit, trium marcarum solucio ad dominum ipsius putei pertinebit. Si uero puteus uniuersorum ciuium communis fuerit, nihil erit hoc nomine persoluendum.

Ch. 52 That half as much is paid in compensation for a freedman as for a freeborn man.

Half as much is paid in compensation for the homicide of a freedman, be it committed by him or against him, than for the homicide of a freeborn man, born by a free woman. The compensation must be received or paid by him who took him into his family when freedom was given at the assembly and who promised to be responsible for his acts; however, of the compensation only a third is either to be added to his property or paid from his property, whereas the remaining two-thirds should be kept or paid by the freedman himself; if he cannot pay in other ways during the three following years everything that he owns down to his belt shall be taken away from him, or, if he refuses to accept the burden of such compensation, he shall not omit to save his life with the help of flight: and this compensation is called *lindabot* [47] in our common language. And he will be obliged to the same if all the compensation is incumbent upon him alone, for instance when he has neither any freeborn kinsman nor has been taken into kinship by someone as mentioned earlier. When someone is summoned for having taken the freedman as kinsman, he shall deny it by an oath of twelve. But when, against the denying of others, someone maintains this with regard to himself, or compensation for a freedman pertains to him due to family relation, he must make an oath as to his assertion with two witnesses and an oath of twelve.

Ch. 53 If a tree that has been cut down kills someone.

If a tree that was cut down crushes someone to death, those who cut it down shall compensate his nearest heir with three marks in money for a calamitous outcome of this sort. [48] And if by accident a piece of wood has slipped from someone's hand and strikes someone to death, he who was holding it will be liable for the entire compensation for homicide.

Ch. 54 What the law is if someone falls into someone's private well or into one that is common to everyone.

If anyone ends his life after having fallen into a well, payment of three marks will be made by the owner of the well. If, however, the well was common to all of the villagers, [49] there will be nothing to pay on this account.

55. Que sit iuris distancia, utrum ferocis an mitis nature animalia, agrestia tamen, sed domita, alicui uulnus siue mortem intulerint.

Pro illata morte ab animalibus quadrupedibus uel uolatilibus, que, cum essent indomita et naturaliter uitarent hominum conuersacionem, assumpta sunt tamen ad domandum, tantum assumens secundum antiquas leges persoluere tenetur, quantum si facinus in propria persona commisisset; pro morte autem cuiquam illorum illata, si soluta incederent, nichil esset penitus exsoluendum; at si huiusmodi animali detento in uinculis mors a quolibet inferretur, animalis domino tantum ab occisore contemptus precium deberetur. Secundum nouam uero regis Waldemari constitucionem pro illata morte ab illis animalibus, que atrocis sunt nature, ut ursus, lupus, aper et aquila et huiusmodi, tantum nouem marce numorum ab eorum domino sunt prestande, et tres marce pro uulnere, si ab eorum aliquo illud constiterit inflictum fuisse. Ceterum pro morte illata uel inflicto uulnere ab illis, que miciorem habent naturam, ut ceruus et accipiter, tantum tres marcas dominus eorum persoluet.

56. Si bos uel equus uel canis hominem occiderit.

Pro morte cuiquam illata uel a boue uel equo uel cane uel quouis alio, quod mansuetam naturam et cum hominibus conuersacionem habeat, animali, tres tantum marce denariorum a domino prestabuntur. Quicumque uero tale aliquod factum negare uoluerit, negacionem suam probet manus duodecime iuramento; confessus uero eo nomine regi uel antistiti nil persoluet.

57. De occulto homicidio.

Nullo uolente reatum homicidii confiteri, hominis occisi proximus tribus diebus iuridicis in communi audiencia coram omnibus in iure de criminis inquirat auctore, et eum sibi deposcat instancius indicari; qui si non fuerit indicatus, excommunicacionis gladio percellatur. Hiis peractis, duobus diebus iterum in iure coram omnibus illum, quem suspectum habuerit, reum deferat homicidii perpetrati; deinde in ius faciat eundem citari, sibi tercio die iuridico super homicidio responsurum, ibique sex testibus ad minus fulciatur, duobus, qui super legitime facta citacione possint testimonium perhibere, duobus, qui testificentur diem illum esse tercium illorum, quibus in iure fuerat accusacio celebrata, duobus, qui suo affirment testimonio accusatum uere sibi crimen impositum commisisse.

Ch. 55 What difference the law makes whether animals are of a ferocious or a mild nature, wild but nonetheless tamed, and cause a wound or death to someone.

For death caused by a four-legged or winged creature, which, even if they are undomesticated and by nature avoid contact with men, nevertheless have been caught for the purpose of domestication, the person taking them is obliged according to the old laws to pay as much as if he had committed the act himself; however, for the death of any one of these animals absolutely nothing is to be paid if they were walking around unfettered; but if someone kills an animal of this kind held in chains, only a fine for contempt will be owed by the killer to the owner of the animal. According to a later statute by King Valdemar, only nine marks in money are to be paid by their owner for death caused by those animals which are of a savage nature, such as a bear, wolf, boar and eagle or something similar,[50] and three marks for a wound, if a wound has been inflicted by any of them. On the other hand, with regard to death or wounds caused by those which are of a milder nature, such as roes or hawks, their owner shall only pay three marks.

Ch. 56 When an ox, a horse or a dog kills a man.

For death caused to anyone either by an ox or a horse or a dog or by any other animal that has a tame nature and is in contact with men, only three marks in money will be paid by the animal's owner.[51] Anyone who wishes to deny such a deed shall do it by an oath of twelve; he who has confessed shall pay nothing on this account to the king or the bishop.

Ch. 57 On concealed homicide.

When no one will confess to the crime of homicide committed, the kinsman closest to the man who was killed shall on three days when the assembly is gathered to the attention of everybody present ask who did it and demand that he instantly makes himself known to him; and if he is not identified, he shall be struck by the sword of excommunication. When this has been done, the kinsman shall then on two further days before everyone at the assembly accuse the one he holds under suspicion as guilty of the homicide committed; then he shall on the third assembly day have him summoned to the assembly to answer for himself concerning the homicide, and there he shall be supported by at least six witnesses: two who can testify that the summons were lawful, two who will testify that the day is the third of those on which the accusation was proclaimed, two who by their testimony will affirm that the accused in fact committed the crime imputed to him.

75

Ubi si reus factum inficiando comparuerit, negacionem suam probare tantum ferri candentis iudicio permittatur, quod in lingua patria *scuz iern* inde meruit appellari, quod ipsum, postquam uestigiis nouem processerit, iactare portitor teneatur. Si uero citatus noluerit comparere, accusator obtineat, ut pacis commodo suus aduersarius communi iudicio denudetur; nec, ut iudicium istud ferri subeat accusatus, accusatoris oportet precedere iuramentum super imposti homicidii ueritate, quod *asswerueth* in lingua patria nominatur. Post hoc si presenciam suam adhuc 4° die iuris exhibeat accusatus, accusatore non habente testes ad probandum celebrate in prioribus diebus ordinem accusacionis, duodeno fidem faciens iuramento se uenire nullatenus potuisse uel minus legitime citatum fuisse, pacem obtineat, quam amisit. Si uero testes habeat accusator, amissam pacem restitui sibi reus nullatenus sine predicti candentis ferri iudicio mereatur, et si per ferrum candens pacem obtineat, pro causa nichilominus principali subire iterato ferri predicti iudicium compellatur, quamuis non debeat accusatoris, ut predictum est, precedere iuramentum. Sin autem prioris ferri candentis iudicio conuincatur exustus, in principali causa succubuisse pariter censeatur. At si reus obtinuerit utrobique, permittatur heres adhuc octo uiros eodem ordine, singulos singulis uicibus, accusare. Postremo, si nullus eorum conuictus fuerit, decimum eodem ordine accusatum hoc modo ad calcandum uomeres ardentes compellat, ut iuret cum uiris xii, quod nec lucri nec odii causa ei homicidii reatum imponant, sed quia uere sciunt eum illud homicidium perpetrasse; illorum xii ad minus quilibet sex marcas in facultatibus habere tenetur, ut si calcatis uomeribus inculpabilis et innocens apparuerit qui calcauit, ad soluendum tres marcas illi et tres marcas antistiti eorum quilibet compellatur.

58. Quod non solum homicida, sed etiam qui comites exstiterint, pecunia multentur.

Non solum homicidii principales auctores, uerum quoque comites rex Kanutus sua dignum duxit persequi constitucione, sic animaduertens in quemuis homicide comitem, ut pro comitatu solo in tribus marcis regi et in tribus marcis heredi occisi comes quilibet, quamuis consanguineus occisoris, satisfacere teneatur; quicumque uero deneget comitatum, negacionem suam duodeno corroboret iuramento. Si quis uero comitum accusetur, quod uulnus inflixerit interfecto, si duos super hoc testes habeat accusator, accusatus tantum ferri candentis iudicio se defendat; si uero testes deficiant, falsum esse, quod imponitur sibi, probet tribus iuramentalium duodenis. Si uero inflictionem fateatur uulneris, tantum tres marcas emendet regi, sed heredi pro uulnere nouem marcas.

If the accused appears there in order to deny the act, he shall be allowed to prove his denial with the proof of hot iron, which in the native language is called *scuz iern* because after having taken nine steps he who carries the iron shall throw it. If, however, the man summoned does not appear, the accuser can obtain that his adversary by a general decision is bereft of the benefit of peace; and in order to have the accused subjected to the iron proof it is not necessary that it is preceded by the oath of the accuser on the truth of the accusation of homicide, which in the native language is called *asswerueth*. If after this the accused does appear on the fourth day and the accuser does not have witnesses to testify the procedure followed on the foregoing days, the accused can recover the peace that was taken from him by an oath of twelve that he was unable to come or that he was summoned in a less lawful way. If, however, the accuser has witnesses, then the accused cannot recover the peace taken from him without the aforementioned proof of iron, and even if by carrying iron he recovers his peace, he is forced to subject himself to the aforementioned iron again in the main case, but the oath of the accuser, as mentioned before, need not precede it. If, however, he is defeated and burnt by the proof of hot iron, he shall also be considered to have lost the main case. But if the accused wins on both occasions, the heir shall be permitted to accuse another eight men one at a time following the same procedure. At last, if none of them is convicted, he can compel a tenth accused to walk upon glowing ploughshares if he swears with twelve men that they do not accuse him for the sake of gain or hate but because they really know that he has committed the homicide; those twelve must possess a fortune of at least six marks, because if he who walks on glowing ploughshares comes out without guilt and as innocent, they can be forced to pay him three marks and three marks to the archbishop.

Ch. 58 That not only the killer but also companions are fined.

In his statute King Knud held not only the main perpetrator of a killing worthy of prosecution but also their companions, and regarding the companion in whatever homicide he decreed, that for merely being in the company any companion, even if he is a kinsman of the killer, must pay three marks to the king and three marks to the heir of the victim; he who denies that he was in the company shall strengthen his denial by an oath of twelve. If anyone is accused of having been in the company and having inflicted a wound on the victim, and the accuser has two witnesses to this, then the accused must defend himself with the ordeal by hot iron; if witnesses are lacking, he can prove the accusations against him false by three oaths of twelve. If he confesses to infliction of the wound, he shall pay only three marks to the king, but nine marks to the heir of the victim.

59. Si quis aliquem occiderit in domo propria uel in agro uel in aliquo loco in campo, ubi sibi quietis hospicium elegerit.

Si quis aggrediatur aliquem uiolenter et occidat eum uel in eius domo uel in agricultura uel in campo, ubi uel fixa lancea uel sella posita uel erecto clipeo sibi hospicium quietis elegit, preter iustam homicidii satisfaccionem quadraginta marcas regi et quadraginta marcas de bonis propriis persoluet consanguineis interfecti. At quisquis comitum tres marcas regi et tres marcas consanguineis emendabit.

60. Quid iuris sit, si quis domum cuiuspiam uiolenter confregerit.

Si quis cum comitibus quinque et armis quinque, que *folcwapn* in lingua patria nominantur, alicuius domum uiolenter confringat, et inde quamlibet rem asportet, si super hoc cum testibus duobus fuerit accusatus, tantum candentis ferri iudicio se defendet. Si uero testes defuerint, factum cum tribus iuramentorum inficiabitur duodenis. Si uero defensio iusta defecerit, uel reatum reus sponte confessus fuerit, tam regi quam aduersario in xl^ta marcis obligabitur persoluendis.

61. Qui sunt excessus, quorum auctores perpetua pace priuantur.

Quorundam excessuum magnitudo deposcit, ut eorum auctores pacis perpetuo quiete priuentur, puta si post homicidium quis offerre renuat satisfaccionem; si post prestitam emendacionem sumatur uindicta; si per homicidium cimiterium uioletur; si turbata pace coram omnibus in iure mors cuiquam inferatur; si sponsa cuiquam per uiolenciam auferatur; si coniunx cuiuspiam uel mater uel soror uel filia ob stupri turpitudinem rapiatur; si hospes a domino uel ab hospite in domo propria domus dominus occidatur; siquis uoluntarie ignem imponat domui aliene, ut ad iniuriam et dampnum domini domus incendio consumatur; si presente rege et in dyocesi commorante quis presumat homicidium perpetrare, secundum nouam a rege Waldemaro editam constitucionem; uerum pro uulnere tune inflicto xl marce regi et xl marce prestande sunt uulnerato.

62. Quod omnia mobilia delinquentis priuati pace ad regem pertineant, uel eciam immobilia, si lese crimen imponitur maiestatis.

Ubicumque propter reatum suum a iuridicis in iure pacis commodo priuatur delinquens, ad regem pertinet quidquid de mobilibus delinquentem contingit; in quodam tamen casu eciam immobilia bona cum mobilibus adiudicanda sunt regie maiestati, puta quando quis ad impugnandum regem regnum eius hostiliter intrare presumit.

Ch. 59 If anyone kills someone in his own home or in the field or in some other place in the countryside where he has chosen a quiet place for himself.
If anyone attacks someone violently and kills him either in his house or while he is cultivating his field or in the countryside, where he has chosen a quiet place for himself[52] by planting his spear, setting down his saddle or erecting his shield, he shall, in addition to just compensation for homicide, pay forty marks to the king and forty marks of his own property to the kinsmen of the victim. But each of his companions shall pay three marks to the king and three marks to the kinsmen.

Ch. 60 How to proceed when someone violently breaks into someone's house.
If anyone, with five companions and those five weapons which in the native language are called *folcwapn*,[53] breaks into someone's house and carries any property away from there, and if he is accused of this with two witnesses, he can defend himself only with the ordeal by hot iron. If witnesses are lacking, he can deny the deed by three times twelve oaths. If the legal defence does not work for him, or if the person accused voluntarily confesses to the crime, he will have to pay forty marks to the king as well as to the opposing party.

Ch. 61 What the offences are whose perpetrators are perpetually deprived of peace.
The seriousness of certain offences demands that their perpetrators are deprived of the quietness of peace in perpetuity, as, for instance, if someone refuses to offer compensation after a homicide; if revenge is taken after compensation has been paid; if a cemetery is violated by homicide; if death is inflicted on someone in front of everyone at the assembly thus disturbing the peace; if someone's bride is carried off by violence; if the wife or mother, sister or daughter of someone else is taken away for the foul purpose of sexual intercourse; if a guest is killed by his host or the host is killed by a guest in his own house; if anyone on purpose sets fire to the house of another person so the house is consumed by fire to the injury and loss of the owner; if someone presumes to commit homicide when the king is present and sojourning in the diocese, according to a recent statute by King Valdemar; and for a wound that has been inflicted on such an occasion, forty marks are to be paid to the king and forty marks to the wounded.

Ch. 62 That all movable property of an offender who has lost his peace belongs to the king, and even his immovable property in the case of high treason.
Whenever an offender is deprived of the benefit of his peace by the men of the assembly because of his crime, the movable belongings of the offender belong to the king; however, in a certain case both the immovable property and the movable property are to be awarded to the royal majesty,[54] namely when someone presumes to enter his realm as an enemy in order to attack the king.

79

63. Que iniqua consilia quibusmodis emendari debent.

In tribus tantum casibus potest quis pro iniquo consilio conueniri, puta si reus deferatur, ut ille, de cuius morte agitur, ipsius consilio fuerit interfectus, aut quod funiculo ignominiose consilio ipsius fuerit quis ligatus, aut quod ad inuadendum possessiones alicuius iniuste et diripiendum bona ipsius diues et prepotens inductus fuerit, cui non esset tutum resistere aut propter generis claritatem aut officii dignitatem, qualem *hetwarthreman* in lingua patria nominamus. In primo casu nouem marcis reatum consilii emendabit, aut accusacioni tres iuramentorum obiciet duodenas; in utroque posteriori casu aut tres marcas persoluet, aut duodeno se negabit dedisse consilium iuramento.

64. De uerberacione et uulneracione et iniuriis et aliis molestiis, que infliguntur libero homini uel seruo uel bruto alicui animali.

Propter uarietatem uulnerancium et uarietatem uulneratorum et uarietatem uulnerum et modos uarios infligendi et uarietatem instrumentorum ledendi uariari necesse est pro uulnerum inflictione satisfaccionem pariter et defensionem.

65. Quid iuris sit, si liber homo ledat liberum hominem uel aliquam iniuriam inferat.

Igitur liber homo uulnerat liberum hominem, uulnerat seruum, uulnerat et animal brutum. Eodem modo seruus uulnerat liberum hominem, uulnerat seruum, uulnerat animal brutum. Eodem modo brutum animal uulnerat liberum hominem, uulnerat seruum, uulnerat et animal brutum. Quando igitur liber homo uulnerat liberum hominem, interdum uulnus infligitur sine membri cuiuslibet amputacione, interdum membrum eciam amputatur. Ubi uulnus infligitur sine membri detruncacione, aut descendit in concauum et ad interiora penetrat aut non. Si non descendat, quod uulnus in lingua patria *wathwasar* apellatur, trium marcarum exigit satisfaccionem, et si uulnus negetur, confirmabitur per duodenum negacio iuramentum. Si uero descendit ad interiora, puta in capite usque ad cerebrum, in pectore usque ad iecur uel pulmonem, in uentre usque ad uiscera, quod uulnus *holsar* dicitur in uulgari, duplo maiorem et satisfaccionem exigit et defensionem; idem obseruandum est, ubicumque telum ita pertransit partem aliquam, quod in carne duas facit aperturas. Hec autem locum habent, ubi caret testibus accusator. At ubi duos testes habet inflicti uulneris, secundum nouam regis Kanuti felicis memorie constitucionem accusatus tantum ad candentis ferri iudicium admittetur. Sciendum preterea, quod pro quolibet osse, quod fuerit extractum de uulnere, donec v ossa extracta fuerint, preter uulneris emendacionem sint xxx denarii emendandi; hoc quoque sciendum est, quod uulnerum huiusmodi accusacio solutis v marcis argenti uel xv marcis nummorum, quotcumque fuerint inflicta uulnera, finiatur.

Ch. 63 Which wicked advice should be compensated and how.

In only three cases can someone be sued for wicked advice; namely, if the defendant is accused because the man, whose death the case concerns, was killed on his advice, or because someone was disgracefully bound with a rope on his advice or because a rich and influential man was induced to invade someone's possessions illegally and plunder his property – a man of the sort we call *hetwarthre man* in the native language, whom it is not safe to resist either because of the distinction of his family or the dignity of his office. In the first case he must pay nine marks for the crime, or he must answer the accusation with three times twelve oaths; in both of the latter cases he must either pay three marks or deny that he gave the advice by an oath of twelve.

Ch. 64 On beating and wounding and injuries and other annoyances that are inflicted upon a free man or a slave or some brute animal.

Because of the variety of aggressors, the variety of victims, the variety of wounds, the ways of inflicting them and the variety of instruments of doing harm, it is also necessary to vary the compensation and the defence.

Ch. 65 How to proceed if a free man harms a free man or causes any injury.

So a free man can wound a free man, he can wound a slave and he can wound a brute animal. In the same way, a slave can wound a free man, he can wound a slave and he can wound a brute animal. And in the same way a brute animal can wound a free man, it can wound a slave and it can wound a brute animal. Accordingly, when a free man wounds a free man, sometimes the wound is inflicted without cutting off any of his limbs and sometimes a member is cut off. When a wound is inflicted without the maiming of a member, either it sinks deeply into a concavity and penetrates to the interior or not. If it does not penetrate, for the type of wound called *wathwasar* in the native language, compensation of three marks is demanded, and if the wound is denied, the denial must be confirmed by an oath of twelve. If, however, it penetrates into the interior, for example, into the head as far as the brain, into the chest as far as the liver or lung, into the belly as far as the entrails – the type of wound called *holsar* in the common language – then twice as much is demanded in compensation and defence; the same is to be observed whenever a missile pierces some part in such a way that it makes two openings in the flesh. This applies when the accuser lacks witnesses. But when he has two witnesses to the wound that has been inflicted, then according to the new statute of King Knud of blessed memory, the accused is only granted the ordeal by hot iron. Moreover it is worth noticing that for each bone that is extracted from the wound until five bones are extracted, thirty pennies are to be paid on top of the compensation for the wound; it is also worth noticing that, regardless of the number of wounds inflicted, there can be no more accusations for wounds of this kind when five marks of silver or fifteen marks in money have been paid.

Quia sepe monete precium uariatur et modo uilior et modo carior reputatur, statutum est, ut semper pro tribus marcis numorum, que nominantur in satisfaccione, sit una marca argenti uel ipsius estimacio in solucione, in superiori uel inferiori summa semper eadem proporcione inter argentum et denarios obseruata; hoc tamen ad episcopale ius uel regium non procedit, ubi ad summam numorum debitam minuendam supplicacionibus pocius quam allegacionibus est utendum.

In menbrorum abscisione refert, quod membrum fuerit amputatum; quorum enim amputatio maiorem generat deformitatem, ampliorem requirit eciam emendacionem. Unde cum amputatio nasi plurimum hominem dedeceat et deformet, statutum est, ut homicidio in emendacione debeat adequari. De lingue quoque, qua carere plurimum est dampnosum, idem est iudicium amputacione. Item eadem, que pro homicidio, satisfaccio est prestanda, si ambo oculi eruantur, si ambe manus abscindantur, si ambo pedes cuiquam amputentur, si uirilia resecentur; duplo autem minus pro unius tantum quam duorum prestabitur amputacione. Est tamen unum de uirilibus, cuius abscisio debet homicidio comparari. Multi enim magis mortem eligerent, quam post amissionem menbrorum uitam ducerent ignominiosam. Unius item manus abscisio in emendacione homicidio duplo minor est, amputacione pollicis duplo maior, item pollicis satisfaccio duplo maior indicis satisfaccione. Sed ulterius ista subduplacio non procedit, ne pro uulnere minor quam trium marcarum numorum uel unius marce argenti satisfaccio debeatur. Licet autem uno ictu plures digiti uel plures partes corporis uulnerentur, uniuscuiusque tamen digiti uulnus, quantumcumque modicum, trium marcarum exigit emendacionem. Ubicumque autem ipso uulnere maior, secundum prudencium uirorum estimacionem a die uulneris post annum et diem factam, deformitas iudicatur, ibi solius deformitatis estimacio est prestanda. Ex eo autem articulorum et aurium minor debet deformitas iudicari, quod operti pannis et crinibus oculorum aspectibus subtrahuntur.

Duplo minus pro manu uel pede uel quolibet membro tali prestabitur, licet prorsus inutili ex inflicto uulnere, si qualitercumque corpori dependens adhereat, quam si penitus a corpore separetur. Item a libero si liber homo fuste aliquo uerberatur, ictu quamuis unico feriatur, locum habebit emendacio sex marcarum aut negacio duplicato iuramentorum duodenario confirmata; maior enim uerberatum ex uerbere quam uulneratum ex uulnere solet infamia comitari, que potest merito corporali lesione grauior iudicari, et idcirco uerberato satisfaccionem maiorem deposcit racio debere prestari.

As the value of money often varies and at one moment is reckoned to be lower, at another moment to be higher, it has been established that in the place of the three marks in money, specified as compensation, one mark of silver or its equivalent must always be paid; with greater or lesser sums, the same proportion is to be kept between silver and money; this, however, does not extend to what is due to the bishop or the king, where the diminishing of the amount of money owed can rather be obtained by using supplications than by claims.

With respect to the severing of members, it is of importance which member is cut off, for cutting off those that produce a major deformity also requires greater compensation. Thus, because cutting off the nose is what disgraces and deforms a man in the highest degree, it has been established that the compensation must be the same as for homicide. And it is the same when it comes to cutting off the tongue, which is very impeding to be missing. Likewise, the same compensation as for homicide is to be paid if both eyes are plucked out, if both hands are cut off, if someone has both his feet cut off or if the manly parts are cut off; but half as much shall be paid for cutting off just one part than for cutting off two. There is, however, one of the male parts whose cutting off must be treated equally as homicide. For many would be more likely to choose death than to lead an ignominious life after the loss of their members. The compensation for cutting off one hand is also half as much as homicide, and the double of cutting off a thumb; likewise, compensation for a thumb is twice as much as for a forefinger. But this halving of compensation does not continue further, in order that the compensation for a wound shall not be less than three marks in money or one mark of silver. And even though several fingers or several parts of the body are wounded with a single blow, nevertheless the wounding of each finger, however trifling, leads to compensation of three marks. And moreover, whenever, according to the estimation of prudent men, a year and a day after the day of the wounding a deformity caused by the wound in itself is judged to be more than the wound, the deformity alone shall be compensated. And a deformity of the limbs and the ears should be judged to be minor because they are removed from eyesight by the garments and hair.

If a hand or foot or any such member still sticks to the body, hanging from it in any way, half as much will be paid as when it is completely divided from the body even though it is utterly useless due to the wound that has been inflicted. Likewise, if a free man is beaten by a free man with any kind of stick, even if he is hit with just a single blow, he is entitled to a compensation of six marks or a denial confirmed by two oaths of twelve; for normally a beating brings more dishonour upon him who is beaten than a wound upon him who is wounded, and as this can rightly be considered more serious than bodily harm, reason requires that greater compensation is paid to a man who is beaten.

66. De appellacione fustis.

Fustis autem appellacio uirgam et baculum, hastam, securis malleum, clauam et uaginatum gladium comprehendit. Item a libero si liber pugno uel osse uel lapide feriatur, uel irato animo ad terram trahatur, uel tractis crinibus affligatur, trium marcarum prestabitur emendacio, uel accusacionem elidet duodeni negacio iuramenti. Est sciendum preterea, quod emendans solus in istis casibus solum equalitatis iuramentum debeat exhibere, et in illa forma, in qua dictum est illud pro homicidio cum uiris xii exhibendum. Item si quis ad nocendum alii arma sua concesserit, aut in tribus marcis satisfaciet uulnerato uel eius heredi, forte letali suscepto uulnere, aut concessionem negabit manus duodecime iuramento. Item siquis tentus fuisset, cum in alium insultum facere conaretur, aut pro reatu suo tres marcas persoluet ei, cui nocere uoluit, aut reatum conaminis duodeno inficiabitur iuramento.

67. Si casu quis alium uulnerauerit.

Siquis non uoluntarie, sed casualiter cuiquam uulnus infllixerit, non idcirco minus integram uulneratus recipiet emendacionem, cuius dolorem lenire non nouit casus pocius quam propositum infligendi, nec ipsius multum interest ex casu pocius quam ex proposito lesum esse; ex casu tamen hoc beneficium prestatur auctori, ut nihil eo nomine regi uel antistiti debeatur, quorum non est casum inopinum, quem nullus potest hominum preuidere, in aliquo castigare, sed iniquam punire pocius uoluntatem, quatenus metu pene illicita et iniqua decetero caueantur. Si tamen uulnus, quod auctor asserit casuale, exactor regis uel pontificis uoluntarium constanter affirmet, assercioni sue auctor uulneris primo suo fidem faciat iuramento. Deinde uulneratus ipse idem suo comprobet iuramento, post quos tandem x uiri, quales inueniri poterunt, ad complendum iuramentorum duodenarium admittuntur; et hic est casus unicus, in quo pro iure regio unius nominati uiri, puta ipsius uulnerati, requiritur iuramentum.

68. Si plura penalia simul concurrunt.

Quando plura penalia concurrunt opera, eodem tempore perpetrata, actor, aduersus quem perpetrata sunt, debet eligere pro quo uno ex omnibus penalem exigat satisfaccionem, nisi forte occisi cadauer armis et uestibus spolietur, in quo casu heres occisi simul et pro homicidio et pro spoliacione iustam recipiet emendacionem, uel nisi simul plura uulnera infligantur, quorum penales emendaciones nullatenus se consumunt, donec v marce argenti fuerint persolute, quibus solutis nihil erit pro pluribus ultra uulneribus persoluendum.

Ch. 66 On the word stick.

The word stick includes rods and staffs, spear shafts, axe shafts, clubs and sheathed swords. But if a free man is beaten by a free man with a fist or a bone or a stone or is dragged to the ground in an angry mood or is thrown down by having his hair pulled, a compensation of three marks shall be paid, or the accusation be struck down by an oath of twelve. It should also be noted that in these cases only the one paying compensation is required to give an oath of equality and with twelve men in the same way as mentioned in cases of homicide. Likewise, if anyone has given someone his weapon in order to harm others, he must pay a compensation of three marks to the wounded man or his heir; if the wound was fatal, or he must deny that he handed over the weapons by an oath of twelve. Likewise, if anyone has been held back when he tried to assault another, he must either pay three marks for his crime to the one whom he wished to harm, or he must deny that he attempted a crime by an oath of twelve.

Ch. 67 If someone wounds another person by accident.

If someone accidentally and not voluntarily inflicts a wound on someone else, then the wounded person should not for that reason get less than the full compensation, because accident is no better at softening his pain than intentional infliction, and therefore it does not make much difference to him whether he was harmed by accident or on purpose; however, when it is by accident, the wrongdoer has the advantage, that nothing is due on that account to the king or the archbishop, for whom it is not to chastise the unexpected accident, which no man can foresee, but rather to punish the wicked will, so that illicit and injurious acts may thereafter be prevented out of fear of punishment. If, however, there is a wound that the perpetrator asserts was accidental and the king's or the bishop's official assiduously asserts it to be intentional, then he who inflicted the wound shall first make his claim trustworthy by his oath. Thereafter, the wounded man shall himself confirm the oath and after them ten men, who can be found, shall be admitted to complete the oath of twelve; and this is the only case in which the oath of a single nominated man, namely the wounded person himself, is required with respect to what is due to the king.

Ch. 68 If several punishable acts concur.

When several punishable acts concur, inflicted at the same time, the plaintiff against whom they have been inflicted must choose from among them the one for which he will ask compensation, unless arms and clothing have been taken from the corpse of the person killed – in that case the heir of the victim shall have just compensation, both for the homicide and for the spoliation at the same time – or unless many wounds have been inflicted at the same time; the penal compensation for these wounds continues until five marks of silver have been paid, but after that nothing more is to be paid for a plurality of wounds.

Excluduntur eciam interdum propter unius tantum uulneris emendacionem ceterorum uulnerum satisfacciones, puta quando propter deformitatem abscisionis unius membri, ut manus uel pedis, v marcas argenti excederit emendacio persoluta; nihil enim super aliis uulneribus deformitate carentibus persoluetur. Si uero in membris pluribus plures deformitates fuerint, sicut contingit manibus ambabus abscisis uel ambobus pedibus amputatis, plures prestabuntur eciam emendaciones, ita tamen ut satisfaccionem homicidii non excedant. Si quis ergo simul et ab eodem fuerit uerberatus et uulneratus et spoliatus rebus suis in uia publica uel quamuis aliam passus iniuriam, equo eius uel boue uel tali quouis alia animali uerberato uel eciam interfecto in eius aspectu, si primo ceperit pro uerberacione requirere satisfaccionem, nihil pro uulneracione postea uel spoliacione uel quouis alio penali opere obtinebit. Res tamen, quibus spoliatus fuit, poterit uendicare, et ad restitucionem estimacionis agere dampni dati; eodem modo per eleccionem alterius accionis penalis omnes alie perimuntur.

69. Si liber homo seruum leserit, que satisfaccio sit prestanda.

Nunc uidendum, que satisfaccio sit prestanda, si seruum membris mutilauerit aut uulnerauerit aut uerberauerit liber homo. Igitur sicut se habet occisio ad membri amputacionem, ita se debet habere occisionis satisfactio ad amputacionis satisfactionem, uerbi gracia, sicut tribus marcis emendandis pro serui cuiuslibet interfectione tantum debet apponere interfector, ut possit cum manu duodecima secure iurare, quod occisi mancipii ualorem omnem illa satisfaccio comprehendat, ita marce et dimidie pro abscisa manu uel amputato pede uel oculo tantum uno eruto emendandis auctor tantum debet addere, ut secure super hoc duodenum exhibeat iuramentum, quod omne dampnum amputacionis in illa satisfaccione domino compensetur; pro duorum autem illorum membrorum amissione eodem modo et ordine, quamuis duplo maior, emendacio est prestanda. Uerum pro serui uulnere uulnerator duas horas domino emendabit, preciumque insuper prestabit medici et operarum, quibus interim fraudabatur dominus, estimacionem, et nihil amplius, nisi forte ex uulneracione uel uerberacione fuerit exorta deformitas, secundum prudencium uirorum estimacionem, que tamen tres marcas non excesserit, emendanda. Si tamen mancipium uulneratum uel uerberatum fuerit in aspectu domini, maior contemptus presencie iuxta quorundam sentenciam maiorem, uidelicet trium marcarum, exiget satisfaccionem.

Sometimes compensation for other wounds is also excluded due to compensation for a single wound only – for example, when the compensation paid for cutting off a member such as a hand or foot exceeds five marks of silver due to the entailed deformity; nothing will then be paid for other wounds which entail no deformity. But if there are several deformities in different members, as happens when both hands are cut off or both feet, more compensation will be paid, provided, however, that this does not exceed the compensation for homicide. Therefore, when someone is beaten and wounded and robbed of his property simultaneously and by the same person on a public highway, or suffers any other injurious acts whatsoever, and his horse or his ox or any other such animal has been struck or even killed in his sight, and he has first undertaken to seek compensation for the beating, he will get nothing afterwards for the wounding or the looting or any other punishable act. However, he may claim the property of which he was despoiled and claim restitution for the estimated value of the loss; in the same way by the choice of one out of several penal actions all others are extinguished.

Ch. 69 On the compensation to be paid if a free man wounds a slave.

Now we shall see what compensation must be paid if a free man mutilates the members of an unfree man or wounds him or beats him. The relation between the compensation for killing someone and for cutting off a member should be the same as the relation between killing and cutting off a member; for instance, just as a killer must add to the three marks for the killing of any slave so much that he can safely swear with twelve men that it covers the entire value of the slave who has been killed, in the same way the perpetrator must pay a mark and a half as compensation for cutting off a hand or a foot or plucking out only one eye, and add so much that he can safely provide an oath of twelve that all of the damage of the severing is paid for with this compensation to the master; and for the loss of two of these members, compensation is to be paid in the same way and order, although twice as much. For wounding a slave the person who wounds shall pay two ounces to the master and additionally pay the assessed value of a doctor and the working capacity of which the master will in the meantime be deprived, and no more; unless the wounding or beating leads to a deformity may have occurred, which must be according to the value assessed by prudent men, but that compensation cannot exceed three marks. If, however, a slave is wounded or beaten within the master's sight, the greater contempt of doing it in his presence, according to the opinion of some, demands compensation on a greater scale, namely of three marks.

70. Quid iuris sit, si liber homo brutum animal leserit.

Liber homo si brutum animal mansuete nature, equm puta uel bouem uel pecus uel quodcumque tale animal, uel uerberando uel percuciendo leserit, omne dampnum inde proueniens domino restitnet animalis, iuxta dampni estimacionem, cum iuramentalibus suis de dampni fidem faciens quantitate, si super ea fuerit dubitatum; duas horas numorum insuper contemptus precium emendabit, uel contemptum cum iuramento manus tercie denegabit, si lesi dominus animalis conqueratur dampnum datum ex iniuriandi animo et contemptu, eodem iure circa lesionem et interfeccionem huiusmodi animalis, quantum ad omnis dampni restitucionem et duarum horarum emendacionem, per omnia conseruato; nec miretur aliquis, si, quod prestandum est pro huiusmodi animalis lesione uel interfeccione iuxta dampni estimacionem, interdum excedat homicidii satisfaccionem, continentem eandem semper in omnibus quantitatem, cum ab ea, multo minus continendo, frequencius excedatur; locum autem contemptus emendacio non habebit, nisi duas horas numorum ad minus ualens in absencia, uel quantumcumque uile in presencia et aspectu domini, uel interficiatur animal uel ledatur. Si quis preterea equum equitauerit alienum contra domini uoluntatem, duas horas numorum, si non pertransierit eiusdem domini uille terminos, atque dimidiam marcam, si per secunde uille loca processerit, et sex horas, si adhuc ultra progressus fuerit, emendabit.

71. Si seruus liberum hominem leserit, que satisfaccio sit prestanda.

Quocumque modo uulnerando uel percuciendo seruus in ingenuum manum miserit uiolentam, tres marcas dominus emendabit, aut negacionem suam iuramentorum duodenario confirmabit. Et si seruus unius seruum alterius uel quodcumque animal mansuete nature uel uulnerauerit uel uerberauerit uel quouis alio modo leserit, ledentis dominus lesi domino dampnum omne tenebitur resarcire fidemque facere super dampni quantitate cum sufficienti iuramentorum numero, iuxta dampni, quod datum dicitur, estimacionem, uel dando seruum noxe se ab omni poterit tam dampni quam iuramenti prestacione penitus liberare.

Ch. 70 How to proceed if a free man harms a brute animal.

If a free man harms a brute animal of a tame nature, such as a horse or ox or cattle or any such animal whatsoever, either by lashing or beating, he shall pay the owner of the animal for all loss resulting from it according to the assessed value of the loss, confirming the extent of the loss along with his oath givers if it is in doubt; additionally he shall pay two ounces as compensation for contempt, or he shall deny contempt by an oath of three; if the owner of the injured animal complains that the damage was done with the intention to offend and out of contempt, and the same law concerning injury and killing of such an animal is followed in every respect, the size of the restitution of the entire loss and the two ounces' compensation; nor should anyone be astonished if the payment for the harming or killing of such an animal made according to the assessed value of the loss sometimes exceeds the compensation for homicide, which is always of the same quantity, although it is more often exceeded by it because it covers much less; but compensation for contempt does not apply unless an animal worth least at two ounces in money is killed in the absence of the owner, or an animal of however small a value is killed or injured within the owner's sight and presence. Moreover, if anyone rides someone else's horse against the owner's will, he shall pay two ounces in money, as long as he does not pass the boundaries of that same owner's village, and half a mark if he proceeds to the village, and six ounces if he proceeds farther than that.[55]

Ch. 71 What compensation shall be paid if a slave harms a free man.

In whatever way a slave lays a violent hand on a freeborn man by wounding or beating, his owner shall pay three marks, or he shall confirm his denial by an oath of twelve. And if someone's slave either wounds or beats or by any other means harms someone else's slave or any animal of a tame nature, then the owner of the perpetrator shall restore the entire loss to the owner of the harmed one and give an oath with a sufficient number of oath givers that the damage is according to the estimation of the damage said to have been suffered; or else he can free himself completely from the liability for both penalty and oath by noxal surrender of the slave.[56]

72. Quid iuris sit, si brutum animal ledat liberum hominem uel seruum uel brutum animal.

Nunc uidendum, quid iuris sit, si cuiquam dampnum detur a quadrupede mansuete nature, et reuera, siue liber homo siue seruus ledatur a quadrupede, boue uel equo uel cane uel apro uel tali quolibet mansuete nature, precium pro curacione lesi medico dabit ledentis dominus, insuperque precium operarum, que domino deperibant propter mancipii lesionem; et si qua deformitas exorta fuerit uel in ingenuo uel in seruo, iuxta prudencium uirorum emendabitur estimacionem, ita tamen, ut pro dampno dato ab huiusmodi animali satisfactio facienda tres marcas nummorum uel unam marcam argenti, computatis omnibus, non excedat. At omne dampnum, quod infra summam istam contigerit, est prestandum, nec quidquam amplius, licet equs ualens xx marcas uel amplius uel a cane uel quouis alio quadrupede perimatur uel inutilis omnino reddatur. Illius autem, qui debet satisfacere, est cum suis iuramentalibus, secundum estimacionem dampni, super dampni dati fidem facere quantitate, si super ea dissensio generetur.

73. Qualiter libertas debeat seruo dari.

Quando mancipio libertas a domino uel confertur uel uenditur uel relinquitur causa mortis, ut libertas irreuocabilem habere ualeat firmitatem, debet in iure dominus libertatem uel collatam uel uenditam protestari et renunciare priori coram omnibus seruituti. At illius, qui relinquit causa mortis suo mancipio libertatem, debet heres per se uel per alium coram cunctis, qui ad tumulandum defunctum conueniunt, relicte libertatis beneficium propalare; frequenter eciam sacerdos coram conuentu parrochianorum in ecclesia sic datam pronunciat libertatem. Statim autem post factam protestacionem libertatis et renunciacionem pristine seruitutis habet auctoritas consuetudinis approbate, ut ingenuorum aliquis sic adeptum libertatem suo coniungat generi, eum in suum consanguineum eligendo, et pro factis eius se spondeat responsurum; et hoc facto pro parte tercia prestande satisfaccionis onus senciet, uel pro parte tercia recipiende satisfaccionis lucrum percipiet cum liberto, duplo minore semper liberto quam ingenuo satisfactione pro homicidio attinente. Matris condicionem sequitur semper partus, ut sit liber partus ex uentre libero procreatus, licet pater seruilis condicionis onere premeretur, uel sit seruus ex uentre seruili progenitus, quantumcumque pater inter ingenuos nobilitatis genere prefulgeret.

74.

Duplo minor pro liberti occisione quam ingenui prestanda est satisfaccio, licet patrem ingenuum habuisset. Si redemptus ab ingenuo patre a miserabili seruitute in fauorabilem libertatem, ancilla matre progenitus, perimatur, tantum dimidiam satisfaccionis homicidii porcionem prestabit occisor, parenti libero et ex eo coniunctis consanguineis attinentem.

Ch. 72 What the law is if a brute animal harms a free man or a slave or a brute animal.

Now we shall see how to proceed when damage is done to anyone by a quadruped of tame nature, and in fact, when either a free man or a slave is harmed by a quadruped, such as an ox or a horse or a dog or a boar or any such animal of tame nature, the owner of the damaging animal shall pay for medical treatment of the wound, and in addition to that, the value of the working ability lost to a master because of his slave's injury; and if a deformity has arisen for either a freeborn man or a slave, it shall be compensated for according to the assessment of prudent men, however so, that for harm caused by an animal of this kind the compensation to be paid may not all in all exceed three marks in money or one mark of silver.[57] But all loss below this sum is to be paid for and no more, even if a horse worth twenty marks or more is killed or rendered entirely useless by either a dog or any other quadruped. But if disagreement about it arises, then it is up to the person liable to pay compensation to swear with his oath givers that the penalty paid accords with the estimation of the damage.

Ch. 73 How freedom shall be given to a slave.

When a master gives or sells to a slave his freedom or relinquishes it to him at his death, for the freedom to stand with irrevocable strength, the master must confirm in the assembly that freedom has been given or sold to him and renounce the prior servitude before everyone.[58] And the heir of someone who has granted freedom to his slave by his death must himself or by another person announce before everyone who has come to the deceased person's burial that the benefit of freedom was given; and often it is a priest who announces the freedom that has been thus given before a gathering of parishioners in church.[59] Immediately after the affirmation of freedom and renunciation of the former servitude, the authority of acknowledged custom demands that a freeborn man takes the one who has thus acquired his freedom into his own family by choosing him as his kinsman and promises to be responsible for his acts; and after this is done he will carry the burden of paying compensation to a third party, or he will receive the gains from compensation paid by a third party along with the freedman; but the compensation for homicide is always half as much for a freedman as for a freeborn man. A child born always follows the mother's status, so that free offspring are born to a free woman even if the father was burdened by servile status, and it is a slave when it is born to a servile woman no matter how brilliant the father may seem among freeborn men due to his noble kin.

Ch. 74.

Half as much is to be paid as compensation for killing a freedman as for a freeborn man, even if he had a freeborn father. If a man, who was born by an enslaved mother but redeemed to freedom from miserable servitude by his freeborn father, is killed, the killer shall pay only half the portion of the compensation due for homicide to the free parent and the kinsmen who are related to the victim through him.

75. Casus, in quo pro occisione serui integra satisfaccio est prestanda.

Si redemptus ab hostibus utroque parente libero procreatus, licet ab emptore deten-
tus in miseria seruitutis, occidatur ab aliquo, agnatis et cognatis integra summa
prestabitur satisfaccionis, a quibus tamen a totali satisfaccione redemptori redemp-
cionis precium est prestandum.

76. Qualiter liber homo possit fieri seruus.

Liber homo in enormi maleficio deprehensus, sicut in ius adductus ad suspendium
uel ad membrorum detruncacionem uel aliam quamuis corporis lesionem poterit
condempnari, sic quoque poterit adiudicari miserie seruitutis, ut tamen onera seruitutis tantum in regis perferat mansione, in nullius alterius umquam dominium tran-
siturus, uerum ibi uel uitam miseram finiturus uel ad statum ingenuitatis pristine
rediturus; hic si, seruus exsistens, fuerit interfectus, non ad agnatos uel cognatos,
sed ad regem uel ipsius exactorem qualis pro seruo satisfaccio pertinebit.

77. Qualiter quis possit seruo et consanguineo suo libertatem obtinere.

Secundum ius antiqum licuit unicuique filium suum uel consanguineum, existentem seruum ex ancilla matre progenitum, fide prius facta duobus testibus et
duodeno iuramento super coniunccione sanguinis, tribus marcis, quamuis inuito
domino, ab onere seruitutis in honorem redimere libertatis; quod nulli permittitur
nouo iure, sed oportet, ut ad hoc domini sufficienti precio inclinetur uoluntas.

78. Qui petit aliquem in libertatem, qualiter liberum probare debeat.

Si quis existentem in possessione seruitutis alleget liberum et iniuste mancipa-
tum indebite seruituti, duobus testibus hoc idem asserentibus et xii iuramentalibus
suam corroboret allegacionem, et sic, de quo agitur, libertate debita perfruatur;
eciam, si mulier est, cum matre proles eciam libertatis beneficium consequatur.

79. Quod domino liceat ubique comprehendere seruum suum.

Ubicumque dominus seruum suum inuenerit fugitiuum, quamuis in presencia regis
uel pontificis, eum iuste licet uiolentis manibus comprehendere. Requirendi quoque seruum suum, in quacumque domo uel loco uoluerit, non debet ei licencia
denegari.

**80. Qui fugit a possessione seruitutis, redire debet ad dominum, ut ibi cognosca-
tur de sua causa.**

Si quis a possessione seruitutis fugienti affirmet coram domino competere libertatem, requisita prius fidei caucione, ne uel ei propter fugam a domino noceatur
uel iudicio subtrahatur, permittat eum ad domini potestatem redire, et tunc duobus
testibus et duodeno iuramento ei, si potest, obtineat libertatem.

Ch. 75 A case in which full compensation shall be paid for killing a slave.

If a man who is ransomed from the enemy but born of free parents on both sides is killed by someone, then even if he was held in the misery of servitude by the buyer,[60] the full amount of compensation is paid to his maternal and paternal kinsmen, but they must pay the buyer the price of the ransom out of the total amount of compensation.

Ch. 76 How a free man can become a slave.[61]

When a free man has been caught in a serious crime, just as he can be taken to the assembly and be sentenced to hanging or the cutting off of his limbs or to some other bodily harm, he can also be sentenced to the misery of servitude so that he carries the burden of servitude in the king's manor, and he shall never be transferred to the ownership of another person, but he shall either end his miserable life there or return to his former status as a freeborn man; if he is killed while he is a slave, the compensation will not go to his maternal or paternal kin but to the king or his official as for a slave.

Ch. 77 How someone can obtain freedom for a slave who is his kinsman.

According to the old law anyone could with three marks redeem his son or kinsman being a slave born by a slave mother from the burden of slavery to the dignity of freedom, even if the master was unwilling, provided that he had first sworn to the blood relation with two witnesses and an oath of twelve; this the new law allows to no one, but it is necessary that the master's will is made so disposed by a sufficient price.

Ch. 78 How someone who is trying to have someone freed can prove that he is free.

If someone claims that someone who is held as a slave[62] is free and has unjustly been sold into slavery without cause, he may confirm his claim with two witnesses and by an oath of twelve, and he whom it is about may enjoy the freedom due to him; and if it is a woman, the children will also obtain the benefit of freedom along with their mother.

Ch. 79 That a master is entitled to apprehend his slave everywhere.

Wherever a master finds his fugitive slave, be it even in the presence of the king or the archbishop, it is lawful for him to apprehend him by force. He who is searching for his slave in whatever house or place he wants should not be denied permission to do so.

Ch. 80 He who flees from being held in servitude must return to his master for his case to be decided there.[63]

If someone in the presence of his master affirms that someone who is fleeing from being held in servitude should be free, then, after he has been guaranteed that neither will he be punished by his master because of his flight nor that the legal action be impeded, he shall permit that he reverts to his master and then with two witnesses and by an oath of twelve he may, if he can, obtain freedom for him.

81. Quid iuris sit, si petatur quis a possessione libertatis in seruitutem.

Si quis in possessione libertatis conuersatus ad seruitutem ab aliquo requiratur, aut fides inmobilibus, que possessa nullomodo relinqueret, habeatur, aut pro se sufficienter fideiubentem producat, ut legitimum cause finem debeat exspectare, et uel sibi die statuto duobus testibus et xii iuramentalibus libertatem defendat, uel petentis dominium recognoscat.

82. Quantum precium consequi debeat, qui seruum fugitiuum reddit domino suo.

Si quis detineat seruum a domino fugientem, ut suo domino reddat eum, si non egressum terre sue terminis, duas horas, aut dimidiam marcam nummorum, si iam egressum terra sua detineat, a domino, cum eum sibi restituerit, retencionis precium consequatur.

83. Semper eundem habent dominum mancipium et bona mancipii.

Nichil sic potest esse mancipii alicuius, quod non sit illius domini, cuius et mancipium, ut de ipso pro suo libito sibi liceat ordinare.

84. De iure postliminii.

Reuerso ab hostibus iure postliminii debent restitui quecumque tempore, quo captus fuit, constiterit ipsius fuisse; et quecumque sibi iniuste subtracta tunc iuste potuit reuocare, et tempore reuersionis poterit, nulla prescripcione sibi preiudicium generante.

85. De furto.

Quicumque statim a furti tempore perpetrati rerum suarum furem prosequitur, comprehensum cum rebus suis et manibus post tergum ligatis in ius deducat, ibi fide prius facta duobus testibus, quod in furto fuerit deprehensus, pro modo criminis condempnandum. Uerum quando amissum a priori tempore bouem uel equm uel quamcumque rem aliam in possessione alterius recognoscit, non statim manus iniciat possessori, sed qui pro eo sufficienter caueat, ut uel in iure prouinciali compareat uel in domo sua iusticiam exhibendo, fideiussorem sibi postulet assignari; pro quo habendo eum ad uillam proximam et de prima similiter ad 2^{am} et deinde ad terciam prosequatur, et si nec sic haberi ualeat fideiussor, tunc quem cepit cum rebus suis ad domum suam deferat uel inuitum, ibique compedes tradat, quos suis pedibus superponat, aut, nolentem hoc sibi facere, comprehensum eisdem uinciat comprehensor, in iuris exequcione nullam iniuriam committendo; at sic capti nec licet ei trunco pedes infigere, nec manus uinculis colligare.

94

Ch. 81 How to proceed if someone is claimed from freedom into servitude.[64]
If someone who has got freedom is required by someone to turn into servitude, he shall either be trusted when he has immovable goods the possession of which he would never give up, or he shall present someone who will guarantee that he will wait for the lawful outcome of the case, and on the fixed day he shall either defend his freedom with two witnesses and an oath of twelve or acknowledge the authority of the claimant.

Ch. 82 What award he who returns a fugitive slave to his master should get.
Someone who detains a slave who is fleeing from his master in order to give him back to the master shall receive two ounces of money from the master as reward for the detention when he restores the slave to him if the slave had not gone beyond the borders of the province, or half a mark in money if he retained him after he had already left the province.

Ch. 83 A slave and the slave's property always have the same master.
Nothing can belong to someone's slave which does not belong to the master whom he belongs to, so that he is permitted to dispose of it according to his own will.[65]

Ch. 84 On the right of rehabilitation.[66]
Someone who has returned from the enemy shall have all that was his at the time of his capture restored to him in accordance with the right of rehabilitation; and whatever has been unlawfully taken from him and which he could at that time have lawfully claimed back, he shall also be entitled to claim back at the time of his return, and no prescription shall prevent him from that.[67]

Ch. 85 On theft.[68]
Someone who pursues a thief immediately when some of his property is stolen[69] shall bring the detained man along with the stolen property and with his hands tied behind his back to the assembly, and there he shall have him sentenced according to his crime after having sworn with two witnesses that he was caught in theft. When he recognizes a previously lost ox or horse or any other property in some-one else's possession, then he shall not immediately lay hands on the possessor. Instead, he shall ask to have a guarantor assigned who will take sufficient care that the possessor either appears at the district assembly or does what is legally required at his home; in order to find this guarantor he shall accompany the possessor to the nearest village and from this first in the same way to a second and finally to a third. And if a guarantor cannot be found in this way, he shall bring the man he caught with his property to his house, even if he is unwilling, and there he shall give him shackles which the man shall place on his own feet, and if he will not do so himself, the captor may bind the captive with them without doing anything wrong by executing the law; but a man caught in this way can neither have his feet tied to a tree trunk nor may his hands be bound with chains.

Hiis peractis, sic captum non ligatum manus funibus, sed uinctum pedes compedibus ad ius prouinciale conuenientibus representet; ubi si nullus offerat pro eo iusticiam, compeditus ipse uel domum sue nominet habitacionis uel auctorem, a quo rem, pro qua captus est, comparauit, quo uel proficiscatur actor ipse causa iusticie obtinende, uel per nuncium experiatur, utrum quis de ipsius curare uoluerit liberacione; et si nec sic possit iusticiam obtinere, deducat eum in ius generale, ad quod uniuersi de terra conueniunt, audito rerum gestarum ordine pro uoluntate conueniencium iudicandum.

86. Si scrutinium negatum fuerit.

Si uolenti rem sibi furto sublatam in domo requirere aliena scrutinium a domus domino denegetur, adducantur duo uel tres testes, qui possunt super iusticia denegata testimonium perhibere; deinde super hoc in iure ab actore, munito duobus testibus, accusetur, et uel neget factum accusatus, negacionem suam duodeno corroborans iuramento, uel confiteatur et tres marcas regi et tres marcas pariter emendet actori; et tunc furti quanti uoluerit actor eum reum deferat perpetrati, et si super summa petita dissensio generetur, in detestacionem furti quantitatem probare conuenientibus iuramentalibus non reo conueniet, sed actori. Absente uero domino domus si quid per scrutinium inuentum fuerit, non licebit inuentori domine manus inicere uiolentas, sed a conuocatis ciuibus fideiussionis recipiet caucionem super non alienandis rebus inuentis, quousque domus dominus reuertatur, et uel sibi res illas defendat, uel assignet actori cum sufficientibus iuramentalibus uendicanti.

87. Quid iuris sit, si scrutinio facto res inuenta fuerit.

Si quis, ut auertat a scrutinio requirentem in domo sua rem furtiuam, asserat non haberi, si facto postea scrutinio ibidem res fuerit inuenta, inuentor de iure potetit pro fure capere domus illius dominum et ligare, et cum re propria, quam inuenit, duplum eius sumet, non de sola patrisfamilias porcione, sed de bonis communibus, quotcumque fuerint cum patrefamilias in communione. Nam cum omnes lucrum respicerent in retencione, non est mirum, si dampnum in eiusdem rei contingat omnibus restitucione. Deinde sola et tota ipsius patrisfamilias capitalis porcio ad ius regium pertinebit, non uxoris, non filiorum aut filiarum, nisi forte quid de furto possit sub secunda sera uel tercia in uxoris custodia reperiri; in quo casu sicut maritus, sic et uxor furti nomine capietur, sic et illi filii, quos etas tenera non excusat, et qui eiusdem furti rei et conscii possunt certissime deprehendi.

When this has been done, he shall bring the captive with his hands unbound by rope, but with his feet chained with shackles, to those gathered at the district assembly. If no one here offers to intervene, the man in shackles shall himself tell either where he lives or name the vendor from whom he bought the property for which he has been taken, and to whom the plaintiff can go to pursue his case, or he shall send a messenger to find out whether anybody will take care of his release; and if the plaintiff cannot have justice done in this way either, he shall lead the captive to the provincial assembly, where people come together from the entire province, and there he shall be judged, after it has been heard how the case has proceeded, according to the will of those present.

Ch. 86 If a search is denied.

If he who wishes to look for something taken from him by theft in someone else's house is denied a search by the owner of the house, two or three witnesses shall be brought who can give testimony concerning the right that has been denied; then the owner can be accused of this at the assembly by the plaintiff supported by two witnesses, and he can either deny it, confirming his denial with an oath of twelve, or he can admit and pay a fine of three marks to the king and three marks to the plaintiff equally; and then the plaintiff may hold him guilty for having stolen as much as he wishes, and if there is disagreement about the amount demanded, it is, due to the hate of theft, not up to the accused but to the plaintiff to prove the amount with a convenient number of oath givers. But if the owner of the house is away and something is found through a search, the finder is not permitted to use force against his wife, but from men of the village called to be present he shall receive surety that the property found will not be disposed of before the owner of the house has returned and either claims the property for himself or hands it over to the plaintiff, if he claims it with sufficient oath givers.

Ch. 87 How to proceed if the thing is found during a search.

If someone says that something is not in his house in order to keep someone look-ing for his stolen property from searching the house and after the search that thing was found, the finder can lawfully take the owner of the house as a thief[70] and bind him, and together with his own thing which he found he can put on top the double, not only from the householder's portion but from the common property, no matter however many are in partnership with the householder. Because everybody would profit from the retention, it is no wonder that the loss strikes them all when the thing is given back.[71] Thereafter it is only the householder's own portion in its entirety which will be due to the king, not his wife's, not his sons' or his daughters' unless some of the stolen goods are discovered behind the second or third bar[72] in the wife's custody. In that case the wife may be taken for theft just as her husband, and also those sons who are not excused by their tender age and who can also surely be considered guilty and accomplices in the same theft.

Uidetur tamen quibusdam iniqum ob hoc solum pro fure quempiam comprehendi, quod in domo sua esse negauit rem furtiuam, ibidem per scrutinium post repertam, cum hoc de fiducia bone consciencie potuisset negari; uerum licet ei, quamuis ante negauerit, cum duodecim iuramentalibus, quales habere potuit, se tueri, si dimidia marcha nummorum minus ualeat res furtiua. At si dimidiam marcham ad minus ualeat, nominatos tantum habebit xii de sua parrochia et, si non sufficit ipsa sola, de proxima purgatores, quorum si uel unus defecerit, hoc solum ei supererit auxilium, ut candentis ferri iudicio se committat, in hoc casu tamen aduersarii sacramento, quod in lingua patria *asswærz eth* nominatur, minime precedente; et si manus exustione reus impositi sibi criminis conuincatur, non tamen subito capietur, licet statim ipsius bona, sicut dictum est, capi possint, sed ut sibi per fugam consulat, uel quouis alio modo prouideat, unius diei tantum inducias obtinebit, alioquin pauci candentis ferri iudicio consentirent; post hoc in iure coram communi audiencia, enarrato prius rerum gestarum ordine, suus obtineat aduersarius, ut expers pacis et dignus patibulo iudicetur; et si repertus fuerit ab illo tempore, pro sui reatus exigencia punietur impune.

88. Quid iuris sit, si animal suum quis in possessione alterius deprehendit.

Quando ab aliquo suus equs uel bos uel quodcumque tale animal in domo et possessione alterius reperitur, possessor prestet caucionem fideiussoriam petitori, ut iudicio ad ius conueniencium primo die iuridico se presentet; quo cum peruentum fuerit, quintus dies prefigatur a iuridicis possessori, in quo aduersus petitorem sic in domo propria se defendat, ut uel ipse uel auctor suus, a quo rem, que petitur, comparauit, fidem faciat duobus testibus et xii iuramentalibus, quod animal, habens calumpniam, in suo dominio et possessione fuerit procreatum, aut si possessor hoc nequeat adimplere, petitor ibidem tantum sex uirorum exhibeat iuramenta, quod illud animal uel uiolenter sibi sublatum uel furtiue fuerit, et sic obtineat suum animal, quod inuenit. Sed sciendum quod terminus interdum breuior, interdum prolixior, quam diximus, prefigi poterit possessori; propter enim alienigenam petitorem et a remotis partibus uenientem, ne mora diutina crucietur, secundum quosdam tantum trium dierum spacium est prefigendum.

It seems unjust to some, however, that someone can be taken only because he denied that some stolen property, which was found after a search, was in his house, as he might have been in good faith when he denied it; and therefore he is allowed to defend himself with twelve oath givers, whoever he can have, even though he denied it before, when the stolen property is worth less than half a mark in money. If, however, it is worth at least half a mark, he shall have twelve men nominated exclusively from his parish, and if there are not enough there, from the next, to purge him, and if just one will not, his only remaining remedy is that he accepts the ordeal by hot iron, but in this case without the preceding oath by the opposing party, which in the native language is called *asswaerz eth*; and if the defendant is convicted of the crime imputed to him by the burning of his hand, he shall not immediately be seized, even if his property as aforesaid can be taken, but he has one day's respite so that he may save himself by fleeing or make other preparations; otherwise, few would consent to the ordeal by hot iron. After that his opposing party may at the assembly before those gathered there, after it has been explained how the case was handled, have him sentenced to loss of his peace and to be worthy of execution; and from that time, if he is found, he may be punished with impunity as his crime demands.

Ch. 88 How to proceed when someone discovers one of his animals in someone else's possession.

When someone discovers a horse or an ox or any such animal in the house and possession of another person,[73] the possessor shall offer a guarantee to the plaintiff that at the next meeting of the assembly he will present himself for judgment of those who come to the assembly; when this is done, the men of the assembly shall fix a term of five days for the possessor where he shall defend himself against the plaintiff in his own home by having either he himself or his seller from whom he bought the property in case swear with two witnesses and twelve oath givers that the claimed animal was procreated in his ownership and possession. If the possessor cannot fulfil this, the plaintiff can give the oath of only six men that the animal was taken from him violently or by stealth, and thus he will get back his animal that he found. But it worth noting that the appointed term can sometimes be shorter, sometimes longer, for the possessor than what we have said; for according to some a term of only three days is to be set, so that a plaintiff who is foreign and comes from far away shall not be delayed by a longer stay.

At ubi possessor primo suum nominat uenditorem die iuridico, quem constat in remotis partibus habitare, non tamen a nobis per interfluentis maris spacium separatis, puta in Suechia, siue alienigena siue indigena sit petitor, possessor xv dierum inducias obtinebit. At si maris intercapedo illum a nobis separet, quem sibi nominat uenditorem, prestabitur unus mensis. Uerum si terra et regno egressum constet eum, ut uisitet sanctorum limina, unius anni et unius diei spacium prefigatur.

89. Si res non uiua, necdum usui preparata, in domo alterius reperitur, utpote securis sine manubrio.

Quando res non uiua, sed alia reperitur, si nondum est usui necessario preparata, puta securis nondum suo manubrio maritata uel gladius uaginatus, cui nondum balteus est infixus, uel uestis nondum ad usum necessarium informata, possessor tantum xii iuramentalibus fidem faciat se rem illam expositam ad emendum iusto precio comparasse. At si securis habeat manubrium, uel mucro cinctorium alligatum, uel uestis sit formata, oportet, ut possessor suum nominet uenditorem uel fideiussorem ad defendendum, ne res euincatur, uel, si res euicta fuerit, ad soluendum sibi precium obligatum, ut eorum alteruter ei statuto die, si poterit, rem defendat; cum prefixus dies aduenerit, si predictum fideiussorem actor neget antea nominatum, possessor probet xii iuramentalibus eundem esse, quem antea nominauit. At si nec uenditor nec fideiussor statuto die comparuerit, possessor producat, si poterit, duos testes, qui testificentur eum iuste rem, de qua agitur, comparasse, quo facto nihil preter rem suam actor ualeat obtinere. Sed si nec testes comparuerint, licebit actori cum re sua duplum accipere et pro fure comprehendere possessorem. Quando rem quamcumque uenditam tamquam a fure condicit uenditor ab emptore, emptor, fide facta duobus testibus et iuramentalibus uel conuenientibus estimacioni, quod iusto precio rem eandem comparauerit ab eodem, aduersus suum se tuebitur uenditorem.

90. Si susspectum quis habet alium pro re sibi furtiue sublata.

Quando quis susspectum habet alium, quod furtiue sibi surripuerit rem amissam, in ius prouinciale progrediens, nominando eum deferat furti reum, ibique statuatur, ut ab actore citetur ad proximum diem iuridicum responsurus; et si non uenerit, sicut prius, iterum ei proximus dies iuridicus prefigatur, et si nec tunc aduenerit, regi eum in tribus marcis actorique in restitucione amisse rei uel eius estimacione iuridici condempnabunt, et ut nullus ei communicet per totam prouinciam, indicabunt sub pena trium marcarum iuri regio soluendarum, quod iudicium *matban* lingua patria nominare consueuit;

But when the possessor at the next gathering of the assembly names a seller who is known to live far away, however not in a place separated from us by a span of sea flowing in between, such as Sweden,[74] not regarding whether the plaintiff is foreign or native, the possessor will be given a term of fifteen days. But if an interval of sea separates from us the man whom he names as his seller, he will be given one month. But if he is known to have left the region or the realm in order to visit the shrines of the saints, he shall be given a term of a year and a day.

Ch. 89 If lifeless property that is not yet ready for use is found in someone else's house, such as an axe without a shaft.

When something other than living property is found, and it is not yet made ready for use, such as an axe not yet coupled with a shaft, or a sheathed sword to which a sword belt is not yet attached or a garment not yet shaped for its intended use, the possessor shall swear with only twelve oath givers that he bought the property for a fair price while it was displayed for sale. But if the axe has a handle, or the sword is bound to a sword belt or the garment is shaped, the possessor must name his seller or a guarantor for his defence in order that the property is not taken from him, or, if the property is taken from him, in order to get back the price he had agreed to, so that one of those two, if he is capable of it, can claim the thing for him on the day assigned; when the fixed day has come and the plaintiff denies that the guarantor is the one previously named, the possessor must prove with twelve oath givers that it is the same one as he named before. If neither the seller nor the guarantor appears on the designated day, the possessor shall have, if he can, two witnesses who testify that he bought the property in question; if this is done, the plaintiff will not get anything but his own property. But if the witnesses do not appear either, the plaintiff shall be allowed to take double the value of his property along with it and to seize the possessor as a thief. When a seller claims back some sold property from the buyer as from a thief, the buyer shall swear with two witnesses and oath givers corresponding to the value of the property that he bought the thing for a fair price from the seller and thus protect himself against him.

Ch. 90 If someone suspects that someone else has taken something from him by theft.

When someone suspects that another has furtively taken a thing from him which disappeared, he shall go to the district assembly and name him and accuse him as a thief, and there it shall be decided that the plaintiff shall summon him to respond at the next gathering of the assembly; and if he does not come, the next assembly will again be fixed for him as before and then if he does not come, the men of the assembly shall sentence him to pay three marks to the king and to restore to the plaintiff the missing property or its estimated value, and they shall publicly declare that no one may have contact with him throughout the entire district under the penalty of paying three marks to the king, a sentence which usually in the native language is called *matban*.

quo iure si contentus noluerit actor esse, uel adiudicatum sibi non potuerit obtinere, in ius generale procedat, et, rerum gestarum ordine uniuersis sub bonorum uirorum testimonio recitato, reo nondum comparente, obtineat, ut a iuridicis talis sentencia proferatur, ut et a reo rex tres marcas accipiat et actor non solum estimacionem, sed duplum pariter estimacionis, et ut ipse reus communis pacis expers ab omnibus habeatur, quem lingua patria *frithløs* appellat, et tam uerbis quam collisione armorum et contactu euidenter exprimitur, ut eum cuilibet cum armis inuadere sit permissum. Uerum si tunc reus tandem 4ª uice comparuerit, uel citatus uel ad suam innocenciam comprobandum, licet nullum precedere debeat actoris iuramentum, quod *asswærueth* dicitur, tantum ad candentis ferri iudicium admittetur, quod *scuzsiærn* in lingua patria nominatur, et si manus exustione conuictus fuerit, per omnia iuridicorum proximo supradicte sentencie subiacebit; si uero per illesam manum innocenciam suam poterit declarare, a cunctis in eum latis, sentenciis absoluetur, sed actori de nouo licebit aduersus eum furti iudicium instaurare.

91. Quod citatus in ius duos mittere debet, qui testentur eum legitima causa prepeditum.

Citatus in ius, licet iustam causam habeat residendi, debet tamen pro se duos transmittere, qui, non tacto sacro libro, sed contactu manuum, utroque scilicet manu sua manum alterius contingente, testificentur eum, ne ueniret, causa legitima prepeditum. Uerum multum refert, qua causa eum docuerint prepeditum; nam propter infirmitatem ei xv dierum inducias impetrabunt, quibus finitis, si non conualuerit, supplebit aliquis proximorum ipsius absenciam et defectum, ipsum, licet per candentis ferri iudicium, defendendo, ita tamen ut ex illesa manu gestantis ferrum non gestantis innocencia comprobetur, et, si manus exusta fuerit gestatoris, solus non gestans furti reus imposti conuincatur; si tamen reus, priusquam ferrum gestatum fuerit, moriatur, eius heres, si uoluerit, negare poterit defunctum uel aliquem pro eo ferri iudicio consensisse, negacionem suam manu xiiª iuramentalium confirmando, et si actor in accusacione defuncti perseuerauerit, heres, hoc inficians, tantum cum xii iuramentalibus se defendat. Quando uero qui citatus non uenit, propter absenciam excusatur, multum refert, in quibus commorari partibus doceatur; quippe si fuerit in uicino, tribus diebus iuridicis sibi continuis, sicut prius dictum est, conuincetur. Si uero transierit ad loca parcium remotarum, dabuntur inducie aut dierum xv aut unius mensis aut unius anni et unius diei secundum iam dictam diuersitatem distancie spaciorum.

If the plaintiff is not content with this decision, or he cannot get what was given to him by the sentence, he can proceed to the provincial assembly. And after everybody with the supporting testimony of good men has been told how the case has been handled and the defendant still does not appear, the plaintiff can obtain that the men of the assembly make a decision to the effect that the king shall have three marks from the defendant and the plaintiff not only the value, but double the value, and that the defendant himself shall be considered by everyone as being outside the common peace, the kind of person called *frithløs* in the native language; and this will be clearly expressed both by words and by the visible striking together and touching of arms, so that anyone is permitted to assault him with arms. If the defendant finally appears the fourth time, either because he was summoned or to prove his innocence, even if the oath shall not be given beforehand by the plaintiff which is called *asswœrueth*, he will only be permitted the ordeal by hot iron, which is called *scuzsiœrn* in the native language, and if he is convicted by the burning of his hand, he will in all respects be subjected to the aforesaid judgment by all the men of the assembly; but if he is able to prove his innocence by an uninjured hand, he will be freed of all sentences imposed upon him, but the plaintiff is permitted to start a new action for theft against him.

Ch. 91 That someone summoned to the assembly must send two to testify that he is impeded due to a legitimate cause.

A man who is summoned to the assembly, even if he has just cause for staying at home, must nevertheless send two men on his behalf who, without touching a sacred book[75] but by the contact of their hands, i.e., one taking hold of the other's hand with his own, shall testify that he who has not come has been impeded for a legitimate cause. Much depends, however, upon the reason they give for his being impeded; for by reason of illness they will obtain for him a grace period of fifteen days, after which, if he has not recovered, one of his closest kinsmen shall fill in for his absence and failing and even defend him by the ordeal by hot iron,[76] and thus by the uninjured hand which carried the iron, the innocence of the one which did not carry it may be proved; but if the hand of the carrier is scorched, only the person accused of theft but not carrying anything is convicted of the accusation. If, however, the defendant should die before the iron is carried, his heir can, if he wishes, deny that the dead man or anyone on his behalf had consented to the ordeal by hot iron confirming his denial by twelve oath givers, and if the plaintiff should persevere in his accusation against the dead man, the heir who denies this can again defend himself with twelve oath givers. When he who has been summoned does not appear and has been excused for his absence, much depends upon the place where he is said to be staying; if in fact he is in the vicinity, he will be convicted after three consecutive gatherings of the assembly as was aforesaid. If, however, he has travelled to distant places, a grace period will be given of either fifteen days or one month or a year and a day according to the aforementioned variety in remoteness of distance.

92. Si de furto accusatus 1° uel 2° die iuridico non comparuerit.

Accusatus de furto si compareat primo die iuridico uel 2°, et pro se offerat per iurisiurandi religionem defensionem uirorum xii, quos actor uoluerit de tota prouincia nominare, oportebit actorem iuri adquiescere nominacionis, et cum xii uiri fuerint nominati, licebit reo tantum tres uiros inimicicie causa sibi suspectos recusare de xii nominatis, in quorum locum actor statim alios tres nominabit; quo facto uel eodem die, si omnes presentes fuerint et in hoc omnes consenserint, uel proximo die iuridico nominati xii ab iniuncto negocio se absoluent; et si omnes iurauerint, et accusati consequenter innocencia comparebit, sin autem uel unus iurare noluerit, reus habebitur pro conuicto, nisi candentis ferri iudicio se committat, in quo casu tamen non debet actoris exigi iuramentum, sicut exigeretur, si statim ab exordio ferri iudicio consensisset. Quando uero ad sequentem diem iuridicum nominatorum defensio prorogatur, si statuto die tantum tres uiros nominatorum numero deesse contingat, uniuscuiusque trium, duorum testimonio de numero nominatorum, reus absenciam excusabit, et tunc actor alios in locum absencium nominabit; licet autem reus prius consenserit, si tribus diebus uel duobus ante prefixum diem nominacioni renunciet, audietur, ut, actoris precedente iuramento, per igniti ferri iudicium se defendat; quod *truxiœrn* in lingua patria nominatur. Hec est forma iuramenti, quod candentis ferri iudicium antecedit, ut affirmet actor sub iurisiurandi religione, quod non odii causa nec lucri gracia reo imposuerit furti crimen, sed quia scit eum ueraciter rem ad minus ualentem dimidiam marcam nummorum sibi furti uicio subtraxisse.

93. Si sponte quis confessus fuerit se rem inuenisse, que furtiue subtracta putatur.

Si quis, priusquam de furto fuerit accusatus, sponte confessus fuerit crimen suum, uel, iam accusatus, si fidem fecerit ad 2^{am} uel 3^{am} citacionem in iudicio duobus testibus et xii iuramentalibus, quod rem illam, que ab eo requiritur, coram ciuibus et parrochianis et omni cetu populi, cui eum contigit interesse, se pronunciauerit inuenisse, ut ad noticiam ueri domini eius inuencio perueniret, a furti crimine se mundabit et ab actoris se peticione pariter liberabit, cum rem restituerit et duodenum exhibuerit iuramentum, quod nihil amplius habuerit uel cum ea restituere teneatur, si super inuente rei fuerit orta dissensio quantitate.

Ch. 92 If a man accused of theft does not appear at the first or second gathering.
If he who is accused of theft appears on the next gathering of the assembly or at the second, and he offers as defence on his own behalf the oath of twelve men, whom the plaintiff may nominate from the entire district, then the plaintiff should be content with his right to nominate; and when twelve men are nominated, the defendant is then permitted to reject just three of the twelve men nominated for enmity towards him, and in their place the plaintiff shall immediately nominate three others; when this is done, either on the same day, if everyone is present and all consent to this, or on the next gathering, the twelve men nominated shall fulfil the task given them; and if they all swear, the innocence of the accused will also be evident, but if, however, just one man will not swear, the defendant will be regarded as convicted, unless he takes upon him the ordeal by hot iron, in which case, however, the plaintiff's oath will not be required as it would have been required had he consented to the ordeal by hot iron immediately and from the beginning. If, however, when the defence by those nominated is postponed to the next gathering of the assembly and on the appointed day it should happen that just three men of the number nominated fail to appear, then the defendant with the testimony of two of those nominated shall excuse their absence, and then the plaintiff shall nominate others in the place of those absent; and even if the defendant has consented first, if two or three days before the day appointed he gives up the nomination, he will be heard, so that after the oath given by the plaintiff he may defend himself by the ordeal by hot iron, which in the native language is called *truxiærn*. The oath that precedes the ordeal by hot iron takes this form: the plaintiff affirms by his oath that he does not accuse the defendant of the crime of theft by reason of hatred or for profit but because he knows him truly to have taken from him a thing worth at least a half-mark by the vice of theft.

Ch. 93 If someone by himself confesses that he has found a thing that is believed to have been taken by theft.
If someone before he is accused of theft voluntarily confesses his crime, or, when he is already accused, swears in the assembly at the second or third summons with two witnesses and twelve oath givers that in order that the true owner might hear of his finding he has declared to the people of the village and the parish and at all gatherings of people where he has been that he has found the thing demanded from him. If he swears to this, he can cleanse himself of the crime of theft and will likewise free himself from the plaintiff's claim when he restores the thing and, if disagreement arises concerning the quantity of what was found, gives an oath of twelve that he kept nothing else nor should give back anything besides that thing.

94. Si coram multis furti crimen imponitur, quod nequit probari.

Si quis in iure coram communi audiencia furti quemquam accusauerit, nisi furti causam fuerit prosecutus, et ad tres marcas regi et ad tres marcas persoluendas obligabitur accusato.

95. De condempnacione furis.

Furis condempnacio iuridicorum, non exactoris subiaceat potestati; pro minore autem quam dimidie marce nummorum furto ad amissionem uite non debet aliquis condempnari, sed aut detruncacionem membrorum aut impressi faciei stigmatis adnotacionem in signum et memoriam deprehensionis aut seruitutem in regis curia tolerandam aut per uerbera castigacionem condempnacionis sentencia comprehendet; licet autem furtum committat, qui eciam unum denarium domino contrectat inuito, pro minori tamen quam v nummorum furto non est quispiam uinciendus; interdum eciam magnitudo sceleris non solum in amissionem uite, sed in exquisitum genus dire mortis acerbam sentenciam iuste dirigit condempnacionis, ut uel ecclesiarum effractor, qui manus sacrilegas in res sacras extendere non ueretur, in furto sacrilegium exercendo, uel sicarius, qui, ut possit predam et spolia per latrocinia obtinere, uite non parcit bestiarum more, tamquam humane societatis immemor, aliene, uel incendiarius, qui consueuit turpis lucri gracia domos incendere alienas, in rota distento corpore suspendatur, uel lapidibus obruatur, uel incendio concremetur. Sciendum preterea, quod furem, quem iuridici noluerint morti uel suspendio condempnare, si noluerit regis exactor soluere, de iuridicorum sentencia iuste qui cepit eum rumpet uel scindet uincula colligati, ut non possit super hoc ab actore regio conueniri.

96. Quantum uxor iure alienare permittitur.

Ius permittit uxorem alienare rem ualentem v denarios et nihil amplius, ignorante marito; uerum quia frequens alienacio quamuis exigue rei tandem immensam poterit afferre iacturam et abundanciam in penuriam commutare, licet marito, suspectam habenti uxorem suam super alienacione frequenti, in ius procedere et uxori sue omnem alienacionem efficaciter prohibere, ut, si postea uxor aliquid de facto presumpserit alienare, maritus possit idem, tamquam alienatum non fuerit, reuocare, licet precium, quod uxor accepit, refundere non cogatur. Eodem modo licet patrifamilias, quod filiusfamilias uel filiafamilias de bonis suis alienauerit, non refuso precio reuocare; licet autem qui cum talibus personis lege contrahunt prohibente, que mercantur restituere compellantur, furti tamen infamiam non incurrunt. Sed si rem quamlibet ab ignorantis domini presumunt mancipio uel mercenario comparare, non tantum restituere sunt cogendi, sed et eo nomine de furto poterunt accusari.

Ch. 94 If in the presence of many an accusation of theft is raised which cannot be proven.

If anyone accuses someone of theft in the assembly to the common attention of all present and the case of theft is not pursued, he will be under obligation both to pay three marks to the king and three marks to the person accused.

Ch. 95 On the condemnation of a thief.

The power to condemn a thief belongs to the men of the assembly, not to the official; moreover, no one should be sentenced to loss of life for the theft of less than half a mark in money, but such a condemnation shall result in either the amputation of limbs or the marking by a brand impressed upon his face as a sign and to remember his capture, or slavery to be suffered in the king's manor, or the punishment of being beaten. However, even though he who takes just one penny against the owner's will also commits theft, no one is to be bound up for the theft of less than five pennies. In some cases, however, the seriousness of the crime leads not only to the loss of life but to a just condemnation to the harsh sentence of a specifically gruesome kind of death. For instance, a sacrilegious man who is not afraid of reaching out his sacrilegious hands towards holy things and commits sacrilege by the theft; or the murderer who in order to obtain booty and spoils through robbery, not refraining from the manner of beasts as if unmindful of human society, does not spare the life of others; or the incendiary, who is used to setting fire to other people's houses for the sake of filthy gain.[77] They will all have their body stretched on the rack, or be struck down by stones or be consumed by fire. It should also be known that when the men of the assembly do not wish to sentence a thief to death or hanging, and the king's official does not want to release him, then the man who captured him can according to a lawful judgment of the men of the assembly break or cut the chains that are binding him, and he cannot be charged by the king's official for this.

Ch. 96 How much a wife may dispose of.

The law allows a wife to dispose of property of five pennies' value and nothing more without the knowledge of her husband; but because repeated disposal, albeit of small property, can in the end bring immense deprivation and turn abundance into penury, a husband suspecting his wife of frequent disposal is permitted to go to the assembly and validly prohibit his wife from all disposal, so that if afterwards his wife should in fact presume to dispose of something, the husband can recover it as though it had not been disposed of and he shall not pay back the price that the wife accepted. In the same way, the householder may recover any of his property that a son or daughter of the house has disposed of without paying back the price; yet although those who contract with such people when the law prohibits it are compelled to restore what they have bought, they nevertheless will not incur the infamy of theft. But if they presume to buy anything whatsoever from a slave or a hired servant without the owner knowing it, not only are they compelled to make restitution, but on the same account they can be accused of theft.

97. Si quis super furto serui sui conuentus fuerit.

Quando quis super furto serui sui conuenitur, si confiteatur, quantum uoluerit persoluendum proponat, et quod maior non fuerit illius furti quantitas, duodeno fidem faciat iuramento, insuperque pro suo libito uel ad cedendum seruum suum uirgis actoris subiciat potestati, uel xxx denariis ipsius redimat uerberacionem, nequaquam ad alterutrum obligatus, si compertum serui sui furtum prius indicare curauerit, quam conueniretur. At si diffiteatur dominus furtum serui, manum eius subiciat ferri candentis iudicio, nullo tamen precedente aduersarii iuramento, et si manus conuictus fuerit ustione, quantum uoluerit persoluat dominus, et quod nihil amplius persoluere teneatur, duodenum exhibeat iuramentum. At si minus dimidia marca nummorum furti nomine requiratur, ferri iudicium, si uoluerit, euitando poterit, quod impositum est seruo suo, cum suis iuramentalibus denegare, ad minus cum xii secundum quosdam propter furti detestacionem, quantumcumque modicum requiratur, secundum alios cum iuramentalibus conuenientibus estimacioni, ut duas horas uel minus neget triplici iuramento, atque seno, si transcendat in aliquo actoris peticio duas horas, ne sic pro facto alieno serui sui sicut pro proprio grauaretur.

98. Quid facere debeat, qui alienum seruum in furto deprehenderit.

Si quis in furto seruum deprehenderit alienum, in ius deducat ligatum, dominoque denunciet, ut occurrat, et oblato quod debetur fideque facta duodeno iuramento, quod pro furto illo nihil amplius debeatur, probacioneque facta duobus testibus, quod in fuga constitutus commiserit furtum illud, recipiat seruum suum, sic tamen, ut uel ab actore, sicut dictum est, uerberetur, uel xxx nummis uerberacio redimatur. Si uero dominus uocatus noluerit aduenire, probato furto duobus testibus seruum illum iuridici iuxta furti magnitudinem condempnabunt.

99. De iudicio candentis ferri.

Gestaturus ferrum lota manu nihil debet contingere, priusquam ferrum leuet, nec caput nec crines nec aliquod uestimentum, ne, per tactum alicuius succi uel unguenti, per fraudem pocius quam per innocenciam ferri candentis effugiat lesionem. Triplex autem ferri iudicium, quod usus recipit, inuenitur. Unum, quod in xii ignitis uomeribus calcandis consistit; quibus personis conueniat, qualiterque debeat exerceri, sufficienter credimus declaratum. Est item aliud ferri iudicium illi soli conueniens, qui pro furti crimine conuenitur, quod *truxiœrn* in lingua patria nominatur, ab alueolo, qui per xii pedum uestigia debet a baculis, quibus ferrum superponitur, elongari;

Ch. 97 If someone is summoned for his slave's theft.

When someone is summoned for his slave's theft and he admits it, he can offer to pay as much as he wishes and he shall swear an oath of twelve that the extent of the slave's theft was no greater, and besides that he can choose either to hand over his slave to yield to the power of the accuser's rod, or he may redeem him from such beating with thirty pennies; but he is in no way obliged to do either thing if after having discovered his slave's theft, he has taken care to make it known before he was summoned. But if the master denies his slave's theft, the slave must subject his hand to the ordeal by hot iron with no oath of the opposing party taking place beforehand, and if he is convicted by the burning of the hand, the master shall pay as much he wishes, and to prove that he should pay no more, he shall give an oath of twelve. But if less than half a mark in money is demanded due to theft, he can, if he wishes to avoid the trial of iron, deny what is imputed to his slave with at least twelve oath givers, however trifling the theft, according to the opinion of some, due to the abhorrence of theft or, as others hold, with a number of oath givers according to the assessed value, so that he shall not be burdened by the act of someone else, namely his slave, in the same way as it if it were his own. He will thus deny two ounces or less by an oath of three, and by six if the plaintiff's claim exceeds two ounces in anything.

Ch. 98 What he should do who catches someone else's slave in theft.

Anyone who catches someone else's slave in theft shall lead him in bonds to the assembly and summon his master to appear. After he has offered what is owed and sworn by an oath of twelve that nothing further is owed for the theft and proof has been made by two witnesses that the slave committed the theft after he had run away, he may recover his slave, however in such a way that he is either to be beaten by the plaintiff, as has been said, or is redeemed from the beating by thirty pennies. If the master who was summoned does not wish to appear, then after the theft has been proven by two witnesses the men of the assembly can sentence the slave according to the amount stolen.

Ch. 99 On the ordeal by hot iron.[78]

He who is about to carry iron must not after having washed his hand touch anything before he raises the iron, neither his head nor his hair nor any of his clothing, in order that he may not by touching some kind of moisture or unguent avoid the harm of the hot iron due to fraud rather than innocence. And there are three different trials of hot iron which custom allows. One, which consists of walking on twelve red-hot ploughshares; we think that it has been sufficiently explained to which people this is applicable and how it should be carried out.[79] Then, there is a second ordeal by hot iron which is applicable only to those summoned for the crime of theft, which in the native language is called *truxiærn* from the trough, which must be twelve footsteps removed from the staffs upon which the iron is placed.

quod accensum, prius prestito ab aduersario iuramento, quod *assweraeth* appellatur, sumptum a baculis in ipsum alueolum nuda manu debet immittere reus ipse, et immissum, si forte resilierit uel extra ceciderit, resumet iterum et proiciet, donec ipsum ibi contigerit contineri. Est item tercium ferri iudicium illis gestaturis ferrum attinens, quibus predicta iudicia non incumbunt, quod ignitum sumptum a baculis reus ipse, donec processerit ix uestigiis, deferre tenetur et tunc primo a se iactare, a quo iactu ipsum lingua patria *scuziærn* appellat; et si dicatur ab aduersario insufficienter uel minus legitime detulisse, probet duobus testibus se deferendi modum legitimum obseruasse. Hoc est autem circa quodlibet ferri iudicium obseruandum, ut nullum eorum debeat in septimana, que diem festum habeat, exerceri; duobus quidem primis diebus, in 2^a uidelicet et 3^a feria, reus in pane et aqua et uestimentis laneis ieiunabit, et in 4^a subibit iudicium; hoc completo in continenti uel pedes, si uomeres calcati fuerint, uel manus, si ferrum gestatum fuerit, panno aliquo inuoluentur, cui diligenter astricto sigillum eciam apponetur, ne quid adueniat fraudulenter, quod uel possit extinguere ustionem uel auferre saltem apparenciam ustionis; hoc uelamen in pedibus uel manibus usque ad sabbatum permanebit, eodem die coram actore aduersario usque ad solis descensum post meridiem exspectando et, si nec tunc aduenerit, coram astantibus auferendum, qui statim, cum nudam manum uel pedes conspexerint, uel innocentem reum uel culpabilem iudicabunt; et si fuerit innocens iudicatus, persoluet laboris sui precium sacerdoti, si uero culpabilis, ad actorem illius mercedis solucio iuxta ecclesie uel prouincie consuetudinem pertinebit. Hiis de causis statutum est, ut septimana candentis ferri nullum habere debeat diem festum, ne diei festo aliqua uideatur iniuria per ieiunium uel huiusmodi operibus irrogari. Preter hec eciam sciendum, quod in detestacionem furti solum medium ferri iudicium exerceri ualeat, non extrema duo, in illis temporibus, in quibus debet pax ecclesiastica conseruari, a uigilia uidelicet sancti Olaui martiris usque ad festum sancti Michaelis et proximum diem sequentem, ab aduentu Domini usque ad octauam epyphanie, a septuagesima usque post festum pasce, et diebus rogacionum et septimana penthecostes; in quibus quoque temporibus, licet super aliis causis cuncta silere debeant iuramenta, licet cuilibet, ut possit res suas iniuste sublatas repetere uel a fure aut latrone condicere, iuramenta prestare, ne mora diuturnior detrimentum aliquod uel iacturam inferat exspectanti.

After the iron has been heated and the oath which is called *assweraeth* has first been provided by the plaintiff, the accused must take the iron from the staffs and throw it into the trough with his bare hand; and if it should bounce back or fall outside after it has been thrown, he must take it up again and throw it, until he succeeds in getting it in there. Finally there is a third trial of iron for those who are going to carry iron and upon whom the aforesaid trials are not incumbent. By this the accused must take up the iron from the staffs and carry it until he has advanced nine steps and not until then throw it away from him, and from the throwing it is called *scuziærn* in the native language; and if it is claimed by the plaintiff that he carried it insufficiently or not lawfully, the accused shall prove with two witnesses that he carried it out in a lawful manner. With any trial of iron it shall be observed that none of them are carried out in a week with a festive day; on the first two days, that is to say on Monday or Tuesday, the defendant will fast on bread and water and be wearing woollen garments, and on Wednesday he will undergo the trial; and immediately after this has been completed and, either the feet, if plough-shares were walked upon, or the hand, if iron was carried, will be bound up in a piece of cloth, to which a seal will also carefully be affixed to avoid that any fraud takes place, which can either quench the burning or at least remove the appearance of burning; this covering will remain on the feet or hands until Saturday and on the same day in the presence of the opposing party who shall be waited for until the descent of the sun after midday, and if he does not come it shall be removed in the presence of those who are present, and when they examine the bare hand or feet they shall immediately judge the defendant either innocent or guilty; and if he is judged innocent, he shall pay the priest the cost of his labour; if he is guilty the payment of this fee will fall on the plaintiff according to the custom of the church and the district. It has been decided that a week for hot iron must not have any holiday to avoid that the holiday is disturbed by fast or that kind of activity. Apart from this it shall also be known that due to the abhorrence of theft only the kind of the ordeal by hot iron mentioned as the second, not the first or the last, may be performed during those times in which the peace of the church should be kept, that is from the eve of St. Olaus the Martyr until the feast of St. Michael and the next day; from Advent until eight days after Epiphany; from Septuagesima until after the feast of Easter, and the Rogation days[80] and the week of Pentecost; and on those days, although all oaths concerning other cases must wait, it is permitted to anyone, in order to take back his property that has been unjustly taken away by a thief or robber, to give oath so that further delay shall not cause harm or loss to him because he was waiting.

100. Quod omnes pisces, qui reperiuntur in litore maris, usui conceduntur inueniencium preter sturgionem et totum cetum.

Omnes pisces, sine sunt mortui siue uiui, sic casu uersus terram appulsi, ut manus hominum non possint effugere, occupantibus conceduntur preter sturgionem integrum, qui iuri regio, a quocumque repertus fuerit, totus cedit, preter quoque cetum, de quo quicumque primo aduenerit, si pedes uenerit, fascem suis sufficientem humeris, si eques, onus equi, si auriga, quantum currus suus trahere poterit, si nauta cum naui uenerit, quantum nauis sex remorum deferre poterit, deportabit, euentumque rei exactori regio nunciabit. Alioquin tres ei marcas nummorum persoluet, uel duodeno suam omissionem inficiabitur iuramento.

101. De rebus per mare ad terram propulsis.

Licet cuique, rebus suis quibuslibet per mare uentorum rabie uel quouis infortunio propulsis ad terram, pro earundem collectione uel quauis alia disposicione adiutores, quoscumque uoluerit uel habere potuerit, prece uel precio aduocare, nullatenus obligato ad auxilium exactoris regii declinare, ne afflicto superaddatur maior affliccio in coacta grauis auxilii comparacione; quando uero tales res suas dominus derelinquit, desperans sibi aliquod super eis auxilium profuturum, per legem ad earum dominium rex uocatur, ut eas subito exactori suo liceat uendicare. Quando uero, rebus ad terram proiectis, earum dominus non comparet, inuentor earum debet euentum hominibus nunciare, ut super rebus suis certioratus dominus, sex iuramentalibus prius de dominio fide facta, rebus suis potiri libere permittatur. Si uero dominus nusquam compareat, per annum et diem res reperte in regii exactoris custodia seruabuntur, ut si uel dominus uel ipsius heres infra illud tempus adueniat, res amissas secundum predictum modum, probato prius dominio et in eis factis utiliter restitutis sumptibus, consequatur.

102. De agraria defensione et circa agros sepibus faciendis.

Tam communis uniuersorum quam priuata poscit utilitas singulorum agros tante securitatis munimine roborari, ut que dei solius munere producunt beneficia, ad utilitatem suorum peruenire ualeant dominorum; quapropter prouida constitutum dinoscitur racione, ut post sementem soli uisceribus commendatam diem sibi prefigant uniuscuiusque uille incole uniuersi, in quo quicumque pro parte sua agros sepire noluerit seminatos, unam horam denariorum pro sua negligencia puniendus emendet. Itemque alius prefigatur, in quo, si sepire noluerit, duabus horis satisfacere teneatur.

Ch. 100 That all fish which are found on the seashore except sturgeon and a whole whale are allowed to be used by the finder.

All kinds of fish, whether dead or alive, which are accidentally driven towards land so that they cannot flee the hands of men, are granted to those who take them except for whole sturgeon, which by law shall be yielded wholly to the king by whomever it is found; and also except for a whale, of which, whoever arrives first shall carry away, if he comes on foot, the load he can carry on his shoulders, if by horse, what a horse can carry, if a driver, as much as his cart can carry, if a sailor comes with a boat, as much as a six-oared boat can remove; and he shall report the matter to the king's official. Otherwise, he must pay him three marks in money or deny this omission by an oath of twelve.

Ch. 101 On objects cast from sea to land.

Anyone may call in as many helpers as he wishes or is able to have by prayer or payment in order to collect any of his property or for some other measure when it has been cast to land from the sea by the savagery of the winds[81] or a misfortune of any kind, and he shall by no means be under the obligation to ask the king's official for assistance, in order that the greater affliction of forced payment for expensive assistance shall not be superimposed upon the already afflicted. However, if the owner abandons such property of his because he has given up the hope that any assistance with it will be of use to him, then the king is called to their ownership by the law, so that his official is permitted to claim them immediately. Moreover, when things are washed ashore, and their owner cannot be found, he who finds them must report it to the people so that the owner when he has been notified, after having first sworn an oath to his ownership with six oath givers, can freely seize his belongings. If the owner does not appear, then what was found will be kept in the custody of the king's official for a year and a day, so that if the owner or his heir should arrive within that time he may acquire the lost things according to the aforesaid procedure after his ownership has first been proven and the necessary expenses spent on them have been paid for.

Ch. 102 On the protection of acres and the making of fences around fields.

Everyone's common interest as well as the particular interest of every single individual[82] require that acres are protected with a fence so secure that the benefits, which they produce as a gift from God, may only come to the use of their owners; and therefore it seems to be a prudent and cautious decision that after the planting of seed in the interior of the soil[83] all those who live in the village shall fix a day for themselves on which any person who for his part has not wanted to fence the sown fields shall be punished and pay one ounce in money for his negligence. And after that another term shall be fixed upon which he shall compensate with two ounces if he declines to put up a fence.

113

Tercioque dies tercius statuatur, in quo, si nec tunc paruerit, ad persoluendam marcam dimidiam obligetur. Deinde si parere nolens in sua perstiterit obstinacione, in
ius cum sua querimonia procedentes ceteri talem a iuridicis deportent sentenciam,
ut eis impune liceat, per subtraccionem bonorum, aduersariorum suorum contu-
maciam utilitati communi contrariam castigare.

103. Quod ad agrorum uel pratorum dominos bona propria tueri pertinebit.
Agris et pratis unius uille coniunctis alterius uille pascuis solis animalibus deputatis, onus faciendarum sepium non ad pascuorum, animalium racione, ne dampnum
inferant, sed ad agrorum et pratorum dominos, ut bona tueantur propria, pertinebit.

104. De sacione et custodia siliginis.
Si seratur siligine totum illud terre spacium, quod ante fuit ordeo seminatum, sicut
ante sepes sunt ab omnibus eiusdem terre possessoribus faciende. Uerum tantum
parte aliqua totalis spacii sementem siliginis admittente, tantum partis illius domini
eam includentibus studebunt sepibus faciendis.

105. Quod nulli licet sepem propriam uel alienam a custodia agrorum uel pratorum remouere, donec segetes et fenum collecta fuerint.
Sepes fiunt agrorum uel pratorum ad arcendum animalia et fenum et segetes conse-
ruandum, unde non licet cuiquam, donec fenum uel seges collecta fuerit et ab agris
omnes manipuli deportati, alienam sepem uel propriam ab agrorum uel pratorum
custodia remouere. Siquis autem ante, ut in curru uel equo per agrum uel pratum
incedat, uel alia quauis causa alienam sepem demoliri presumpserit aut auferre,
preter omnis dampni restitucionem duas horas nummorum pariter emendabit, aut
hoc se fecisse terno inficiabitur iuramento. Sunt et sepes, quarum demolicio uel
ablacio trium marcarum exigit satisfactionem, puta quibus fundus includitur et
munitur edificiis deputatus.

106. Quod pro furto unius manipuli fur possit ligari.
Ex quo propter annone periculum uiolatores multantur sepium, racione suadente
multo sunt atrocius puniendi non uerentes rapinam uel furtum in ipsa anona cus-
todienda sepibus exercere. Quapropter qui de agro uel unum furatur manipulum,
licet forte non ualeat unum denarium, de iure comprehendi poterit et uinciri et
uinctus in ius adduci, pro reatu tali a iuridicis condempnandus, licet pro furto
commisso in rebus aliis, quod v denarios non ualeat, nullus sit per legis licenciam
uinciendus.

114

Then, a third day shall be fixed, and if he does not appear there, he shall render half a mark. If after that he still unwillingly persists in his obstinacy, the others shall bring their complaint to the assembly, and they shall have the judgment by the men of the assembly, that they may punish their opponents' obstinate rejection of the common interest by taking their property without being punished themselves.

Ch. 103 That it is for the owners of acres or meadows to protect their own property.

When acres and meadows of one village adjoin the pastureland of another that is intended for their animals alone, the burden of fencing shall not be carried by the owners of the pastureland in order to keep the animals from causing damage, but rather by the owners of the fields and meadows, in order to protect their own property.

Ch. 104 On the sowing and care of rye.

If an entire stretch of land that was previously sown with barley is sown with rye, fences are to be made by all the owners of this land as before. But if only a portion of the total area is reserved for the sowing of rye, only the owners of that part shall see to it that it is fenced in.

Ch. 105 That no one is permitted to remove his own or another's fence from the protection of fields or meadows until crops and hay have been harvested.

Fences of fields and meadows are made for keeping off animals and preserving hay and crops, and therefore no one is allowed to remove another's fence or his own from the protection of fields or meadows until the hay or crops have been harvested and all sheaves are taken out of the fields. If, however, anyone at an earlier date presumes to demolish or carry away another's fence so that he can come forward either in a cart or on a horse through a field or meadow or for any other reason whatsoever, he shall in addition to paying for the damage equally give compensation of two ounces in money or deny that he has done this by an oath of three. And there are even fences whose destruction or removal demands compensation of three marks, namely those with which the curtilage of the houses is enclosed and which protect the land belonging to the buildings.

Ch. 106 That a thief may be bound for the theft of a single sheaf.

As violators of fences are fined because of the danger to the crop, it is reasonable that those who do not hesitate to engage in plunder or theft of the same crop must be punished more harshly. Therefore, he who steals just a single sheaf from the field, even if it should be worth less than a penny, by the law may be taken and bound and carried off to the assembly in bonds to be condemned by the men of the assembly for such a crime, even though nobody can lawfully be tied up for the theft of other things worth less than five pennies.

107. Qualiter puniantur qui animalia sua tollunt hiis, qui ea in agro suo uel prato comprehenderint.

Ad arcendum animalia pastum affectancia licet sepium prosit custodia, non tamen sufficit usquequaque, nisi custodie ipsorum animalium cura diligencior impendatur; et idcirco, ut studeat unusquisque animalia sua diligencius custodire, ne dampnum inferant in anona, sustentacioni hominum reseruanda, utilitate communi persuadente lege constat indissolubili constitutum, ut unicuique liceat animalia comprehendere que in messe sua repererit aliena, et impune, donec per ea fiat dampni restitucio, retinere; in uiolatores huius constitucionis pro uarietate presumpcionis pena quoque uaria constituta, ut siquis animalia comprehensa manu ducenti rapuerit, tres marcas nummorum, aut si a propellente ipsa coram se abigendo fugauerit, duas horas, aut si a domo comprehensoris uel curia iam inclusa extraxerit, tres marcas eciam nummorum emendet, aut duarum horarum reatum cum trino et trium marcarum cum duodeno deneget iuramento.

108. Qualiter dominus animalia sua debet redimere, et quando preter restitucionem dampni dati tenetur satisfacere, et quantum.

Multum refert, quot animalia et utrum domini uoluntate an domino nesciente in agrum uel pratum ueniant alienum, si quidem estimacioni dampni dati tres marcas numorum adiunget dominus, si gregem suum aut equicium ad minus xii capitibus constitutum in agrum uel pratum cum pastore et cane dirigat alienum, uel consensu suo dampnum datum duodeno inficiabitur iuramento. Si uero casu, preter domini uoluntatem, constat a tot animalibus dampnum datum, dato prius pignere, quod dimidiam marcam nummorum ualeat, super estimacione dampni dati prestanda, facta a duobus uel tribus et probata trium hominum iuramentis, a dampnum passo dominus animalia, que dampnum intulerant, consequatur. Si uero numerus animalium minor fuerit, solius domini, si conciuis fuerit dampnum passi, super estimacione dampni sufficiat iuramentum. Si uero, cum animalibus dampnum inferentibus, uille alterius inhabitator fuerit, duobus sociis indigebit, ut super estimacionis dampni quantitate fidem terno faciat iuramento. Eodem quoque sociorum et iuramentorum numero se defendet, si dampnum in presenciarum passus se dampnum sepius ab eius animalibus conqueratur perpessum. Si uero dominus contendat animalia sua non in agris uel pratis quibuslibet, sed innoxia comprehensa, dampnum passus, quod ea iuste ceperit, trium probet hominum iuramentis, aut animalia cum duarum horarum nummorum reliberat emendacione. Excepto primo casu nihil addendum est estimacioni, nisi accusetur dominus animalium ea furtiue in agrum uel pratum alterius induxisse, in quo casu uel duas horas nummorum addet dominus estimacioni, uel trium hominum iuramentis a furti uicio se purgabit.

Ch. 107 How to punish those who take their animals away from others who have seized them in their field or meadow.

Although the protection of fences is helpful to keep away animals seeking food, nevertheless it is not always sufficient unless the utmost care is expended in the guarding of these animals. Therefore, it is stated by irrevocable law for the common advantage that anyone is permitted to seize other people's animals that he finds in his crops and to keep them with impunity until restitution is made for the damage, so that every man strives to keep his animals with the utmost care so they do not damage the harvest, which is meant for human sustenance; and for those who violate this law there are different punishments according to the variety of seriousness in the violation, so that anyone who forcefully seizes his animals when they are being led by hand shall pay three marks in money, or if he makes them flee from the person who is driving them in front of him, he shall pay two ounces, or if he takes them away from the home of the apprehender or his farm where they have already been enclosed, he shall also pay three marks in money or else he must deny the two-ounces crime by an oath of three and the one of three marks by an oath of twelve.

Ch. 108 How an owner shall redeem his animals and when he is liable to pay compensation besides the restitution for the inflicted loss and how much.

Much depends on the number of animals and whether they go into another's field or meadow at their owner's will or without the owner's knowledge. If he directs his flock or his troop of horses numbering at least twelve into another's field or meadow with a shepherd and dog, the owner will have to add three marks in money to the assessed value of the damage inflicted, or else he must deny by an oath of twelve that the damage was done with his consent. If it is decided that damage by this many animals was done by accident contrary to the owner's will, then the owner will get the animals back from the person who suffered the damage after a pledge worth half a mark has first been given in addition to the assessed value of the loss inflicted as determined by two or three men and confirmed by the oaths of three. If the number of animals is less and the owner comes from the same village as the man who suffered the damage, the oath of the owner alone regarding the assessed value of the loss will suffice. If it is someone from another village whose animals caused damage, then he will need two companions so that he may swear his oath regarding the assessed value of the loss by an oath of three. But he must also defend himself with the same number of companions and oaths if he who has suffered the damage complains that he has often suffered damage from his animals. But if the owner contends that his animals were in no fields or meadows whatsoever and were blameless when taken, then the man who has suffered the damage shall prove by the oath of three men that he took them justly, or else he must release the animals along with compensation of two ounces. With the exception of the first case, nothing is to be added to the assessed damage unless the owner of the animals is accused of having led them furtively into the field or meadow of another man, in which case the owner can add two ounces to the assessed damage or purge himself from the vice of theft by an oath of three.

117

109. Inter regem uel episcopum et alios, item inter regis uel episcopi uillicum et alios, que sit differencia et que conueniencia in iure comprehendendi uel redimendi, in quantitate satisfaccionis uel estimacionis prestande uel sumende.
In iure comprehendendi aliena et propria redimendi animalia et in quantitate satisfaccionis uel estimacionis prestande uel sumende inter exactorem uel uillicum regis uel episcopi et quemuis alium nihil differt. At in mansione sua rege uel episcopo existente, si sibi dampnum in suis agris inferatur ab animalibus scientis domini et uolentis, estimacioni dampni dati, propter contemptam presentis regis uel presulis honorificenciam, in tribus marcis nummorum contemptus precium adiungatur. Si uero casu, domino ignorante, fuerit dampnum datum, nihil preter estimacionem dampni dati terno probandam iuramento, licet presens, rex uel episcopus obtinebit; in hoc autem solo exactor uel uillicus regis uel antistitis differt ab aliis, quod si taliter sibi dampni dati ad multorum audienciam in ius deferat accusacionem, aut trium marcarum satisfaccionem ab aduersario preter estimacionem, si confessus fuerit, aut duodenum iuramentum, si negauerit, consequetur.

110. Quid iuris sit, si dampnum passus perimat animalia dampnum inferencia.
Licet licite possint animalia in alienis agris dampnum inferencia comprehendi, non tamen perimi, sed seruari, donec estimacione prestita liberentur. Uerum si quod propter talis dampni iacturam animal occidatur, post omnis dampni prestitam estimacionem probatam manus tercie iuramento, licet conciuis fuerit occisoris dominus animalis, occisor prestabit precium animalis occisi probatum iustum et sufficiens tribus trium hominum iuramentis, deinde contemptus precium duas horas nummorum uidelicet emendabit, si duas horas nummorum ad minus ualens in absencia uel quantumcumque parum ualens in domini presencia et aspectu fuerit interfectum; nec confesso interfectionem licet in hoc casu contemptus precium diffiteri, nisi iuret occisor cum duobus sociis occisum animal absente domino duas horas nummorum minime ualuisse; in quo casu nihil prestabitur racione contemptus, sed tantum precium animalis occisi, fide facta trino iuramento super sufficienti precii quantitate. Si uero super occisione accusatus se deneget occidisse, per iurisiurandi religionem aut cum duobus sociis aut cum v aut cum xi se defendet, puta uel trino uel seno uel duodeno hominum iuramento, iuxta quantitatem precii animalis, quod dicitur interemptum, trino si duarum horarum nummorum uel minus, seno si sex horarum uel minus quantumlibet usque ad duas horas, duodeno si sex horis maius precium opponatur.

Ch. 109 What differences and similarities exist between the king and the bishop and others, and between the bailiff of the king or of the bishop and others, in their right to seize and redeem, and in the amount of compensation or assessment to be given or obtained.

No difference exists in law between a king's or bishop's bailiff or official and any other man as to the seizure of another's or the redemption of one's own animals and in the amount of compensation or the assessed value to be offered or taken. But when the king or the bishop resides in his manor, compensation for contempt consisting of three marks in money will be added to the assessed value of the loss inflicted if damage is inflicted by animals in his fields with the knowledge and at the will of the owner due to contempt for the honour of the king or bishop present. When the damage happens by accident and without the owner's knowledge, the king or the bishop, even if present, will get nothing in addition to the assessed value of the damage inflicted, which shall be confirmed by an oath of three; and only in this alone does the king's or bishop's official or bailiff differ from others, that if one of them brings an accusation for a damage he has suffered before the assembly in the presence of many people, he will, besides the assessed value, get a compensation of three marks from his adversary, if this one admits, and if he denies, this must be followed by an oath of twelve.

Ch. 110 How to proceed if he who suffered damage kills the animals that caused the damage.

Even if animals caught doing damage in another's fields may lawfully be taken, they may not, however, be killed but must be kept until they are released by the payment of the assessed value. If an animal is killed due to the loss incurred through such damage and the owner is from the same village as the killer of the animal, then after payment of the assessed value of the entire damage has been confirmed by an oath of three, the killer shall pay the worth of the killed animal, confirmed as just and sufficient by three times the oath of three men, and thereafter he shall pay compensation for contempt, which is two ounces in money if an animal valued at least at two ounces is killed in the owner's absence, or regardless of how little value if it is killed within his presence and sight; nor in this case is someone who has admitted the killing allowed to deny compensation for contempt unless the killer swears with two companions that the animal killed in the owner's absence had a value of less than two ounces; in that case he shall pay nothing for contempt but only the value of the killed animal when he has sworn by an oath of three that the value is sufficiently large. If, however, he who is accused of the killing denies having killed, he shall defend himself by an oath, either with two companions or with five or with eleven; namely with either an oath of three men or an oath of six men or one of twelve men, in proportion to the worth of the animal killed, and an oath of three if the price is two ounces or less, an oath of six if the price is six ounces or any lesser amount down to two ounces and an oath of twelve if the price is estimated at more than six ounces.

Est et casus, in quo specialitas interfectionis, que *gornithings werk* lingua patria nominatur, puta quando sic lancea uel quouis alio instrumento nocendi ad minus dimidiam marcam ualens animal perforatur, ut horrende per uulnus uiscera emanare cernantur, trium marcarum nummorum exigit satisfaccionem preter occisi precium animalis, de cuius iusta fidem facient quantitate estimacioni animalis conueniencia iuramenta. Si uero huiusmodi denegetur interfeccio, negacioni duodenum fidem faciat iuramentum. Si quis dicat alium furtiue suum animal occidisse, dimidiam marcam ualens, iuramentum exhibeat, quod *asswærueth* patria lingua dictum est appellari, et sic reum ferri candentis iudicium subire compellat, et si reus manus conuictus apparuerit ustione, pro reatu suo iusto animalis precio duplum addat.

111. Quod animalia comprehensa non debeant post oblatam iusticiam retineri.
Non licet eciam dampnum passo animalia comprehensa post oblatam sibi iusticiam retinere; postquam enim dominus in compensacionem dampni dati annonam obtulerit exhibendo, et de sufficienti compensacione suum prestiterit iuramentum, si noluerit eum dampnum passus in restitucione animalium exaudire, eiusdem uille aliquot inhabitantibus conuocatis dominus protestetur coram eis et dampnum passo sibi iusticiam denegari; deinde cum testimonio conuocatorum ciuium in ius deferat querimoniam suam ad iuridicorum audienciam, ibique in accusatum feratur sentencia, ut aduersario suo pro negata iusticia uel trium marcarum offerat satisfaccionem uel, quod illud non egerit, duodenum exhibeat iuramentum. Item si post iusticiam denegatam animalia moriantur, preter eorum precium iniustus detentor uel tres marcas nummorum emendet uel iniuste detencionis accusacioni duodenum obiciat iuramentum.

112. Quod dominus teneatur redimere animalia sua.
Nec licet quoque domino nolle animalia sua redimere comprehensa; nam eo nolente comprehendens eum, ut redimat, primo die, missis duobus hominibus, deprecetur. Idemque tam 2° die, missis aliis duobus hominibus, quam die tercio, missis quoque tercio nouis duobus hominibus, operetur; eo perseueranter redimere recusante, deinde procedens in ius cum suis testibus uniuersis uniuersum rerum gestarum ordinem coram omnibus protestetur, talemque contra suum aduersarium latam a iuridicis reportet sentenciam, ut in nullo teneatur ei de cetero de illis animalibus, quidquid de ipsis contigerit, respondere. Si uero super iniusta comprehensione uel detencione detentorem dominus instanter accuset, iuramentorum numero conuenienti animalium estimacioni detentor probet, quod dominus animalia sua iuste capta redimere supersedit post predictam trinam legitimam admonicionem. Si uero deficiat in probacione, tantum animalia, si possit, uel, si non possit, precium eorum restituat, post dampni dati prestitam estimacionem ab omni alia satisfactione propter assercionem suorum testium excusatus.

There is also the particular case of killing called *gornithings werk* in the native language when, for instance, an animal worth at least half a mark is pierced with a lance or another injurious instrument, so that its intestines may be seen to issue from the wound in a horrible way; this demands compensation of three marks in addition to the value of the killed animal, the just amount of which is fixed by oaths corresponding to the estimated worth of the animal. But if a killing of this kind is denied, an oath of twelve shall confirm the denial. If anyone says that someone else has furtively killed his animal which is worth half a mark, he shall swear the oath, which is said to go by the name of *asswaerueth* in the native language, and thus compel the accused to submit to the ordeal by hot iron; and if the accused is found to be convicted by the burning of his hand, he shall add for his crime the double to the just value of the animal.

Ch. 111 That animals that have been seized must not be kept after what can be demanded has been offered.

After what can be demanded has been offered, the man who has suffered damage is not allowed to retain for himself animals that have been seized. If he who suffered the damage does not want to comply with the owner of the animals by restoring them after he has offered and paid the compensation for the damage inflicted in grain and given his oath that the compensation was sufficient, then after a number of the inhabitants of the same village have been called together, he must affirm before them and before him who suffered the damage that he is not being treated lawfully; then, with the testimony of the villagers gathered in the assembly, he shall present his complaint to be heard by the men of the assembly, and there the sentence shall be given against the accused, that for not treating him lawfully he shall either offer compensation of three marks or give an oath of twelve that he did not do it. Also, if the animals should die during unlawful treatment, the unjust detainer must pay on top of their value either three marks in money or counter the accusation of unjust detention by an oath of twelve.

Ch. 112 That an owner is obliged to redeem his animals.

Nor is it allowed for an owner to omit to redeem his seized animals; for if he is unwilling, the seizer shall on the first day send two men to the unwilling man and ask him to redeem. The same shall happen on the second day, two other men being sent, and on the third day for a third time, with two new men being sent; if he perseveres in his refusal to redeem, then at the assembly with all his witnesses the seizer shall explain before everyone the entire order in which the case has proceeded, and he shall obtain from the men of the assembly a judgment against his adversary so he will in no way be held responsible for anything else with regard to the animals, no matter what happens to them. If, however, the owner expressly accuses the detainer of unjust seizure or detention, the detainer shall prove with a number of oath givers appropriate to the agreed-upon value of the animals that the owner did not redeem his animals when they were lawfully captured, after the aforesaid triple legal admonition. But if he is deficient in proof, he shall restore the animals, if he can, or if he cannot, their value, but except for the estimated damage inflicted, he shall not pay any other compensation because of the declaration of his witnesses.

113. De tempore, quod animalium custodie deputatur.

Non est totus annus animalium custodie deputatus, uerum illud tempus totum et solum, quod a uigilia penthecostes inchoatur et in uigilia sancti Michaelis archangeli terminatur; unde alio quocumque tempore, si reperiantur in agris et pratis, non possunt animalia comprehendi, sed absque aliqua lesione depelli; quippe si per inuia et lutosa loca propulsa uitam finierint, propellentes simul omnes omne dampnum restituent, et sue presumpcionis iniuriam expiando tres marcas prestabunt insuper satisfaccionis nomine. At si factum maluerint diffiteri, quemcumque super hoc dampnum passus detulerit furti reum, premisso iuramento, quod lingua patria *asswærueth* nominatur, candentis ferri iudicium subire compellet, et a conuicto per manus ustionem preter omnis dampni restitucionem tres marcas satisfaccionis nomine reportabit.

114. De nemorum defensione.

Ne siluis suis domini cotidianis usibus ualde necessariis defraudentur, iuris censura prohibet alienum nemus succidi contra domini uoluntatem, in succidentem quantitati succisionis penam constituens competentem, ut si ligna succisa uel uno curru uel duobus uel tribus uel pluribus, donec occurrat duodenarius, deferantur, preter restitucionem lignorum duas horas nummorum domino succidens persoluat, uel succisionem trino deneget iuramento; si uero xii currus uel plures lignorum fuerint succisorum, et ligna restituat et tres marcas prestet nomine satisfaccionis, uel accusacioni duodenum obiciat iuramentum. At si reum in ipsa succisione dominus deprehendat, de sex horarum emendacione prestanda pignus ab eo suscipiat, ne conuentus ex postfacto se diffiteri ualeat debitorem. Non dato pignore, si oblatam satisfaccionem exactus uoluerit diffiteri, trinum ei sufficiat iuramentum. Si nihil secum ad impignerandum habeat deprehensus, ad uillam proximam profectus cum domino succisi nemoris procuret ei uel pignus uel fideiussorem, ut oblate fidem habeat satisfaccioni. Eo uero neutrum procurante, ibidem dominus protestetur omnem sibi iusticiam denegari, et, cum uoluerit, istam iniuriam in solemnis deducat querimoniam accusacionis, ut trium marcarum obtineat satisfaccionem, nisi, sue saluti rem preferens temporalem et affectans in anima puniri pocius quam in pecunia, illam aduersarius accusacionem duodeno presumat elidere iuramento. Eodem dominus utatur remedio protestacionis ad uillam procedens proximam, si, cum possit, nolit succisor lignorum ei rem suam pignori obligare, ne, rem ei per uiolenciam auferendo et ius sibi dicendo, non ad minus aduersario quam sibi suus aduersarius ob illatam iniuriam obligetur.

Ch. 113 On the period when animals shall be guarded.

The entire year is not intended for the guarding of animals, but only the whole period that begins from the eve of Pentecost and is ended on the eve of St. Michael the archangel; from this it follows that at any other time whatever animals discovered in fields and meadows cannot be seized but must be driven out without doing any harm; if on the other hand they end their life by being driven into an impassable and muddy location, all of those who drove them shall pay damages for the total loss collectively and as atonement for their preposterous breach of the law they shall in addition pay three marks as compensation. But if they choose to deny the deed, the one who has suffered damage on this account shall accuse each of them of being a thief; and after the oath, which is called *asswærueth* in the native language, has been offered in advance, he can compel him to undergo the ordeal by hot iron, and on top of the damages for all loss obtain three marks as compensation from him who has been convicted by the burning of his hand.

Ch. 114 On the protection of woods.

In order that the owners shall not be fraudulently deprived of their woods which are so necessary for daily use, the law prohibits cutting in someone else's woods without the owner's permission, and the penalty shall correspond to the amount of the cutting, so that if cut timber is carried off either in one cart or in two or three or more up to the twelfth, the person who did the cutting must pay two ounces in money to the owner on top of the restitution for the timber or deny the cutting by an oath of three; if in fact there were twelve carts or more of cut timbers, he shall both make restitution for the timber and pay three marks as compensation or counter the accusation by an oath of twelve. But if the owner catches the culprit in the very act of cutting, he can take a pledge from him for the six ounces to be paid as compensation, so that when he is later summoned he cannot deny that he is in debt. If a pledge is not given, and he will deny that he offered compensation, an oath of three will suffice for him. If the person apprehended has nothing with him with which to pledge, he shall go with the owner of the cut wood to the nearest village to get for him either a pledge or a guarantor, so that the owner can be assured of the compensation that has been offered. But if he gets neither one nor the other, the owner shall declare that he was denied what is due to him, and when he wishes he can turn this breach of the law into a formal accusation to get three marks' compensation, unless his adversary dares to counter his accusation by an oath of twelve, thus preferring temporal property to his salvation and being less affected by punishment to his soul than to his purse. When the owner has gone to the nearest village and the cutter of wood, even though he can, will not give him any of his things as a pledge, the owner can make use of the same declaration in order that he shall not, by removing something by violence and taking the law into his own hands, make himself just as guilty towards his adversary as his adversary is towards him.

Cum extractis corticibus necesse sit, ueluti succise fuissent, arescentes arbores deperire, de subtraccione corticis et succisione arboris idem erit iuris iudicium obseruandum, ut iacture quantitati iuxta capacitatem curruum estimate predicto modo respondere pena debeat emendacionis. Idem quoque obseruabitur, si ad pastum animalium alieni nemoris contra domini uoluntatem arbores succidantur, licet nullis curribus deferantur.

115. De hiis, que sumi licite possunt ex nemore alieno.

Humane societatis liberalitas quedam concedit ex nemore alieno, licet domini conniuencia non accedat; ut quotquot axes franguntur in curribus per nemus transeuncium alienum, tot ex ipso possunt nemore restaurari. Si quid tamen preter ipsos axes ex lignis succisis fuerit deportatum, duarum horarum exigit emendacionem, uel succisum esse de nemore alieno tercio negabitur iuramento. Licet quoque de fructu nemoris, puta de nucibus auellanis uel aliis, dum transit, edere transeunti, licet quoque deferre, sed quantum pugnus uel sue capiunt cyrotece. Pro hiis autem, que sinu suo uel hora uestis sue deportauerit, duas horas tenebitur emendare uel factum per iurisiurandi religionem cum manu tercia diffiteri. At si curru uel equo detulerit, estimacionem dampni prestabit, uel factum inficiabitur iuramentis conuenientibus estimacioni.

116.

Falcones et accipitres et quelibet aues indomite licenter accipiuntur in nemore alieno, ita tamen ut nemus succisione aliqua non ledatur; nidum accipitrum et falconum siquis primo repererit, quamuis in nemore alieno, si pullorum pedes innexos laqueis sic affixerit, ut non possint, cum creuerint, auolare, si quis postea superueniens eos amouerit, duas horas, si palam factum indicauerit, emendabit; si uero celauerit, accusari poterit furti reus. Apes suas auolantes siquis ad nemus prosecutus fuerit alienum, aut ibidem apes inuenerit nullius dominio mancipatas, licenter eas auferat, sed absque nemoris lesione. Si uero arborem ab eis occupatam succiderit, consensu domini non obtento, tres marcas nummorum prestabit nomine satisfaccionis, aut factum suum duodeno diffitebitur iuramento; equitatis autem persuadet racio, ut obtineatur uoluntas domini, si suo dominio apum medietas assignetur. Uerum ad consenciendum animo suo nullatenus inclinato, si, postquam dominus uel inuentor recesserit, consignata prius arbore ab apibus occupata, ipse silue dominus eas sustulerit, nisi se dominum contra salutem suam cum duobus testibus et duodeno docere presumpserit iuramento, uerus dominus, cum eas ceperit uendicare, postquam sibi sublatas uel furtiue uel uiolenter seno tantummodo iuramento docuerit, obtinebit.

As fresh trees will necessarily die after the bark has been removed just as if they had been cut, the same rule will be observed, so that the penalty will correspond to the amount of compensation according to the capacity of carts in the aforesaid manner. And the same is to be observed if for the pasturing of someone else's animals the trees of a wood are cut contrary to the owner's will, even if they are not carried away in any carts.

Ch. 115 On those things which can lawfully be taken from the wood of another person.

The generosity of human society allows you to take certain things from another person's wood even if the owner does not give his assent, so that no matter how many axles are broken on wagons travelling through someone else's wood, replacements can be retrieved from that wood. If, however, some of the cut timber besides the axles themselves is carried away, it must be compensated by two ounces, or it must be denied by an oath of three that anything was cut in the wood. While passing through a wood it is also permitted for the person passing through to eat from the fruit of the wood such as nuts or other things and to carry away as much as the hand or gloves can seize. But for what he carries away in his bosom or in the folds of his clothing he shall pay two ounces or deny it by an oath of three. And if it is carried away by horse or wagon, he must pay the assessed value of the loss or deny it with oaths according to the assessed value.

Ch. 116.

Falcons and hawks and any other untamed birds may freely be taken in someone else's wood, as long as the wood is not damaged by any cutting. If someone who first finds a nest of hawks and falcons, even in someone else's wood, fastens together the bound feet of the chicks with halters so that they cannot fly away when they grow larger, and someone who comes later takes them away, then he must pay two ounces if he openly makes the act known; but if he keeps it secret, then he can be accused of theft. If anyone follows his bees into someone else's wood, or in the same place finds bees that do not belong to any owner, he may freely take them away, but without damage to the wood. If, however, he cuts down the tree that they occupy without the owner's permission, he must pay three marks in money as compensation or deny his action by an oath of twelve; the reason of equity suggests, however, that the owner's goodwill might be obtained if half of the bees are handed over to him. But if the owner of the wood is not willing to consent and he takes the bees away after the owner or finder has withdrawn and the tree occupied by the bees has previously been marked, then the real owner shall have them when he decides to claim them back if he proves only by an oath of six that they have been taken from him either by theft or by violence, unless the other at the risk of his salvation dares to prove that he is the owner with two witnesses and an oath of twelve.

Si silue dominus apum obiciat inuentori, quod easdem prius inuenerit, non debet audiri, nisi suam assercionem trino corroboret iuramente. Domum alicuius apibus ingressis alterius eas, donec illam domum eligerent, insequentis, si domus dominus se contendat earum dominum, trino se probet dominum iuramento, aut eas insecutus eodem numero iuramentalium de suo facere fidem dominio permittatur; inde tamen sic eas extrahat, ne domui uel parum officiat aliene. Unius apibus super alterius apes descendentibus atque ad spiritus eas confringentibus exalacionem, inferentes dampnum ad alias apportentur, easque domini simul possideant in communi. At si nequiuerint super communi dominio conuenire, accusatus supra dampno a suis apibus irrogato, si negare uoluerit dampnum datum, se iuramentalibus tueatur dampni conuenientibus estimacioni. At confessus restituat, quantum uoluerit, atque residuum iuxta quantitatem eius neget sufficientibus iuramentis.

117. De hiis, que non possunt licite sumi uel fieri in nemore alieno.
Uentorum rabie sine alio quouis modo prostratam arborem si quis a nemore alieno presumpserit deportare contra domini uoluntatem, estimacionem dampni domino prestabit conuentus, aut negabit factum iuramentalibus sufficientibus estimacioni. Racione indaginis facte de nemore alieno cum estimacione dampni sex horarum emendacio locum habet aut per senum defensio iuramentum.

118. Quid iuris sit, si quis in alieno solo fossam fecerit.
Extrahendi fetus uulpini gracia si quis effoderit fossam in nemore uel solo quolibet alieno, ad sex horarum tenebitur satisfaccionem uel defensionem tante pecunie competentem; nullo tamen prohibito fetum uulpinum in nullius dominio permanentem, ubi res aliena non leditur, occupare. Insequenti uulpem suis exagitatam canibus, donec in nemore uel loco quolibet alieno latibulum ingrediatur fouee, licet, quantum ad comprehensionem uulpis opus fuerit, eandem foueam ampliare. Sed nisi foueam illam repleuerit, si quisquam in eam elapsus uitam finierit, tres marcas ob dampni occasionem prestitam emendabit, et omne aliud dampnum prestabit usque ad trium marcarum summam, de quocumque ibi contigerit animali, aut se fodisse negabit iuramentalibus dampni conuenientibus estimacioni.

119. Alieni porci inuito domino de nemare non pascantur alieno.
Persuadet equitas naturalis nullius inuiti bona deseruire usibus alienis, unde non alieni porci admitti debent ad pastum nemoris alieni, circa nemus alienum et agrum alienum ob eandem racionem iuris eadem eciam permanente censura, quantum ad comprehensionem et redempcionem, quantum ad numerum animalium et porcorum, quantum ad scienciam et ignoranciam dominorum.

If the owner of a wood objects to the finder of the bees and says that he found them first, he shall not be heard unless he confirms his assertion by an oath of three. If the house of someone is entered by bees which belong to someone else and they were followed until they chose that house and the owner of the house contends that he himself is their owner, he shall prove his ownership with an oath of three, or else the man pursuing them is permitted with the same number of oaths to prove his ownership; thereupon he must take them away so that he does not in the least damage the alien house. If the bees of one person descend upon the bees of another person and cause so much harm to them that they give up their spirit, those who harmed the others shall be brought together with them, and the owners shall share them in common ownership. But if they are unable to reach an agreement on common ownership, and the one who is accused of the damage inflicted by his bees denies the damage, he shall protect himself with oaths appropriate to the assessed value of the loss. But if he admits, he shall make the restitution he wishes and deny the rest with sufficient oaths according to the amount.

Ch. 117 On the things that cannot licitly be taken or done in someone else's wood.

If anyone presumes to take away from someone else's wood against the owner's will a tree which has fallen because of the savagery of the winds or by any other means, he must pay the owner the assessed value of the loss when summoned, or he must deny the deed with oaths appropriate to the assessment. In the case that a hunting ground is made from the wood of another, together with assessed damages a fine of six ounces or a defence by an oath of six is applicable.

Ch. 118 How to proceed if someone digs a pit on the land of someone else.

If someone who is digging out a fox cub makes a pit in the wood or soil of someone else, he shall, regardless of where it was, give six ounces or a defence suitable to this sum; there is no prohibition, however, against taking a fox cub which is in no one else's ownership when someone else's property is not disturbed. He who pursues a fox with his hounds until it hides itself in a pit in the wood, or in any other place belonging to someone else, may widen this pit so much as is necessary to seize the fox. But if he does not fill the pit up again and someone falls into it and dies, he must pay three marks for having caused the damage, and he must pay up to the sum of three marks for all other harm to animals there or deny that he has dug the pit with oaths appropriate to the assessed loss.

Ch. 119 Someone else's pigs may not feed in another person's wood against the will of its owner.

Natural equity[84] teaches that no one's property may not be used against his will by others; therefore, one person's pigs shall not be allowed to feed in the wood of another, and with regard to other people's wood and other people's fields, the same legal reason leads to the same opinion when it comes to seizure and restoration, the number of animals and pigs and the knowledge and ignorance of the owners.

127

120. De communi nemore.

Uniuersis communi nemore unicuique libito suo licet uti. Uerum ibi succisam arborem, nisi secum deportet succisor continuo uel consignet, licebit uolenti cuilibet deportare. At abscisione utriusque termini consignata per annum et diem exspectabit proprium succisorem; infra quod tempus siquis eam abstulerit, estimacionem, cum eam habere non possit, primo restituet succisori, duasque horas nummorum prestabit nomine satifaccionis.

121.

Siquis in asseres uel columpnas uel aliam formam communis nemoris ligna dolauerit, ea dominio suo subiciet sine temporis prefinicione, ut nec post annum et diem alii preter consensum domini ea liceat sine furti uicio contrectare.

122. De aqua communi uel propria.

Omnis aqua nullo manufacto aggere, sed naturalibus tantum contenta litoribus equitate iuris omnibus est communis, ut in ea piscari nemo de iure ualeat prohiberi. At in aqua, quam ob molendini uel piscacionis usum iure quis facto aggere congregauit, preter eius consensum non licet alii piscacionis officium exercere.

123. De communis aque piscacione.

In aqua communi licet cuilibet piscari liceat, nulli tamen licet in amnem communem piscatoriam sepem inmittere, nisi terram possideat adiacentem, cui sepem suam infigendo profundius superponat; unde si ex una tantum parte amnis solum habeat, sepem ultra amnis medium non extendet. Si uero terras habeat utrimque fluuio accedentes, ex utraque parte fluuii sepes infixa per amnis medium extendetur.

124. Quod nullus a piscacione communis aque debeat prohiberi.

Incremento redundans communis aqua si terras occupat adiacentes, in ea nullus eciam in occupatis terrarum spaciis a piscacione de iure poterit cohiberi.

125. Quod nulli licet a uigilia penthecostes usque ad festum sancti Michaelis aquas ad usum molendini colligere alienis officientem pratis.

Nulli licet a uigilia penthecostes, donec sancti occurrat solemnitas Michaelis, aquas sic ad usum colligere molendini, ut super terras alienas propter retencionis uiolenciam effundantur, feno et ceteris, que prouenirent, commodis suos dominos defraudantes. Si uero dominus molendini iuris parere supersederit equitati, in ius querimonia deportata dies a iuridicis auferendi uel aperiendi portam aquarum constituatur, ne quouis obstaculo ad cuiusquam iniuriam earum transitus retardetur; cui nisi dominus molendini obtemperauerit iussioni, preter estimacionem dampni sex horas nummorum prestabit nomine satisfaccionis, aut seno factum inficiabitur iuramento.

Ch. 120 On common woods.

Everybody is permitted to use a common wood as he pleases. And if someone who cuts down a tree there does not immediately remove it or mark it, anyone who wants can take it away. But if it is marked by cutting off both ends, it shall await the man who cut it down for a year and a day; if someone takes it away during this period he must first pay the estimated value to him who cut it down, because he cannot have the wood, and pay two ounces as compensation.

Ch. 121

If anyone chops the timber of the common wood into stakes or poles or another shape, it will be subject to his ownership without time limit, so that not even after a year and a day may another person take it away against the will of the owner without committing the vice of theft.

Ch. 122 On common and particular water.

All water not dammed by hand but which is contained by any kind of natural bank is common to everyone by the equity of the law, so that no one can lawfully prohibit anyone to fish in it. But in water that someone has lawfully stemmed by damming it for milling or fishing, fishing is not allowed for others without his consent.

Ch. 123 On fishing in common water.

Even though everyone is permitted to fish in common water, no one is allowed to place a fish weir in a common fishing stream, unless he owns adjacent land on which his fish weir can be placed and deeply fastened; this means that if he has land only on one side of the stream, he may not extend the fish weir beyond the middle of the stream. If, however, he has land that reaches to the stream on both sides, a fish weir may be placed and extended into the middle from both directions of the stream.

Ch. 124 That no one is prohibited from fishing in common water.

If common water covers the adjacent lands by overflowing, no one can lawfully be hindered from fishing in the flooded lands as well.

Ch. 125 That no one is permitted to stem water for the use of milling to the detriment of others.

From the eve of Pentecost until the Mass of St. Michael no one is permitted to stem waters for the use of milling in such a way that they pour out upon someone else's lands due to the force of restraining and thus deprive the owners of the benefit of hay and what else is grown there. If, however, the owner of the mill disregards the law of equity and a complaint is brought for the assembly, a day shall be set by the men of the assembly to remove or open the water gate in order that the flow of the waters shall not be impeded anywhere to the detriment of anyone; and if the owner does not comply with this command, he must pay six ounces as compensation in addition to an estimate of the loss or deny what has happened by an oath of six.

126. De adulterio.

Mechum a iure quilibet habet licenciam occidendi, quem in uno lecto cum sua coniuge deprehendit; et in iure facta fide per duorum testimonium et sanguinolentorum culcidre et lintheaminis exhibicionem super interfeccionis huiusmodi qualitate, ob iuste sumptam de tanto facinore ulcionem et ab omni periculo sumende uindicte et ab omni prestande satisfaccionis onere iuridicorum absoluet sentencia peremtorem; et perempti corpus orthodoxorum priuabitur sepultura, nisi forte de reatu suo uulneratus penitenciam agat ante spiritus exalacionem.

127. Quod adulterii reus candentis ferri iudicium subeat.

Amarito adultere rem adulterii delatus adulter solum habet refugium ad candentis ferri iudicium, quod lingua patria *scuzs jærn* nominat, conuolandi; quo si nequierit exortam infamiam abolere, condempnatus in exilium redeundi nullam habebit de cetero facultatem, nisi forte passus iniuriam in thori consorte prestande consenserit satisfaccioni, quam, xl marcas nummorum secundum tamen estimacionis precium continentem, debet quoque ob criminis enormitatem, licet preter solitum in priuatis, comprehendens tres marcas uel unam marcam argenti contemptus precium comitari. Uxori proprie crimen adulterii maritus imponens, si suam muniat duobus testibus accusacionem, uxorem candentis ferri iudicium subire compellat. Quo si queat suam innocenciam demonstrare, et integritate fame gaudebit et mariti consorcium retinebit. Sin autem et infamie respersa macula et bonis omnibus denudata iure legis humane tam a domo quam a thoro coniugis excludetur. Utrique tamen coniugum, quam diu reliquus superstes fuerit, noua connubia contrahendi licencia denegata. Uerum in parte constat huic humane legi, uelud famule obsequenti, uelud pedisseque sequenti domine sue uestigia, per diuine legis preminenciam derogari, que matrimonia iubet non fori, sed poli, non curie secularis, sed ecclesie spiritualis examini atque regimini subiacere, nec permittit eciam separacionem thori per igniti ferri iudicium celebrari.

128. De uiolenta oppressione uirginis uel solute.

Ubicumque quispiam, licet solus, uiolenter uel uirginem humiliauerit uel corruptam oppresserit, duplicata xl marcarum obligabitur satisfaccione, una regi pro uiolacione iusticie alteraque pro irrogacione iniurie procuratori persone passe iniuriam, ad opus ipsius nihilominus, exhibenda. Uerum si crimen inficiatus fuerit, aduersus simplicem accusacionem triplicato iuramentorum duodenario se defendet. At aduersus accusacionem duobus testibus innitentem igniti tantum defensioni iudicii deferetur.

Ch. 126 On adultery.

Everyone has a lawful right to kill the adulterer whom he catches in the same bed with his wife[85]; and when at the assembly he confirms with two witnesses and by showing the blood-stained coverlet and linen that the killing was of this kind, the sentence of the men of the assembly will free the killer from just revenge of the deed and from all risk of retribution and from all burden of paying compensation; and the body of the person killed shall be excluded from burial among true believers, unless after having been wounded he did penance for his crime before he expired.

Ch. 127 That a defendant accused of adultery shall undergo the ordeal by hot iron.

When an adulterer is accused of adultery by the husband, he can only take refuge to that ordeal by hot iron, which in the native language is called *scuzs jærn*; if he is unable to extinguish the infamy that has fallen upon him in this way, being condemned to exile, he will have no possibility to return unless the man who suffered the offence as to his bedfellow should agree to receive compensation, which shall be of forty marks in money according to the value of what is paid, and due to the seriousness of the crime, three marks or one mark of silver shall be added as compensation for contempt, even though it goes beyond what is customary in private matters. A husband who charges his own wife with the crime of adultery and supports his accusation with two witnesses compels his wife to undergo the ordeal by hot iron. If she is able in this way to demonstrate her innocence, she will both rejoice in the integrity of her reputation and keep the partnership of her husband. If not, however, by the rule of human law she will be excluded from her husband's house and bed, carrying the stain of infamy and stripped of all her property. Both of the spouses, however, for as long as the remaining spouse survives, are denied permission to contract new marriages. But for some part it is so that this human law, just as an obedient maid or a female slave follows her mistress's steps,[86] must cede to the pre-eminence of divine law, which dictates that marriages are subject not to the scrutiny and regimen of the assembly but of the Heavens,[87] not of a secular court but of the spiritual church, and which does not permit separation from the marriage bed to be performed by the ordeal by hot iron.

Ch. 128 On the violation of a virgin or a single woman.[88]

Anyone, anywhere who by force either disgraces a virgin or violates a woman already touched shall, also if he was acting alone, pay a compensation of forty marks twice, one part to the king for violation of the legal order and the other for the infliction of injury to the violated woman's guardian, but to be used for her own needs. If he denies the crime, he must defend himself against a simple accusation with three times twelve men. But against an accusation supported by two witnesses, only the defence of ordeal by fire is granted.

131

129. Quid iuris sit, si uirgo uel soluta consenserit oppressori.

Oppressori suo innupta femina consensum prestante, non ad ipsam, uerbere dignam nec munere, ne lucrum capiat ex delicto, sed ad solum eius, presertim in copula maritali, secundum legem proximum prouisorem et in eius persona iniuriam perpessum pudoris sex marcarum nummorum uel duarum argenti satisfaccio pertinebit, nisi xxiiii iuramentalibus illatam sibi reus repulerit accusacionem. Licet autem sit proximus, quem in ipsa mater concepit oppressione, filius, ipsi satisfactio tamen nullatenus attinebit, cum nec pater eo nomine grauaretur, et mater, filii mediante persona, ex reatu suo sortiri commodum uideretur. Ob humiliacionem tantum filie naturalis, quam non est legitime pater suam esse filiam protestatus, neque pater neque agnatus quilibet, uerum habet tantum cognatus proximus actionem.

130. De oppressione ancille.

Siquis ancillam oppresserit alienam, duas horas nummorum domino prestabit nomine satisfaccionis, aut reatum trino diffitebitur iuramento. Ad sex horarum satisfaccionem uel seni iuramenti defensionem interdum illicitus attingit concubitus cum ancilla, puta que, seruilibus exempta operibus, societatis et honoris et obsequii dignioris intuitu assidendi domine sue officium est adepta, unde quoque *sœtis ambut* lingua patria nominatur.

131. De igne.

Sicut ignis ob multiplicem commoditatem est necessarius, sic ob frequens et graue periculum metuendus, unde sicut usum eius commoditatis necessitas cotidiana deposcit, sic et periculi metuenda calamitas ipsius custodiam diligentem requirit; igitur, ut uitetur periculum igne diligencius custodito, circumspecte racionabili lege dinoscitur cautum esse, ut in tribus marcis dampnum passio satisfacere teneatur, ex cuius domus igne adortum incendium, consumendo domum alienam, haut minus sex horis nummorum ingerit detrimentum, et si domus plurium concrementur, non maiorem plures quam unus consequentur incendii satisfaccionem inter se porcionibus equalibus diuidendam, quantumcumque dispar dampnum eis per incendium irrogetur. Preter hec quilibet bonis suis per ignis uiolenciam spoliatus, eciam ille, de cuius domus igne primo tota combustionis iaetura subsequens pullulauit, in iure prouinciali cum duobus sociis, non ab eis tacto sacro libro, sed utroque manum suam in manum alterius immittente, fidem iuratoriam exhibeat se, consumpta domo sua, dampnum ad sex horas nummorum per incendium incurrisse, et hoc facto pro eo feretur sentencia, ut per totam prouinciam unusquisque persoluat sibi uel unum denarium uel unam mensuram ordei uel duas auene in dampni, quod accidit, compensacionem.

Ch. 129 How to proceed if a virgin or a single woman consents to her violator.
An unmarried woman who gives her consent to her violator merits punishment, not reward, and in order that she does not gain any profit from her offence she shall not receive anything. Only the man who, particularly with respect to giving her in marriage, is her closest guardian according to the law and who has endured in full the injury of honour done to her person shall receive a compensation of six marks in money or two of silver, unless the accused refutes the accusation brought against him with an oath of twenty-four.[89] If, however, the nearest relative is the son, who was conceived by his mother by the same act of violation, the compensation will by no means go to him, because in this way his father will not be burdened and his mother would be seen to benefit from her crime through the person of her son. In the case of an abasement like this of a natural daughter, whom her father does not lawfully acknowledge as his daughter, neither her father nor any of his kin but only the nearest kin on her mother's side has the right to sue.

Ch. 130 On the violation of a slave woman.[90]
If anyone violates another man's slave woman, he shall pay her master two ounces in money as compensation or deny the crime by an oath of three. Sometimes, compensation for illicit intercourse with a slave woman extends to six ounces or the defence of an oath of six, namely when it is with one who is exempt from servile duties and in consideration of her social position and her esteem and her more dignified service takes the seat beside her mistress, as a result of which she is called *sætis ambut* in the native language.

Ch. 131 On fire.
Just as fire is necessary for a variety of useful purposes, it is to be feared on account of its frequent and grave danger and therefore, just as everyday necessity requires the use of its convenience, so the frightening calamity of its danger requires diligent custody of it; therefore, in order that danger may be avoided by diligently watching the fire,[91] it seems prudent when by a reasonable law it is prescribed that he from whose house the fire was started which consumed the house of another and thus caused damage of at least six ounces in money is liable for three marks to compensate the victim for the loss and if the houses of many are burned down, the many shall not get higher compensation for the fire than one person, and the compensation shall be divided among them in equal portions, however unequal the damage inflicted on them. In addition to this, anyone despoiled of his property by the violence of fire, even he from whose house the flames' subsequent destruction sprang forth with the first fire, can in the district assembly with two companions, not touching a holy book but each placing his hand in the hand of the other, give his oath that his home was destroyed by fire and that he has incurred damage of at least six ounces in money; and when this is done a sentence in his favour will be given to the effect that throughout the whole district everyone shall pay him either a penny or one measure of barley or two of oats as compensation for the damage that he has incurred.

Quandocumque indeterminate agitur de mensura, illa debet intelligi, que, rotunditatem equalem amplectens et orthogonaliter more cateti per senam pollicis latitudinem a fundo consurgens, duplo maiorem habet instar ypotenuse altitudinem transuersalem, probatam per uirgam, que, habens pollicis duodenam latitudinem in longitudine, ubicumque superponitur extremitati fundi, qua parte coniungitur cum corona, per mensure medium transeundo, summitate sua contingit directe oppositam summitatem corone, ob quam altitudinem hanc mensuram *tolfmynning* ydeoma patrium appellauit. Ad hanc collectam gratis conferre cuipiam respuenti non est prima uice res aliqua subtrahenda, sed in ius querimonia deferenda, ubi condempnabitur qui unius denarii solucioni contumaciter contradixit, ut ad certum diem, prefixum in iure, cum predicto denario xxx persoluat, nisi tribus probet iuramentalibus se prius exactum legitime non fuisse. In eiusdemque iuridicorum conuentu licencia petitori prestabitur adiudicacionis auctoritate subtrahendi rebelli bona sua, si preelegerit in contradiccionis sue contumacia perdurare, ne petitor cogatur sepius ob hanc causam inaniter fatigari. Racione dampni per incendium contingentis dispensator uel uillicus uel quicumque domum inhabitat alienam, non tenetur ad aliquam emendacionem, dummodo manu iuramentalium duodena dampnum illud absque culpa sua doceat euenisse.

132.

Accusatus quispiam, quod uoluntarie domum incenderit alienam, si firmata delacio illa non fuerit iuramento, tribus se tuebitur iuramentalium duodenis. Si uero fuerit iuramenti munimine roborata, tantum ad candentis ferri iudicium, quod proiciendum est in alueolum, admittetur, et si conuictus fuerit, ex ipsius honis, quantum facultas permittit, debet omne dampnum incendii reparari, capitali porcione sua tantum ad ius regium pertinente; conuictus autem gaudebit uno die tantum induciis libertatis, post quem licite, si repertus fuerit, suspendatur.

133. De uillicacionis officio.

Si quis conuenerit cum alio de prestando sibi officio uillicacionis, si prorsus exsequi supersederit quod promisit, pena multabitur sex horarum, uel conuencionem factam seno diffitebitur iuramento. Uerum ad assignatam sibi pertransiens mansionem, si res suas uel in unico curru adduxerit, et si resilierit ab incepto, uel tres marcas prestabit, uel duodeno se tuebitur iuramento. In utroque tamen casu, si cum rege uel pontifice talis conuencio celebretur, uel trium marcarum prestabitur satisfaccio, uel offeretur duodeni defensio iuramenti.

Whenever a measurement is used without specification, this refers to the one that is round and rising upward by six widths of a thumb from the base orthogonally as a cathetus by twice as much has the equivalent to the transverse height of the hypotenuse when tested with a rod, which, having twelve widths of a thumb in linear extent, wherever it is placed over the farthest part from the base, in crossing which part it comes into contact with the rim, through the middle of the measuring stick it touches with its surface directly upon the facing surface of the rim, on account of which width this measure is called *tolfmynning* in the native idiom. If someone refuses to contribute to this collection voluntarily, nothing is to be taken from him at first, but a complaint must be brought before the assembly, where he who defiantly refused to pay one penny will be sentenced to pay along with the aforesaid penny another thirty on a certain day fixed by the assembly, unless he proves with three oath givers that he had not earlier been lawfully asked to pay. In the same gathering of men of the assembly the plaintiff shall be permitted by judgment to deprive the denier of his property, should he choose to persist in his defiant opposition, so that the plaintiff shall no longer be troubled with this matter without reason. As to damage by fire, a household manager or a bailiff or anyone who lives in another person's house will not be held liable for any compensation whatsoever, provided that it is demonstrated by twelve oath givers that the damage was caused without his fault.

Ch. 132.
Anyone accused of having set another person's house on fire with intent[92] can defend himself with three times twelve oaths if the accusation is not affirmed by oath. But if it is strengthened by an oath, then he will only be permitted the ordeal by hot iron, which is to be thrown into a trough; and if he is convicted, all the damage of the fire must be repaid from his property as far as his means allow, and his capital portion is due to the king; if convicted, moreover, he will only enjoy a one-day grace period of freedom and thereafter he can licitly be hanged if he is caught.

Ch. 133 On the duty of the bailiff.
If a man agrees with someone to take upon himself the office of bailiff,[93] and he later will not fulfil what he promised, he shall be punished with a fine of six ounces or deny by an oath of six that there was an agreement.[94] When he has moved to the house assigned to him, even if he has just brought in his things in a single cart and then withdraws from the outset, he must either pay three marks or defend himself by an oath of twelve men. However, if he makes an agreement of this sort with the king or archbishop, in either case he must either pay compensation of three marks or offer the defence of an oath of twelve.

135

134. De deposicione uillicacionis.

Uolens onus deponere uillicacionis, si consensum ad hoc domini sui non ualeat inclinare, obtinere debet, in ius cum sua querimonia proficiscens, ut dies suo domino diuidendi secum bona communia prefigatur, quem diem dominus si noluerit obseruare, idem secundo uillicus debet a iuridicis impetrare; et si nec tunc iusticiam consequatur, ad ius procedat tercio, et tunc nominabuntur uiri prudentes, quot necessarii uidebuntur, ut auctoritate publica certo die diuisioni debeant interesse, attendentes, ne uillicus a suo domino contra iusticiam opprimatur, puniendo multa trium marcarum ad ius regium pertinente, si perstiterit in contumacia contradiccionis; post diuisionem factam ex hiis, que cesserunt uillico in diuisione, si quid dominus auferre presumat, non solum illud restituere, sed et rapine debitam multam persoluere compelletur. Ad uniuersorum quidem euidenter dinoscitur pertinere commodum, si defendatur iusticia et propulsentur iniurie singulorum.

135 a. Quod uillico sufficit pro se duodenum iuramentum, si dominus eius eum pro furto accusauerit.

Aduersus dominum, accusantem suum uillicum in diuisione pro furtiua subtractione uel occultacione rerum, sufficit ipsi uillico duodeni defensio iuramenti. At diuisione facta uolens rem aliquam auferre dominus ei, quem uillicum prius habuit, si rem aliquam occultatam asserat, ne diuideretur, ille, qui uillicus erat, si fidem faciat duobus testibus et xii iuramentalibus, quod res illa sibi cesserit in diuisione, ab accusantis calumpnia suam innocenciam liberabit; sed licebit accusatori testes impetere super perhibiti testimonii falsitate, et uterque uel se duodeno tuebitur iuramento uel penam falsi testimonii tres marcas persoluet. Si uero deficiat accusato testium et iuramentalium predicta defensio, accusator eum candentis ferri iudicium subire compellet, si crimen, quod imposuit, iuramento confirmet.

135 b. De rerum communium specialitate.

Si duorum habencium res communes unus rem aliquam ad suum singulariter contendat dominium pertinere, alter e contrario communem affirmet, debet audiri pocius communem affirmans, si cum xii iuramentalibus sue fidem faciat affirmacioni. Hanc quoque specialitatem omnis habet communio, quod quicumque rem communem accusetur sic uel subtraxisse uel occultasse uel uiolenter contrectasse, quod eam uel eius precium restituere teneatur, quanticumque, quod tamen dimidiam marcam excedat, precii iudicetur, si negare uelit, quod imponitur sibi, sufficiat duodenarius iuramentalium accusato, solus uero senarius, si dimidia marca minus ipsius precium estimetur.

Ch. 134 On the renouncing of a bailiff.

If a man wishes to quit the burden of being a bailiff and he is unable to get his master's consent to this, then he must go to the assembly with his complaint and have a day fixed for dividing common property with the master; if the master will not observe this day, the same bailiff must request a second one from the men of the assembly; and if no decision is made, then he must go to the assembly a third time, and then prudent men shall be named, as many as appears necessary, to be present for the division by public authority[95] on a certain day, in order that the bailiff shall not be unjustly oppressed by his master, and they shall punish him with a fine of three marks due to the king if he should persist in his obstinate opposition; and if the master, after the division is made, presumes to carry away some of those things that were ceded to the bailiff in the division, he shall be compelled not only to restore it but also to pay the fine to be paid for rapine. It is evident that it serves the common benefit of everyone when justice is defended and harm done by particulars is suppressed.[96]

Ch. 135 a. That an oath of twelve is sufficient for a bailiff if his master accuses him of theft.

Against a master who accuses his bailiff of furtively taking away or hiding things when they are being divided up, an oath of twelve is sufficient defence for the bailiff himself. But when the division has been made and the master wishes to take something away from him whom he formerly had as bailiff and he asserts that something had been hidden so that it would not be divided, then he who was bailiff will guard his innocence from the calumny of his accuser if he swears with two witnesses and twelve oath givers that the thing was granted to him in the division; but the accuser shall be allowed to sue the witnesses for giving a false testimony, and each of them must either protect himself by an oath of twelve or pay three marks as penalty for false testimony. If the aforesaid defence of witnesses and oath givers does not work for the accused, the accuser can force him to submit to the ordeal by hot iron by confirming the crime that he imputed to him by oath.

b. On the particularity of things that are held in common.

If one of two who hold things in common alleges that sole ownership of something belongs to him, and the other on the contrary affirms that it is common, he who says it is common shall rather be heard, provided that he affirms it by an oath of twelve. All common ownership has this particularity, that whenever someone is accused of having either taken away or hidden or violently stolen a thing held in common so that he is demanded to restore it or its value, then an oath of twelve will suffice for the accused to deny what is imposed upon him, no matter how much the value is judged to exceed a half-mark, and merely an oath of six if the value is estimated to be less than a half-mark.

137

136. De excepcione remissi debiti uel soluti.

Excepcione debiti remissi gracia liberalitatis opposita creditori, impedietur peticio creditoris, donec excepcionem oppositam sibi falsam duodeno probauerit iuramento; uerum excepcio soluti debiti uel per transactionem sublati, cum eam debitor duobus testibus et duodeno confirmauerit iuramento, peticionem perimet creditoris. Obligante creditore pro solucione debiti obligatam sibi terram alii creditori, si refuso precio petat a primo creditore dominus et primus debitor ypotecam, aduersus suum debitorem precium offerentem non suffragabitur uel prescripcionis excepcio uel empcionis facte cum uero domino creditori 2°, sed oportet, ut ad primum terra per medium reuertatur.

137. Qualiter a debitore creditor suum debitum consequatur.

Debitore respuente satisfacere creditori, si post legitime in ius querimoniam deportatam ex concessa licencia et adiudicacione iuridicorum in sui debiti solucionem creditor bona queuis surripuerit debitori, et coram eodem conuentu iuridicorum debitor super rapine uicio reum detulerit creditorem, si conuentus totus affirmauerit ex adiudicacionis sue auctoritate creditorem bona, de quibus agitur, subtraxisse, ab impugnacione debitoris creditor absoluetur. Uerum in alio quoque loco super hoc creditor accusatus, si duos exhibeat, qui se fecisse illam asserant adiudicacionem, et duos alios priorum duorum assercionem suo testimonio roborantes, a uexacione liberabitur debitoris. At istorum si utrumque defuerit creditori, adiudicacionem illam legitime factam a iuridicis seno negabit debitor iuramento, ut sic et bona sua recipiat et trium marcarum insuper satisfactionem rapine uicio congruentem, nisi se creditor a rapina duodeno excusauerit iuramento.

138. De precario.

Restitucionem precarii uel iusti precii nullus casus de iure poterit impedire. Nec audietur precium uolens restituere, nisi prius probet et se facultatem ipsum restituendi precarium non habere et iustam esse precii, quod offertur pro precario, quantitatem iuramentalibus sufficientibus estimacioni, compellendus nihilominus, si umquam in suam redierit potestatem, ad debitam restitucionem, priore domino ipsum refuso precio postulante.

139. De re qualibet mobili conducta uel locata.

Deterioracionem uel amissionem conducte rei prestare non tenetur probans eam iuramentalibus conuenientibus estimacioni sine facto suo et negligencia contigisse.

140. Quod rei se defendentis est probare quid esse precarium uel conductum.

Licet actor dicat precarium, rens debet audiri, si sufficienti numero iuramentorum probet precio rem conductam; eodem modo si contendat actor rem conductam, audiendus est reus, si probet eam liberaliter et precario concessam fuisse, ut utrobique defendenti se probacio deferatur.

Ch. 136 On a counterclaim that a debt has been remitted or paid.

When a counterclaim[97] is asserted against a creditor that the debt has been remitted due to generosity, then his claim is impeded until he proves by an oath of twelve that the claim brought against him is false; nevertheless, when a debtor confirms with two witnesses and an oath of twelve the counterclaim that a debt has been remitted or settled by a compromise, the creditor's plea is brought to an end. If a creditor gives land pledged to him as security for a debt to another creditor as pledge, and the owner and the first debtor claim back the pledge from the first creditor after having paid the debt, then a counterclaim of prescription or that it was sold by the real owner will not help the second creditor against the debtor who offers to pay the money, but the land shall revert to the first owner through the middleman.[98]

Ch. 137 How a creditor can obtain his debt from a debtor.[99]

When a debtor refuses to satisfy a creditor and the creditor, after lawfully bringing his claim to the assembly and he with the permission and judgment of the men of the assembly, seizes any property from the debtor to have his debt paid, and the debtor accuses the creditor of rapine before the same gathering of men of the assembly, and the entire assembly affirms that the creditor has seized the property in question by the authority of a judgment, then the creditor is absolved from the debtor's accusation. And if the creditor is accused of this in another place and he provides two people who assert that they made this judgment and two others confirm the assertion of the first two with their testimony, he will be freed from the debtor's harassment. But if both procedures fail for the creditor, then the debtor can deny by an oath of six that the judgment was lawfully made by the men of the assembly, and he can thus get his property back and in addition to that three marks as compensation for rapine, unless the creditor by an oath of twelve can excuse himself of rapine.

Ch. 138 On loans upon request.

No incident can justly impede the restitution of a loan or its just compensation.[100] Nor shall a man be heard who wishes to pay compensation when he has not first proven both that he is not able to restore the loan itself and that the compensation offered for the loan is fair in the estimation of a sufficient number of oath givers, and still he shall give it back, as he should, if ever it should come under his power again, when the prior owner demands it and pays back the compensation.

Ch. 139 On any sort of rented movable property.

Nobody shall answer for destruction or loss of something that he has rented when he proves with oath givers corresponding to the estimated value that it happened without his interference or negligence.[101]

Ch. 140 That the accused who defends himself must prove that something was on loan or rent.[102]

Even if the plaintiff says that it is a loan, the defendant shall be heard if he can prove with a sufficient number of oaths that the thing has been rented. In the same way if the plaintiff maintains that it is hired, the defendant shall be heard when he proves that it was given to him out of generosity and as a loan, so in both cases it is up to the defendant to produce the proof.

141. De deposito.

Per hoc solum se liberat depositarius a restituendi obligacione, si eodem infortunio se ostendat res suas et depositum amisisse.

142. Si condicionaliter seruanda recipiuntur.

Quicumque recipit ea condicione quelibet conseruanda, ut in eodem, quidquid eis contigerit, ualore reddantur, que deposita *halzfæ* lingua patria nominantur, facta condicio irrefragabiliter est tenenda, ut nullatenus in restitucione, quecumque restituantur, in conuencione prima facta depositorum bonorum estimacio minuatur. At si depositarius predictam neget condicionem, audiendus est, si negacionem suam duodeno corroboret iuramento.

143. Locati et conducti.

Cum quibusdam locare sit necessarium terras suas, quibusdam conducere alienas, ne uel conductor opprimatur per potenciam locatoris uel locator circumueniatur uersucia conductoris, per certam legum diffinicionem expedit utrumque ab alterius iniuria refrenare. Contractus igitur conduccionis et locacionis solo consensu contrahencium celebratur, sed impune rescinditur, donec iuxta consuetudinem approbatam percussione manus unius in manum alterius roboretur. Contractus conduccionis tantum annuus esse solet, ut sicut singulis annis noua prestatur pensio, et annis singulis noua conductio celebretur. Dies assumpcionis beate uirginis prefixus est celebracioni pariter et solucioni, ut suum commodum in piscacionis nundinis ex soluta pecunia locator ualeat procurare. Idem dies deputatus eciam est renunciacioni, si colonus conduccionis sue continuare recusauerit per sequentis anni spacium habitacionem.

144.

Non licet colono conduccionis relinquere mansionem, donec anno finito 5° die post septimanam pasce tempus aduenerit recedendi; sex horas, si prius recesserit, emendabit, et nihilominus, ut omnes debite prestentur opere usque ad prefixum terminum, procurabit, uel, si penam uitare uoluerit ui horarum, se contra locatoris sui licenciam recessisse seno diffitebitur iuramento. Conduccionis adueniente termino colonus secum non deferet domos suas, a conduccionis successore iuxta prudencium uirorum estimacionem precium pro suis domibus recepturus, hoc ordine persoluendum, ut circa medium quadragesime successori medietatem precii persoluenti pro parte dimidia domus pariter assignentur, et post pascalem ebdomadam die quinto et residuam medietatem precii persoluat accedens, et residuam medietatem domorum liberam dimittat recedens. At si nullus ei successerit in conduccione, quicumque conduccionis terram coluerit, ad eum precii domorum solucio pertinebit, licet sit dominus, qui locauit, aut dabit colono domos suas licenciam deferendi; inhumanum enim esset et iniquum eum et suis domibus et domorum precio defraudari.

Ch. 141 On deposit.

The depositor can free himself from giving back what is due, only if he can show that he lost both his own property and the deposit by the same misfortune.[103]

Ch. 142 If something is taken into deposit on conditions.

He who receives something to be kept by him on the condition that he shall give back its value, no matter what happens to it, a kind of deposit called *halzfæ* in the native language,[104] shall keep the condition without exception once it has been accepted, so that when it comes to restitution, whatever is given back, there shall be no diminishing with regard to the value originally agreed upon. If he who has the goods in deposit denies the condition, he shall be heard if he confirms his denial with an oath of twelve.

Ch. 143 – renting.

For some people it is necessary to rent out their land and for others to rent land that is not their own; it is therefore beneficial that the law states clearly that both parties shall abstain from doing harm to each other in order that the tenant is not oppressed by the power of the landlord nor the landlord cheated by the cunning of the tenant. A contract of rent is made by the mere consent of the parties,[105] but it can, following an established custom, without anything to be paid, be rescinded until it has been confirmed by the parties by giving each other their hand.[106] A contract of renting is usually for a year, so that every year a new rent is paid and each year a new renting is contracted. The day of the Assumption of the Holy Virgin is fixed both as the day of moving in and for payment in order that the landlord can acquire what he needs from the fish market with the money paid.[107] The same day is set for dissolving the contract if the tenant will not prolong the renting of his dwelling for the span of the following year.

Ch. 144.

The tenant is not permitted to give up a rented house until a year has passed and the time to leave has come, which is the fifth day after Easter week; if he leaves before that time, he shall pay six ounces and nevertheless he shall see to it that all necessary work is done until the prefixed term, or, if he wants to avoid a fine of six ounces, he shall by an oath of six deny that he has left without the permission of his landlord. When the period of renting has been terminated, the tenant shall not take his houses with him, but he shall, according to the estimate of prudent men, receive the value of the houses from his successor, and this should be done in the following order, so when the successor by *Laetare* Sunday[108] pays half the price he shall be assigned half the houses, and on the fifth day in the week after Easter he shall pay the other half, and the person leaving shall clear out the other half of the houses. But if nobody succeeds him in the renting, then whoever cultivates rented land, even if it is the owner who rented it out, shall pay the price for the houses, or he shall give the tenant permission to take away his houses, because it is inhuman and unjust to cheat him both out of his houses and of the price of the houses.

Si colonus duos testes habeat super conduccionis contractu percussione manuum confirmato, non licebit a conuencione recedere locatori, et quia tantum annua debet esse conduccio, non potest eciam ultra unum annum huius modi una conduccionis probacio prorogari. Si se duo contendant ab eodem pariter conduxisse, in conduccionis mansione residenti semper est probacio deferenda. At si neuter ingressus fuerit mansionem, cui testimonium locator perhibuerit, audietur. Qui conduxit, si prius uoluerit resilire, quam conduccionis fuerit ingressus mansionem, duas horas tenebitur emendare, aut contractum trino diffitebitur iuramento. Si colonum, a conduccionis mansione uolentem recedere, locator asserat oonduxisse, seno colonus liberabitur iuramento.

145.
Naturalis exposcit equitas, ut colonus, licet conductioni renunciauerit, possit siliginem seminare, cum serendi causa constet eum terram precipue conduxisse; in serendi tamen quantitate debet prouincie consuetudinem obseruare, ut tantum seminet terre feracis siliginis, quantum permittit prouincie consuetudo; in quibusdam enim partibus nihil excipitur, in quibusdam excipiuntur uel due partes uel medietas, in quibusdam excipitur solus fundus.

146.
Non licet colono, in communionem bona sua cum bonis alterius redigendo, in conduccionis mansione se uillicum et prouisorem constituere sine licencia locatoris.

147.
Si colonus non potuerit prefixo die soluere pensionem, rursus petat et impetret, ut sibi solucionis dies alius prefigatur, in quo, si non soluerit, duas horas tenebitur emendare.

148.
Si locator recusauerit statuto tempore oblatam sibi recipere pensionem, et ob hoc colonus adueniente conduccionis termino non soluta recesserit pensione, colonus postea, quod non soluerit accusatus, duobus testibus et xii iuramentalibus oblacionem legitime factam probet, et nihil amplius exsoluet debita pensione. Si uero deficiat in probacione, solucioni pensionis sex horas adiunget nomine satisfaccionis.

149.
Recusante prorsus colono persoluere pensionem, trina querimonia super hoc in ius legitime deportata, consulendi sibi per subtraccionem bonorum coloni adiudicando iuridici dabunt licenciam locatori.

150. Si locator pensionem suscipere negauerit.
Si locator animo uexandi colonum prefixo die a iuridicis nolit oblatam recipere pensionem, adducat colonus ex sentencia iuridicorum duos uiros uel plures, qui possint perhibere testimonium ueritati, in quorum conspectu et pensionem offerat locatori, et si nolit recipere, super larem eius uel limen coram ipsius oculis eandem deponat, et sic ab omni se liberet obligacione.

If the tenant has two witnesses to the contract of rent and confirmation by the shaking of hands, the landlord is not permitted to rescind the contract, and as the renting is for a year, such proof cannot prolong the renting beyond one year either. If two men both claim that they have rented from the same man, proof shall always be produced by the one residing in the rented house. But if neither of them has moved into the house, then he who is supported by the testimony of the landlord shall be heard. If he who has rented wants to rescind the contract before he has entered the rented house, then he shall pay two ounces or deny the contract with three men. If the tenant wants to leave the rented house and the landlord claims that it has been rented, the tenant can free himself by an oath of six.

Ch. 145.

Natural equity demands that the tenant may sow rye even if he will discontinue the contract when it is evident that it was for the sowing that he rented the land; when it comes to the quantity to be sowed, local custom shall be observed, so that he can sow on so much land fertile of rye as local custom permits; because in some places nothing is excepted, in some places two-thirds or half, in some places only the curtilage is excepted.

Ch. 146.

The tenant is not permitted to take goods of others into a common ownership with his belongings and constitute himself as a bailiff or manager without the permission of the landlord.

Ch. 147.

If on the day prescribed the tenant cannot pay his rent, he shall ask for and have another day fixed; and if he does not pay on that day he shall pay two ounces.

Ch. 148.

If the landlord will not receive the rent on the day fixed, and for that reason the tenant has left without paying the rent when the term for renting has come to an end, and he is accused of not having paid, he shall with two witnesses and an oath of twelve prove that he did offer to pay and then pay no more than the rent he owes. If, however, he cannot prove it, six ounces will be added to the rent as compensation.

Ch. 149.

When the tenant has three times refused to pay his rent and three complaints about it have lawfully been brought before the assembly, then the men of the assembly shall permit the landlord to satisfy himself by taking away the belongings of the tenant.

Ch. 150 If a landlord refuses to accept the rent.

If a landlord with the intention of harming the tenant will not accept the rent on the day prefixed by the men of the assembly, then the tenant, according to the decision of the men of the assembly, shall bring two men or more who can give trustworthy testimony and before them he shall offer the rent to the landlord, and if he will not take it the tenant shall place it on the threshold of his house within his eyesight and thus free himself from any obligation.

Notes

1 The Latin text in this edition is based on the publication Jørgen Olrik, trans., "Anders Sunesøns Latinske Parafrase af Skånske Lov/Antique leges Scanie," in *Danmarks gamle landskabslove med Kirkelovene*, vol. 1.2, ed. Johs. Brøndum-Nielsen, Poul Johs. Jørgensen, Svend Aakjær and Erik Kroman, publ. Det Danske Sprog- og Litteraturselskab (Copenhagen: Gyldendalske Boghandel/Nordisk Forlag, 1933–1961), 467–667.

   Compared to the previous edition, consonantal and vocalic '*i*' and '*u*' respectively are not distinguished in this edition, *e.g.*, '*ius*' instead of '*jus*', '*iems*' instead of '*yems*', '*uilla*' instead of '*villa*', and '*uulgariter*' instead of '*wlgariter*'.

2 A corresponding oath is not mentioned in the Law of Scania (hereinafter SkL).

3 That is, the brothers and sisters of the deceased and the brothers' wives.

4 See ch. 14.

5 Normally only an oath of twelve is given when not more than three marks is claimed.

6 In Roman law what was gained or lost (*lucrum* and *damnum*) in a *societas omnium bonorum* was to the benefit or detriment of all members, see e.g. Justinian's *Institutes*, III, 25, 1: "Et quidem si nihil de partibus lucri et damni nominatim convenerit, aequales scilicet partes et in lucro et in damno spectantur."

7 ASun refers to Roman law terminology of emancipation, *emancipatio*, when the *paterfamilias* freed house sons and slaves from his *potestas* to describe the procedure of separation of members of the medieval household from the partnership, which ASun calls *potestas*. According to Justinian law a son could be released from his father's power (*potestas*) by a declaration before a judge or magistrate, see *Inst*. I, 12,6.

8 According to the laws of Zealand, the son had a right to take his lot with him, but such a rule was not accepted in Scania as ASun stresses here.

9 The following sentence is lacking in the Ledreborg MS: "When the householder is dead and relinquishes wife and children, be they in the partnership or the children of the wife only, a lot shall be taken from the common property of the deceased to be excluded completely from the wife and given to the children alone."

10 A similar rule that emancipated children would only inherit if they bring back what they have received or gained after the emancipation, so-called *collatio bonorum*, is found in Roman law.

11 The expression *deviare a iustitiae tramite* is found in the letters of St. Ambrosius, see Otto Faller, ed., *Sancti Ambrosii Opera*, Pars decima. Epistolae et Acta I, Corpus Scriptorum Ecclesiasticorum Latinorum 82. (Vindobonae: Hoelder-Pichler-Tempsky, 1968), 130.

12 In the gloss to *Decretum Gratiani* Dist. 1 c. 7, *viri et femine coniunctio, liberorum successio et educatio* is mentioned as an example of *naturalis equitas*.

13 Cp. *Decr. Grat.* C.16 q.1 c.8: "mundo mortuus est, Deo autem vivit."

14 This is the Roman age limit and not the age of fifteen prescribed by SkL ch. 46. In the following ASun seems to follow Roman law on guardians of minors and the curatorship and tutorship of women. However, the expression provisor is not the Roman law word for a guardian.

15 Cp. *Decr. Grat.* Dist. 1 c. 11: "quoniam necessitas non habet legem." *The Lombard laws of Liutprand* (149.VII) have a similar exception concerning sale of property on behalf of minors at risk from dying of hunger. The expression "Necessitas legem non habet" is well known in later *ius commune*; see e.g. Brian Tierney, *The Idea of Natural Rights, Studies on Natural Rights, Natural Law and Church Law, 1150–1625*, Emory University Studies in Law and Religion 5 (Atlanta: Scholars Press, 1997), 84–85; Cp. *X*. 5.41.4.

16 An *exceptio* in Roman procedural law is a counter-claim made by the defendant against the actor's claim.

17 *Justum pretium* is a concept of Roman law of sale, as are the terms *emptio, venditio* and *venditor*.

18 ASun uses the Roman law concept of *tutela*. Impubes were children under the age of puberty in Roman law determined by Justinian as the age of 14 (girls by 12). Tutors should be men of at least the age of 25.

19 In Roman law more family members of the same degree could be guardians. SkL only admitted one guardian, who would not be sole heir of the ward, however, but would share the inheritance with other heirs. ASun in this and the following chapters uses the terminology of Roman law such as the *Authentica ad Cod.* 5,30,1: "tutelae onus comitatur emolumentum".

20 In Roman law women were under perpetual guardianship – however only to economic dispositions of certain importance.

21 The Latin word used, *convolare*, indicates haste, cp. *Cod.* 5.17.9, also *ad secundas nuptias*, cp. *Decr. Grat.* C.3 q.6 c.14.

22 The concept of a *tutor suspectus* (ch. 23), an untrustworthy guardian guilty of unreliable management, who can be removed, also stems from Roman law, see *Inst.* I, 26. According to the Law of Scania the guardian would take the ward's property into a partnership, whereas in Roman law the ward's property was administered separately. On security from guardians, see *Inst.* I. 24.

23 The meaning is that he will take upon himself to carry out the proof demanded by the law.

24 *Leges* must refer to the earlier and following articles in which prescription is mentioned; see ch. 35 and 37.

25 Cp. *Dig.* 41, 3, 3.: "Usucapio est adjectio dominii per continuationem possessionis temporis lege definiti". In Justinian's law the so-called *longi temporis possessio* (long-term possession) led to *usucapio* (prescription) within ten years between persons present and twenty years between people apart, see *Inst.* 2.6.

26 Cp. *Inst.* 2, 6 that rules on prescription were introduced "ne rerum dominia in incerto essent" (to prevent uncertainty over title).

27 Cp. *Dig.* 41,3,1.

28 In Roman law of sale *evictio* is the term used to describe the situation that someone with a better right takes away from the buyer something sold by a seller who was not the legitimate owner. In that case, and only then, the buyer was entitled to have the price paid back.

29 In Roman law the owner who had lost possession of his property could claim it back by an action of *vindicatio*, cp. *Inst.* 4, 1, 19: "sed vindicatio quidem adversus possesorem est".

30 SkL does not have a similar explanation of how the conveyance of land took place or a name for the procedure, mentioned in SkL ch. 51 as *scøtæ*, cp. DD 1.3.238.

31 The corresponding solemnities in Roman law would be *mancipatio* or in *iure cessio*. However, land could also be transferred by *tradition*, but in that case a period of prescription was needed for the buyer to be able to protect himself against other claims to the property.

32 *Praestare* in Roman law is an elastic term covering several duties arising out of an obligation. Here it refers to the seller having a duty to uphold his disposal of the land.

33 Here the Devil comes in and introduces the following chapters (until 63), which all deal with homicide.

34 ASun in the following sticks to this order: see ch. 44 on division, ch. 45 on composition, ch. 47 on distribution and ch. 48–52 on satisfaction.

35 By the newest statute, ASun refers to a statute of unknown date given by King Valdemar II, the *Ordinance on Compensation*, which changed *Knud VI's Ordinance of Homicide* from 1200 by demanding that the killer himself should offer and pay the whole compensation without the help of his (innocent) kinsmen (see the translation of the Danish laws.). We may suspect that ASun has played a role in the making of this new statute, which, however, seems not to have been accepted by the local people even if according to ASun it was endorsed by the most prudent men of Scania.

36 *Rapina* is the word used by ASun for the Old Danish word *ran*, which basically includes both armed robbery but also the forceful seizure of property, even belonging to the perpetrator, without the criminal intent of armed robbery.

37 This chapter has no parallel in the text of SkL and may be ASun's own explanation.

38 ASun: "curatis per contrariam contrariis". Only apparently opposed to the medical principle of the Greek Hippocrates that *similia similibus curantur*. Galen (a. 150 A.D.) introduced the complementary doctrine that *contraria contrariis curantur*. See also Anders Sunesen, *Andreae Sunonis Filii Hexaemeron, Post M. Cl. Gertz*, ed. Sten Ebbesen and Laurentius Boethius Mortensen. Corpus Philosophorum Danicorum Medii Aevi, vols. 1–2, 11–11.2 (Copenhagen: Det Danske Sprog- og Litteratur Selskab, Gad, 1985–1988), v. 6033–6034. Also in *Knud VI's Ordinance of Homicide* from 1200 we find the metaphor that a wrong needs medicine.

39 Here ASun uses the Roman term *curator*.

40 This distinction between *impubes* and *minores* is taken from Roman law and unknown in Old Danish law.

41 This might be the archbishop himself or his representative, as the following words should be spoken by a cleric.

42 According to the new order mentioned by ASun, this would only be the case if the killer has fled; however, we may supsect that the new order was not easily accepted and therefore the old system of the kinsmen contributing persisted.

43 This last part of the chapter has no parallel in SkL.

44 Noxal surrender is a term from Roman law indicating that the owner of something that caused harm, e.g., a slave or an animal, can discharge himself by handing the thing (slave or animal) over to the person harmed; see *Inst*. 4,8. The reason behind this is that a slave should not be able to commit a master over his own value.

45 The opinion of the king seems well in accordance with the tendency to diminish payment for acts committed by others and thus stress personal responsibility that is also expressed in his *Ordinance on Compensation*, which obliged the killer to pay the whole compensation himself.

46 Killing of a slave in Roman law was regulated by the *lex Aquilia* according to which the killer must pay the highest value within the last year: "quanto ea res in eo anno plurimi fuit"; see *Inst*. 4, 3, 1.

47 ASun explains the expression *lindabot* from the Old Danish word *lindi* meaning a belt. Cp. SkL ch. 126 and 127.

48 In *Decretum Gratiani*, Dist 50 c. 50, in a similar case (of a man being killed by a tree as opposed to a piece of wood that slips out of a hand) the responsibility, as in Roman law, is dependent on intent or negligence, cp. the gloss: "fortuiti enim casus nullo hominum consilio praevidere possunt". ASun thus faithfully renders the same rule of local law, which was not in conformity with canon law. Nor is the following rule on full compensation to be paid in case of accident found in the text of SkL.

49 In this case the situation of the well should be well known and therefore no one is liable.

50 According to Roman law there was no responsibility for wild animals which escaped, as they were not considered under ownership any more; see *Inst*. 4,9. It is also noted l.c. that the edict of the aediles forbids bringing dogs, hogs, boars, bears or lions into

places where people usually come and go. If this was infringed, just and reasonable damage should be paid.

51 Such cases where an animal turns fierce against its nature in Roman law (called *pauperies*) were covered by the noxal surrender; see earlier note. *Inst.* 4,9 gives the example of horses given to kicking and bulls to goring.

52 This chapter renders SkL, ch. 87 and reflects the rules of peace stated at the Third Lateran Council, which included *rustici euntes et redeuntes et in agriculture existentes*.

53 The weapons which, together with a number of people, formed the crime called *herwirki* in SkL were those which were supposed to be carried in case of warfare (*lething*).

54 An offence against *regiam majestatem* is mentioned in *Knud VI's Ordinance of Homicide* from 1200 ch. 9 about taking revenge after compensation has been paid. Cp. to the following, *Dig.* 48, 4, 1 on the crime of *contra rem publicam arma ferre*.

55 Such a case of misusing a right to use someone else's thing in Roman law would be seen as theft, *furtum*.

56 On this influence from Roman law, see earlier.

57 In Roman law paying any damages could be avoided by rendering the animal as noxal, the limit of one mark of silver may correspond to the normal value of an animal capable of causing high damage.

58 This procedure is known in Roman law as *manumission*; see *Inst.* 1, 5. Cp. previous ch. 10 on the freeing of sons from dependence.

59 Not in SkL but known in Roman law since the time of Constantine (*Cod.* 1,13,1) and mentioned in *Inst.* I, 1,5,1.

60 This chapter has no correspondence in SkL. In Roman law free captives became slaves but recovered their former status when they escaped and got back to their own people; see *Inst.* 2. 1,17. A person ransomed from the enemy could be kept as a pledge by his redeemer until the ransom was paid.

61 The following chapters from ch. 76–84 contain substantially more detailed rules on slavery than those found in SkL. The law of slavery thus seems to have been of particular interest to ASun, a slave owner himself, who, apart from talking of slavery as misery, does not comment negatively on this particular status.

62 Cp. to the wording *Dig.* 40.12.1.pr.: "in possessione servitutis constitutus est".

63 No parallel in SkL.

64 No parallel in SkL.

65 Cp. I. 2, 9, 3: "ipse enim servus qui in potestate alterius est nihil suum habere potest".

66 No chapter in the Law of Scania corresponds to this chapter on what in Roman law is called *ius postliminii*, namely the right for someone who returned from captivity to be restored into former possessions, see e.g. *Dig.* 49.15.5. I 1, 12, 5.

67 Cp. *Decr. Grat.* C.16 q. 3 c. 13. Normally those to whom the belongings were transferred would have a right to defend them as their own after three years of possession.

68 ASun uses the Roman term *furtum*; however, the rules of Scanian law differ substantially from those of Roman law.

69 This kind of theft where the thief is caught in the act or pursued immediately corresponds to *furtum manifestum* in Roman law (as opposed to *furtum non manifestum*).

70 This kind of theft where a stolen thing is found in someone's house after a search before witnesses is in Roman law called *conceptum furtum* (theft by receiving).

71 Cp. the principle in ch. 9. ASun does not consider the question of whether the other partners, as ignorant of the theft and therefore innocent, should not be responsible for the double compensation to be relevant with regard to the liability of partnership. However, in relation to what is due to the king the other partners do not pay.

72 The word *sera* can refer to a lock or the bar that could secure a door by sliding into place. The bar in this case seems to indicate the private rooms of the house used

147

exclusively by the women of the house. The third bar or lock may be that of a chest. In this case her complicity is supposed.

73 This is a case of what the Romans would call a *furtum non manifestum*, when the thief has managed to bring the stolen goods away without being pursued.

74 Actually Scania borders with Sweden but due to the borderland being at the time mostly rather impenetrable forest, ASun may refer to marine transport as being the norm as to contacts.

75 Probably the Bible or any shortened version or excerpt of the Bible that may be available. The reason for mentioning that a sacred book shall not be touched may be that such a book was not available in all districts.

76 Cp. ch. 25 on the case of someone offering to defend someone else.

77 The expression *turpis lucri gratia* is found in 1. Peter 5,2 and Tit. 1, 10–11. See also *Gratian*, D.47 c.2, D. 86 d.p.c.25 and 86 c. 26, C.1 q.3 c.2, C.7 q.1 c.33, C.16 q.1 c.64 and other texts in the *Decretum*.

78 A corresponding chapter which summarized the procedure in connection with carrying hot iron is not found in SkL.

79 Cp. ch. 57 i.f.

80 Rogation days are observed on 25 April (the Major Rogation) and on the Monday, Tuesday and Wednesday immediately preceding Ascension Thursday (the Minor Rogations).

81 Cp. Ovid Ex Ponte 1,3,50: "Neve fretum terra laudes magis; aequora semper Ventorum rabie, solibus orba, tument."

82 Cp. Cic. Off. 3,26: "Ergo unum debet esse omnibus propositum ut eadem sit utilitas uniuscuiusque et universorum; quam si ad se quisque rapiet dissolvetur omnis humana consortio."

83 *Viscera*, for *viscera terrae* see Ov. Met. 1.138.

84 Cp. Gloss to *Gratian's Decree* c 2 Dist. 1: "Item aequum et iustum est, ut nemo cum alterius iactura locupletur."

85 In Roman law a similar rule was found in the Augustan *Lex Iulia de adulteriis coercendiis* (18 BC) which permitted a wronged husband to kill an adulterer who was either a slave or an *infamis* (a group not protected by the law comprising criminals, actors and entertainers, gladiators e.a.).

86 Cp. for the same metaphor comparing the position of local law in relation to canon law as a maid to her mistress, see Sunesen, *Andreae Sunonis Filii Hexaemeron* (see note 38, earlier) v. 2985.

87 For the expression *Fori . . . poli*, cp. Stephen of Tournai: *Summa* ad c. 2 XVII qu. 2.

88 The word *soluta* is sometimes used in medieval texts as referring to notorious women of bad reputation; here it seems to be women (widows) who are now single but have been married and thus are no longer virgins. In ch. 5 a widowed woman is *dire mortis imperio soluta*. In this chapter the term may thus aim at widows as well.

89 In Roman law a similar rule in the Augustan *Lex Iulia de adulteriis coercendiis* "punishes sexual intercourse, where, without violence, a man seduces an unmarried girl (*virginem*) or a respectable widow (*viduam honeste viventem*)"; see *Inst.* 4,18,4.

90 The fine is considerably lower than for a free woman; see ch.128. Violation of a slave woman in the Bible was not a capital crime but led to the payment of damages: *Deut* 22:25–27 and *Lev.* 19:20–22.

91 Even if the importance of diligent custody of fire is stressed, there is not, like in Roman law, a difference in liability for accidental and negligently caused damage by fire. However, damages are limited to three marks.

92 Ch. 131 is about fire not caused intentionally, whereas ch. 134 deals with arson (*incendium*) as a crime, which in Roman law also was a capital crime.

93 The word *villicatio*, which denominates a farm overseer or manager of an estate in a countryside, is here rendered by the word bailiff. It should be noted that chs. 133–135 only deals with the private law agreement between bailiff and master as to his appointment and division of the common ownership by the end of his service. Some bailiffs appointed by the king or the archbishop had official duties which are here denominated by the translation of official.

94 *Conventio* is a word used in later Roman law for i.a. private agreements.

95 In Roman law, common ownership (*communio*) was dissolved when the partners disagreed and division made on the basis of a specific *actio communi dividundo* which permitted that claims and counterclaims as to the common ownership could be considered.

96 It is noteworthy that the rules chs. 133–135 aim at protecting the bailiff against the master.

97 Chapters 136 and 137 treat some specific questions of payment. Chapter 136 authorizes as in Roman law a counterclaim (*exceptio*) that it was agreed that debt should not be paid (*exceptio debiti remissi*) which could again be met with the counterclaim (*replicatio*) that this allegation was false.

98 This rule ensures that the owner of a pledge can get his pledge back even if it has been transferred to someone else. Again ASun refers to Roman procedure when he explains how the second creditor cannot claim (as an exception) that he has had the land in possession for the period described (prescription), nor that it was sold to him (*exceptio rei venditae*).

99 This chapter also regulates a procedural question – namely how to prove the authorization by the assembly to seize a debtor's property in order to force him to pay the debt.

100 ASun uses the late Roman term *precarium*, which normally was about land given in use for a tenant. The tenant was responsible for any damage to what was given in *precarium*.

101 Here ASun refers to the Roman contract of *locatio-conductio* in which payment (rent) was given for the use of a thing. The responsibility for the renting part in this case was in later Roman law limited to negligence.

102 Similar conflicts as to different conceptions of the qualification of a contract were described in Roman law.

103 The person who received a deposit according to the Roman contract of *depositum* could in later Roman law free himself from responsibility if he could prove that he had shown the same diligence in handling the deposit as in his own matters (*diligentia quam in suis rebus*).

104 This contract corresponds to the Roman *mutuum* by which the loantaker obliged himself to give back not what was loaned but anything of the same sort.

105 As headline for the following chapters ASun uses the Roman law term *locatio-conductio*, a consensual contract which covered ordinary hire and contracts of work. The chapters only deal with renting of land and the relation between landlord and tenant. The landlord is mentioned as *locator*, tenant as *colonus* or *conductor* corresponding to *locare*, hire out and *conducere*, rent.

106 This means that the contract of renting in local law is not as in Roman law a consensual contract which is binding when an oral agreement has been made.

107 *Nundine piscationis* (143) market to be held yearly, the term of 15 August (the day of the Assumption of the Virgin) for tenants to pay their rent is fixed so that the hirer can buy his necessities at this market, which was held from that day to September 29 in Malmoe.

108 The fourth Sunday of Lent, so called after the beginning of the first word of the introit at the Mass 'Laetare Jerusalem'.

CORRESPONDENCE BETWEEN LIBER LEGIS SCANIAE AND THE LAW OF SCANIA

The following list demonstrating the correspondence of chapters between Liber legis Scania and the Law of Scania is based upon information derived from Erik Kroman and Stig Iuul, Danmarks gamle Love paa Nutidsdansk vols. 1–3 (Copenhagen: Det Danske Sprog- og Litteraturselskab, 1945–48). The chapters of Liber legis Scania are listed below in two columns in numerical order from 1 to 150, and for each chapter the corresponding chapters of the Law of Scania are listed after a hyphen. This is followed by a similar listing of the chapters of the Law of Scania and the corresponding chapters of Liber legis Scania.

Liber legis Scaniae – the Law of Scania

1-_1, 2, 4, 25_
2-_3_
3-_5_
4-_6, 7, 22, 29, 31_
5-_8, 9, 10, 11, 12, 13, 14, 15_
6-_30_
7-_14_
8-_32_
9-_16_
10-_17, 18_
11-_19, 20, 21, 35_
12-_23, 24_
13-_26, 27, 28_
14-_33, 34, 36_
15-_38, 39, 40_
16-_37_
17-_41, 42, 43, 44_
18-_45, 46, 47, 48, 49, 50, 52_
19-_51_
20-_53, 55, 56, 65_
21-_57_

22-_58_
23-
24-_59, 60, 61, 62, 63, 64_
25-_66_
26-_67_
27-_67_
28-_68_
29-_69_
30-_70_
31-_70_
32-_71_
33-_72_
34-_73, 74_
35-_75, 76_
36-
37-_53, 76, 78, 79, 80_
38-
39-_77, 81_
40-_82_
41-_83_
42-_84_

43-
44-
45-*85, 92, 97*
46-*85, 113*
47-
48-*85, 97, 109, 110, 118, 120*
49-*118, 119*
50-*123, 125*
51-*115, 122*
52-*126, 127*
53-*99*
54-*100*
55-*103, 104, 105*
56-*102*
57-*121*
58-*86*
59-*87, 122*
60-*88*
61-*90, 91*
62-*90*
63-*111, 112*
64-*89*
65-*93, 94, 95, 96, 116, 117*
66-*96, 98, 106, 107, 114*
67-*108*
68-
69-
70-*178*
71-*124*
72-
73-*126, 127*
74-*128*
75-*129*
76-*130*
77-
78-*131, 132*
79-*134*
80-
81-
82-*133*
83-*135*
84-
85-*136, 137, 138, 139*
86-*140, 159*

87-*141*
88-*142*
89-*143, 144, 150*
90-*145*
91-*146, 147*
92-*147, 149*
93-*148*
94-*158*
95-*151, 153, 163*
96-*152*
97-*160, 161*
98-*162*
99-*154, 155, 156, 157*
100-*164*
101-*165, 166*
102-*188*
103-*185*
104-*189*
105-*186, 187*
106-*184*
107-*167*
108-*168, 169, 174*
109-*171, 172, 173,*
110-*175, 176, 177*
111-*181*
112-*170*
113-*179, 180*
114-*191, 192, 194, 195*
115-*193, 207*
116-*196, 197, 198, 199, 200, 201*
117-*204, 210*
118-*202, 203*
119-*206*
120-*208*
121-*209*
122-*211*
123-*212*
124-*213*
125-*214*
126-*215, 216*
127-*217, 221, 222*
128-*218*
129-*219, 223, 224*
130-*220*

131-*225, 226*
132-*226*
133-*227, 228*
134-*231*
135-*229, 230*
136-*232*
137-*233*
138-*234*
139-*235*
140-

141-*236*
142-*237*
143-*239*
144-*238, 239*
145-*240*
146-*240*
147-*240*
148-*241*
149-*241*
150-*241*

The Law of Scania – Liber legis Scaniae

1-*1*
2-*1*
3-*2*
4-*1*
5-*3*
6-*4*
7-*4*
8-*5*
9-*5*
10-*5*
11-*5*
12-*5*
13-*5*
14-*5, 7*
15-*5*
16-*9*
17-*10*
18-*10*
19-*11*
20-*11*
21-*11*
22-*4*
23-*12*
24-*12*
25-*1*
26-*13*
27-*13*
28-*13*
29-*4*
30-*6*
31-*4*
32-*8*

33-*14*
34-*14*
35-*11*
36-*14*
37-*16*
38-*15*
39-*15*
40-*15*
41-*17*
42-*17*
43-*17*
44-*17*
45-*18*
46-*18*
47-*18*
48-*18*
49-*18*
50-*18*
51-*19*
52-*18*
53-*20, 37*
54-
55-*20*
56-*20*
57-*21*
58-*22*
59-*24*
60-*24*
61-*24*
62-*24*
63-*24*
64-*24*

65-*20*	**110**-*48*
66-*25*	**111**-*63*
67-*26, 27*	**112**-*63*
68-*28*	**113**-*46*
69-*29*	**114**-*66*
70-*30, 31*	**115**-*51*
71-*32*	**116**-*65*
72-*33*	**117**-*65*
73-*34*	**118**-*48, 49*
74-*34*	**119**-*49*
75-*35*	**120**-*48*
76-*35, 37*	**121**-*57*
77-*39*	**122**-*51, 59*
78-*37*	**123**-*50*
79-*37*	**124**-*71*
80-*37*	**125**-*50*
81-*39*	**126**-*52, 73*
82-*40*	**127**-*52, 73*
83-*41*	**128**-*74*
84-*42*	**129**-*75*
85-*45, 46, 48*	**130**-*76*
86-*58*	**131**-*78*
87-*59*	**132**-*78*
88-*60*	**133**-*82*
89-*64*	**134**-*79*
90-*61, 62*	**135**-*83*
91-*61*	**136**-*85*
92-*45*	**137**-*85*
93-*65*	**138**-*85*
94-*65*	**139**-*85*
95-*65*	**140**-*86*
96-*65, 66*	**141**-*87*
97-*45, 48*	**142**-*88*
98-*66*	**143**-*89*
99-*53*	**144**-*89*
100-*54*	**145**-*90*
101-	**146**-*91*
102-*56*	**147**-*92, 91*
103-*55*	**148**-*93*
104-*55*	**149**-*92*
105-*55*	**150**-*89*
106-*66*	**151**-*95*
107-*66*	**152**-*96*
108-*67*	**153**-*95*
109-*48*	**154**-*99*

155-*99*
156-*99*
157-*99*
158-*94*
159-*86*
160-*97*
161-*97*
162-*98*
163-*95*
164-*100*
165-*101*
166-*101*
167-*107*
168-*108*
169-*108*
170-*112*
171-*109*
172-*109*
173-*109*
174-*108*
175-*110*
176-*110*
177-*110*
178-*70*
179-*113*
180-*113*
181-*111*
182-
183-
184-*106*
185-*103*
186-*105*
187-*105*
188-*102*
189-*104*
190-
191-*114*
192-*114*
193-*115*
194-*114*
195-*114*
196-*116*
197-*116*
198-*116*

199-*116*
200-*116*
201-*116*
202-*118*
203-*118*
204-*117*
205-
206-*119*
207-*115*
208-*120*
209-*121*
210-*117*
211-*122*
212-*123*
213-*124*
214-*125*
215-*126*
216-*126*
217-*127*
218-*128*
219-*129*
220-*130*
221-*127*
222-*127*
223-*129*
224-*129*
225-*131*
226-*131, 132*
227-*133*
228-*133*
229-*135*
230-*135*
231-*134*
232-*136*
233-*137*
234-*138*
235-*139*
236-*141*
237-*142*
238-*144*
239-*144, 143*
240-*146, 145, 147*
241-*148, 149, 150*

BIBLIOGRAPHY

Text

Diplomatarium Danicum. Publ. by Det Danske Sprog- og Litteraturselskab. Copenhagen: Ejnar Munksgaard, 1938–2000.

Faller, Otto, ed., *Sancti Ambrosii Opera*. Pars decima. Epistolae et Acta I. (1958).

Kroman, Erik and Stig Iuul. *Danmarks gamle Love paa Nutidsdansk*, vols. 1–3. Copenhagen: Det Danske Sprog- og Litteraturselskab, 1945–1948.

Olrik, Jørgen, trans., "Anders Sunesøns Latinske Parafrase af Skånske Lov/Antique leges Scanie." In *Danmarks gamle landskabslove med Kirkelovene*, vol. 1.2. Edited by Johs. Brøndum-Nielsen, Poul Johs. Jørgensen, Svend Aakjær and Erik Kroman. Publ. by Det Danske Sprog- og Litteraturselskab. Copenhagen: Gyldendalske Boghandel/Nordisk Forlag, 1933–1961. 467–667.

Sunesen, Anders. *Andreae Sunonis Filii Hexaemeron, Post M. Cl. Gertz*. Edited by Sten Ebbesen and Laurentius Boethius Mortensen. Corpus Philosophorum Danicorum Medii Aevi, vols. 1–2, 11–11.2. Copenhagen: Det Danske Sprog- og Litteratur Selskab, Gad, 1985–1988.

Tierney, Brian. *The Idea of Natural Rights, Studies on Natural Rights, Natural Law and Church Law, 1150–1625*. Emory University Studies in Law and Religion 5. Atlanta: Scholars Press, 1997.

Part III

VOCABULARY

ANDREW SUNESEN'S LANGUAGE

Sten Ebbesen[1]

1. How did Andrew learn his Latin?

Andrew Sunesen was probably no older than 6 when his father, the Sealandic territorial magnate Sune Ebbesen (†1186) – presumably in concert with his cousin Bishop Absalon (†1201) – decided that the boy was to have an ecclesiastic career.[2] Considering the social position of the father, he can hardly have been aiming at any lesser position than abbot for the son, with bishop or archbishop as the desired outcome. The decision must have been taken early in Andrew's life, for it involved that he had to learn to read, write and speak Latin. We know nothing about who was selected to teach the boy, but the pupil's secure grasp of Latin later in life suggests that he had had a good teacher, who – with the assistance of ferule and birch – managed to knock the Lord's Prayer, extracts from the Psalter, Donatus' little morphology from the fourth century, some ancient prose and quite a bit of ancient poetry into the boy's head.

Thus prepared, Andrew was sent to Paris for advanced studies when he was about fourteen, we may presume. There he must have learned some French, but first and foremost he will have had his Latin skills honed. All teaching was in Latin, and Latin, the universal language of Western Europe, is also what he must have used for ordinary communication with his fellow students, although he may have spoken Danish with a few fellow Scandinavians.

Andrew must have stayed in Paris for a decade, and probably more, for he managed to become not only a master of arts, but also of theology, and to actually teach for some time. During his student years Andrew got familiar with the technical vocabulary of the disciplines he studied. In the first years he must have concentrated on theoretical grammar and logic; later it was time for theology and canon law. We can confidently assume that he studied theology under Master Stephen Langton, who later was to become Archbishop of Canterbury (1207–1228) and probably had a leading role in the formulation of the *Magna Carta* of 1215. The study of theology will have required several years, whereas Andrew's initiation into canon law may have been accomplished during a shorter visit to the schools in Bologna, lasting half a year, or at most a whole year. We do not, in fact, have conclusive evidence that he was in Bologna, but according to the historian Saxo,

159

he did travel to Italy, and it is a most reasonable guess that the purpose of the travel was to study law in Bologna, which at the time was famous for its law schools. It is hardly possible to squeeze more than a year into the admittedly not very well anchored time schedule for Andrew's youth.

Already as a boy Andrew would have become familiar with Biblical Latin, both by reading the Psalter and by participating in Mass with its recitals of Biblical texts and singing of hymns influenced by the language of Jerome's *Vulgate* – a thorough revision of earlier Bible translations completed around the year 400. As a theology student he would have been intimately familiar with the *Vulgate*, but he would also have read some Augustine and have become acquainted with his rather more Ciceronian Latin, although perhaps mainly through reading anthologies with excerpts from the church fathers rather than the original works. He would also have read some recent theological literature, both easy readers like Petrus Comestor's Biblical history *Historia Scholastica* ("History for School Use") and highly technical treatises. The study of law – whether civil or canon – would have introduced him to legal Latin.

But Andrew did not only read the Bible and technical literature. He must have been introduced to classical Latin poetry already as a boy, and we can be reasonably certain that he was taught Virgil's *Aeneid* and at least selected passages from Ovid, some Lucan and some Statius. Concurrently with his training in reading Latin poetry, Andrew would have been trained in the art of composing Latin hexameters and pentameters according to the rules of ancient quantitative metrics, which had never been an easy art to master and had only become more difficult when the underlying phonetic basis, the distinction between long and short syllables, was eroded in late antiquity so that no medieval poet could tell the length of a syllable solely by paying attention to his own pronunciation. However, Andrew's 8040-hexameter-long theological poem *Hexaemeron*, which in all probability dates from his time as a Parisian master of theology in the early 1190s, demonstrates that he fully mastered Latin versification. It furthermore reveals that his reading had ranged over more texts than were obligatory for his elementary and university education. Thus there are clear cases of influence from a very recent work, John of Hauville's moralizing *Architrenius* ("The Arch-Lamenter") from 1184/85.[3]

As will by now be clear, young Andrew acquired broad Latin competences within several disciplines and styles: the lean and factual styles of philosophy, theology and law, as well as the ornate styles of poetry. At the latest when he became chancellor to the king of Denmark in 1195 (or slightly earlier), he must also have begun to familiarize himself with the technical language and style used by the chancelleries of lay and ecclesiastical princes. That cannot have cost him much trouble. It is not possible to see from his preserved official correspondence whether he personally formulated his letters, but he quite probably did so if the subject was not a trivial matter of administrative routine. We should probably imagine him dictating the central part of the letter, the one that carries the real message, to a secretary, who could afterwards add the obligatory introductory and valedictory formulas.

2. Pronunciation and spelling

2.1 How did Andrew's Latin sound?

We cannot, of course, reconstruct Andrew's pronunciation in any detail, but we can say *something* about it.

First and foremost, he will have used a fairly literal pronunciation, basically assuming that each letter should be pronounced separately. Second, his phonetic interpretation of the written language will have been heavily influenced by the habits of Romance, and in particular French speakers. This implies, among other things, that:

- the sound *[h]* is non-existent, as the letter *h* is a mute letter. In principle, it is written that in republican Rome there was an *[h]* sound, and thus in classical orthography an *h*, but sometimes it is omitted in cases where classical norm requires it; thus *ortus* for classical *hortus* "garden" and *yle* for *hyle* "matter" both occur in the medieval manuscript of *Hexaemeron*, in all likelihood a faithful reproduction of Andrew's own spelling. Inversely, *h*s turn up in places where they have really nothing to do. *Lex Scaniæ*, the manuscript on which the edition is based, consistently uses an *h* in *hore*, which represents the Danish *øræ*.

- *c* is pronounced *[t͡s]* or *[s]* before *e, i* and *y. Pacis* "of the peace" is thus read *[pa:t͡sis]* or *[pa:sis]*. The *t͡s* pronunciation (preserved in traditional German pronunciation of Latin words) is the older of the two; around 1200 it may already have become obsolete in Paris.

- *t* and *c* are pronounced identically when followed by an *i + vowel*. As a consequence, in such cases *c* often replaces a classical *t* in writing: *violenciam [violɛn(t)siam]* = classical *violentiam*.

- no distinction is made between single and geminated consonants, or between short and long vowels, so *sume* and *summe* would be pronounced identically. It is, however, just possible that someone with Andrew's training in versification would make an audible difference in some circumstances.

- the classical digraphs *ae* and *oe* are both pronounced *[ɛ]* (much like *e* in English *red*] and spelled *e: aliene, pena* = classical *alienae, poena*.

- *i* and *y* both spell *[i]. yeme* = classical *hieme*. In classical Latin *y* was only used in Greek loan words containing an upsilon. In Medieval Latin it is also often used in Greek loan words, but as few Westerners knew Greek, a *y* often appears in places where it really has nothing to do. It is etymologically correct when *Lex Scaniæ* uses *y* in *ypoteca* "pawn" (classical *hypotheca*), but not when it has *y* in *dyocesis* "diocese" and *ydioma* "language", which in a correct transliteration would have appeared as *dioecesis* and *idioma*.

- *m* and *n* can be realized as a nasalization of a preceding vowel: *diligam [diligã]*. This phenomenon cannot be directly observed in any of Sunesen's works, but Latin poems written by twelfth-century Frenchmen sometimes

161

use rhymes that presuppose it. Thus Andrew must at least have known this type of pronunciation, and quite possibly used it.

2.2. How did Andrew spell Latin?

We have no documents in Andrew's own hand, but there is every reason to believe that his spelling habits were not much different from what we find in the manuscript that has preserved his *Hexaemeron* and the one on which the edition of *Lex Scaniæ* is based. Both manuscripts exhibit the same sort of standard medieval orthography with, generally speaking, the same range of acceptable variation, although the former was copied just a generation or two after the author's death, whereas the latter was produced 200 years after his time.[4] The scribe of the *Lex Scaniæ* manuscript is:

- consistent in using *e* for classical *ae* and *oe*, so *pene* = classical *poenae*.
- fairly consistent, but not always following classical norms, in the use of *h*. In particular, *th* appears both in places where it is etymologically appropriate (*anathematizare, orthodoxorum, orthogonaliter*) and in places where etymology demands a simple *t* (*lintheamenta thorus penthecoste*). Inversely, etymology would prescribe *th* in *cyrotece*. Twice a paratitic *h* appears in *marcha*, which is otherwise spelled *marca*.
- inconsistent in choosing between *cia, cio* and *tia, tio*. Thus both *satisfaccio* and the classical *satisfactio* occur.
- inconsistent in choosing between *mpn* and *mn*. Both *condempnandus* and the classical *condemnandus* occur.
- inconsistent in choosing between single and double consonants. There are thirty-three examples of the correct *nummorum* and twelve of the incorrect *numorum*. In this matter Andrew's extensive training in writing Latin verse may have resulted in his being consistent, and in accordance with classical norms, because the distinction between single and geminated consonants is relevant to versification.

Unfortunately, the 1933 edition of *Lex Scaniæ*, which according to the editors renders the text exactly as it is spelled in the manuscript, creates an illusion of spelling habits that were neither the scribe's nor Andrew's. Being confused by the fact that in their own time, the twentieth century, *j, v* and *w* are elements of the alphabet in the same way that *a, b* and *c* are, they write *j, v* or *w* whenever the manuscript offers something that looks like that. But to the scribe these were not independent letters (*graphemes* in modern linguistic terminology); they were just alternative ways of writing *i, u* and *uu*, the choice between the letter shape being determined by aesthetic considerations and considerations of readability. As *i* did not obligatorily have a dot above it, a sequence of two *i*s – *ıı* – could easily be mistaken for an *n*, and a sequence of two *u*s could look like *ıııı*, which could mean *ini, iui, im, mi, un* or *nu*. Hence the preference for a long *i* after a short one (in the edition represented as *ij*) and for the wedge-shaped *w* over *uu* – in the latter case the *w* shape was particularly useful in the beginning of words, where the risk of misreading was greatest, and where there was also, apparently, a feeling that even a single *u* looked better if it had the wedge shape.

The scribe is not consistent in his choice between these equivalent letter shapes, and why should he be so? Whether he chooses the *u* or the *v* shape, the value of the sign is the same, just as it does not make a difference whether he uses a long *ʃ* or a short *s*, an *a* or an *a*.

Due to these considerations, the reprint of the 1933 edition included in the present volume has eliminated its use of *j* and *v*.

3. The vocabulary, syntax and style of *Lex Scaniæ*

3.0 Introduction

Andrew was a learned man, and his learning is palpable in the language of *Lex Scaniæ*. The vocabulary is richer and the syntax more elaborate than strictly necessary. Generally speaking, his Latin is classicizing, but moderately so. In that respect he distances himself from the contemporary school of rigid classicists and its Danish representative Saxo Grammaticus.

Whereas most lexical items come from the basic vocabulary of classical prose, several words with a background in ancient poetry also appear, as do expressions originating in Roman law or in ecclesiastical language. When a slightly unusual, but classical, word turns up in the law, there is a high probability that it is also attested in Andrew's *Hexaemeron*, to which references will be provided later when relevant.

The syntax follows, in the main, the classical rules of construction. Without being overly complex, many periods are quite long, containing several subordinary clauses and other subordinary syntagms. Syntactic breakdowns do not occur.

Stylistic embellishment, *amplificatio*, that lifts the text to a higher literary level than required by the information to be conveyed, is obtained in a variety of ways. Nouns are equipped with adjectives that add no real information, as when death is called *dira mors* "fearful death" instead of just *mors*. A spade is not always a spade; if it is referred to several times, it is likely to appear under several other designations as well (*variatio sermonis*). Words that syntactically belong together may be separated from one another (*hyperbaton*). And so on. Andrew clearly wanted to – and did – elevate *Lex Scaniæ* to a stylistically more sophisticated level than that of the down-to-earth vernacular text that was his starting point. Whoever his intended public were, he did not want them to turn up their noses at Danish lack of mastery of Latin style.

The remaining part of this essay will consist of annotated examples illustrating Andrew's choice of words, constructions, stylistic figures etc., without any aspirations to exhaustivity.

163

3.1 The vocabulary

3.1.1 Old and new meanings, words for non-classical phenomena

The core of Andrew's vocabulary is ancient, and the words usually have their ancient meanings. Sometimes, though, the meaning has been modified. Thus *satisfacere* does not mean "to satisfy" but "to pay an indemnity to", and whereas *emendare* is used in its classical sense of amending in §26, in §21 *emendari* means "be paid as a fine" and in §37 *emendatio* is a sum of money to be paid as damages.

In §115 Andrew calls a glove a *cyroteca*. Strangely, there seems to have been no word for a glove in ancient Latin, so the medievals used a home-made Greek word *chirotheca* "hand-case", which is apparently not attested in either ancient or medieval Greek.

Andrew did not have to be innovative to find a way to say "glove", but he will not have had much tradition to build on with regard to the Latinization of specifically Nordic measures or institutions. The Germanic word *mark* was used for a measure of value over a wide area and had already been Latinized as *marca*. It was also established custom to use *denarius* to mean "penny" (Old Danish *pænning*). But what to do about the Nordic *øræ*? The word is now generally believed to be an old loan from Latin *aureus* "golden coin", but the Latin origin was no longer perceptible in Andrew's days. He calls it an *hora* (with a mute *h*, of course) – whether he coined the loan word himself or inherited it, the choice was not a very happy one. Someone from central or southern Europe would be likely to completely misunderstand §7, which states that if somebody does not show up after having been summoned to the *Thing* he is *condemnandus in duabus horis*. In standard Latin this would mean that the man should be condemned within two hours, *hōra* "hour" being an old loan word from Greek, but the sense intended in the law is that the absentee should be fined two *øræ*.

Notice, by the way, the law's repeated use of the proposition *in* to introduce the size of a fine. Thus in §27 we find *illo in tribus marcis regi condempnando* "the person is to be fined three marks payable to the king" and in §60 *tam regi quam aduersario in xl^{ta} marcis obligabitur persoluendis* "he will be obliged to pay forty marks both to the king and to his adversary". This non-classical use of *in* is not a calque from Danish.

Whereas marks, pennies and øræ are not deemed worthy of explanation, Andrew has inserted in §131 a lengthy definition of a *skæppæ* "bushel", which he renders *mensura*. The description of the vessel used as a bushel measure gives him the opportunity to show off his acquaintance with the vocabulary of elementary geometry: *orthogonaliter, catetus, ypotenusa.*

Andrew has no consistent policy regarding Nordic institutions. Sometimes he just accommodates a Danish word to Latin morphology and uses the loan word without offering any explanation. Thus *bondæ* ("independent farmer", and more generally "free man with full citizen rights") makes its appearance as *bondo* in §5 and is repeatedly used afterwards without any explanatory comments[5] (at the beginning of §5, where it is the man's status as a husband that matters, *bondæ* is rendered *maritus*). At other times an explanation is offered, but not necessarily on the first occurrence of the Latinized vernacular term. *Scotatio* ("transference of property, symbolically marked by the old owner placing some earth in the new owner's lap") makes its appearance in §16 and is then repeatedly used before, finally, being explained in §38.

Andrew uses the Latin phrase *candentis ferri iudicium* for "ordeal by fire" no less than twenty-five times, four times with the addition that this is what in our paternal tongue is called *scuz iærn*, but only after several occurences of the term does he explain the custom in §38.

He does better with *mansus*, which makes its first appearance in §26. The text describes how the land of a village can be measured into units "which people popu-larly call *bool* in our maternal tongue, and which we may call *mansi* in Latin". The phrasing suggests that Andrew is aware that *mansus* is really a foreign measure (of Frankish origin), but §26 makes it clear what is to be covered by the term in the context of the law.

The Danish *lanbo*, that is, a tenant who leases a farm from someone else, is ren-dered *colonus* on its first appearance in §143 and used several times in the following paragraphs. It is not explained, but, for one thing, the sense is clear from the context, and for another, the word was also used about people in similar circumstances else-where in Europe. In the same way, there was no great need to explain exactly what the Danish administrative unit *hæræþ* was – the imprecise *provincia* would do. But *hæræzmen* needed some explanation, so they became *XII bondones de prudentibus tocius provincie* in §29. Almost the same formulation turns up in §33 *XII de pruden-tioribus tocius provincie*, but this time with the addition that the Latin phrase is meant to cover *aldungebønder*. When later in the same paragraph Andrew has to introduce *opolbøndær* he gives up, and just says *XI quos hotolbønder materna lingua nominat* "eleven [men] whom our maternal tongue calls *otolbønder*".

The law time and again stipulates the recourse to an oath (*eþ*) sworn by a certain number of men, usually twelve. One might have expected a consistent rendition of this key term with one and the same Latin word, but in fact Andrew uses *iura-mentum* and *sacramentum* indiscriminately.

Even more remarkably, Andrew did not think he needed to decide on one par-ticular word for that most important institution, the Thing (*þing*). In §7 "to sum-mon (*stæfnæ*) someone to the Thing" simply becomes *ad ius citare*, in §93 "at the Thing" becomes *in iudicio* and in §95 *þingmæn* "Thing-men" are called *iuridici*, but in §127 the Thing is called *forum* and described as a *curia secularis, curia* here clearly meaning "court of law" – in §95 *curia* it is used about the king's court (*garþ*) and in § 107 about an ordinary courtyard (*garþ*).

3.1.2 Terms borrowed from Roman law

Lex Scaniæ does not contain many obvious lexical borrowings from Roman law texts, but there are some, as the following examples will show:

The verbs *certiorare* (§101) and *irritare* (§39) and the adverb *licite* "lawfully" (four occurrences) are in ancient literature only found in the *Digests*. Other words which Andrew certainly owes to Roman legal literature include *adiudic-are, -atio* "adjudic-ate, -ation" (nine occurences), *depositarius* "'depository" (§§141–2), *fideiubeo* "go bail" with the derivatives *fide-iussio, -iussor* (eight occurrences in all), *inflictio* (§§58, 64) "infliction".

In §2, which is about inheritance, the Danish legal term *full lot* ("full lot") becomes *uirilis porcio*, a loan from the *Digests*.[6] The expression returns in §§14 and 24, but in §24 *porcio integra* is also used (cf. the section about *variatio sermonis*, later).

In §§95, 121, 135 we find *contrectare* in the unusual sense "lay hands on, steal", which is attested several times in the *Digests*. §95 *licet autem furtum committat, qui eciam unum denarium domino contrectat inuito* "even though someone who lays hand on just a single penny against the owner's will is committing theft" is clearly inspired by *Digests* 13.1.20.pr *qui primo inuito domino rem contrectauerit*. The Danish text has the ordinary word for stealing (§151 *æn þo ær han ok þiuf um han **stial** en pænning*). In *Hexaemeron* 2884 Andrew uses *contrectare* in its common sense of handling.

Convolare "take refuge" is not among the top ten Latin verbs, but Sunesen is fond of it. It occurs four times in *Lex Scaniæ* (§§ 22, 37, 127) and once in *Hexaemeron* (5920). The occurrence in §22 stands out, because the notion of taking refuge somewhere has been watered down to that of entering: *Matre vero ad secundas nupcias conuolante* "If a mother enters into a second marriage". This is undoubtedly a loan from a section in the *Pandects* which, like §22, deals with the economical consequences of a second marriage[7] *De poenis quae viro aut mulieri ad secundas nuptias convolantibus communes sunt* "About the economical consequences applicable to both a man and a woman if they contract a second marriage".

In these cases, inspiration from *Corpus Iuris Civilis* seems undeniable, although it may possibly have reached Andrew through some intermediary. A less certain case is his use of the not-too-common verb *deperire* "be lost, die", which occurs three times in *Lex Scaniæ* (§§ 45, 71, 114) and once in *Hexaemeron* (5793). *Deperire* is used no fewer than fifteen times in the *Digests*, but also four times in Ovid, who could thus be Andrew's source for the word. A similar doubt concerns the rare adverb *furtive* "furtively" (seven occurrences), which is used three times in the *Digests*, but also occurs once in Ovid (plus a few texts that Andrew is unlikely to have read).

3.1.3 The language of the church

It is hardly surprising to find a Biblical tag like *turpis lucri gratia* "for filthy lucre" (*Ep. 1 Pet.* 5.2, *Ep. Tit.* 1.11) in §95, but there are not many of them, nor much properly theological language. The law did not offer much scope for it. There was, however, a place for words relating to the daily running of church business: *ecclesia, dyocesis, episcopus, monasterium, sacerdos, parrochia, parrochianus, religionis causa monasterium introire, mundum relinquere*.

166

Andrew's fondness of circumlocutions also manifests itself in this lexical field. A justly killed adulterer may not be buried in the church yard unless he manages to express repentance before expiring (§126). The Danish text says *liggi han utæn kirkiu garþe* "he is to lie outside the church-yard", which Andrew could have rendered *iaceat extra cemeterium*, but instead he chose *perempti corpus orthodoxorum priuabitur sepultura* "the body of the man slain shall be deprived of the burial of the orthodox".

Andrew only puts his mastery of the language of theology on display in two passages, both of which are his own additions to the law. See section 3.2.3.

3.1.4 Embellishment: poetic words

Andrew uses a number of words that are rare or non-existent in the classical prose authors whom he is likely to have read, but do occur in poets whom he is likely to have read. A few examples:

> *Conamen* "exertion, attempt" occurs once in *Lex Scaniæ* (§66) and three times in *Hexaemeron* (94, 1888, 1929). The word is repeatedly used by Ovid and Statius.
>
> *Confringere* "break (into)" occurs three times in *Lex Scaniæ* (§§60, 116) and once in *Hexaemeron* (6178). There are three occurrences in Lucan.
>
> *Inopinus* "unexpected" is found once in *Lex Scaniæ* (§67), twice in Virgil, twice in Ovid and more than ten times in Statius.
>
> *Pullulare* "sprout" occurs twice in *Lex Scaniæ* (§§ 37, 131) and once in *Hexaemeron* (6221). In all three cases the verb is used in a metaphorical sense: in §37 it is harm (*noxia*) that sprouts, in §131 it is destruction by fire that sprouts from somebody's hearth and in *Hexaemeron* it is the corrupted nature of man that sprouts forth due to the tinder left by original sin. A comparison of the first of the occurrences in *Lex Scaniæ* with a passage from Virgil makes it rather obvious in which context Andrew had learned the word:

>> § 37 consultum videtur tempestiue *radicem* malorum, ante quam *ex ea contingat pullulare* noxia, resecari "it seems well-advised to cut the root of evils in time before harm sprouts from it"
>>
>> *Georgica* 2.17: *pullulat ab radice* aliis densissima silua "in the case of other trees a dense forest [of suckers] sprout from the root"

It is conceivable that Andrew did not think of such words as poetical, but more likely he made deliberate use of them to raise the stylistic level of the law.

3.1.5 Variatio sermonis and circumlocutions

The historian Saxo, who dedicated his *Gesta Danorum* to Andrew, is famous for his classicizing Latin, in which unclassical words are eschewed even when there is no classical word for a medieval phenomenon. In his vocabulary the words *episcopus* and *archiepiscopus* simply do not exist, nor does the word *apostolicus*, which was commonly used to designate the pope, so he resorts to old titles of pagan priests, using *antistes, pontifex* and *presul* indiscriminately of popes, archbishops and bishops. Andrew had no problems with calling a spade a spade, so the pope is *apostolicus* and the (arch)bishop is an *episcopus* – most of the time, that is, for no less than seven times he uses *antistes*, five times *pontifex* and once *presul* instead. In Andrew's case the choice of those words was not the result of pathological classicism but of a wish to embellish his text by means of *variatio sermonis*, employing now this, now that, of two or more synonyms.

Such *variatio* can hardly be called a virtue in a law text, but it is a rather pervasive trait in *Lex Scaniæ*. Some examples have already been given in section 3.1.1.

Sometimes there is *variatio* on a small scale, as when scotation is sometimes just called *scotatio*, at others *scotationis solemnitas* "the ceremony of scotation", and the latter is once replaced with *scotationis solemnia*. Or when in §126 three different verbs (or their respective deverbal nouns) are used about exactly the same act, namely that of killing an adulterer caught *in flagranti* (*occidere, interficere, interimere*), whereas the corresponding Danish text only uses one verb, *drepa*. But *variatio* on a grander scale also occurs.

The Danish language never occurs under its proper name, *lingua Danica* (which is actually found in Saxo in spite of the lack of Danes in classical Roman literature). When Andrew wants to tell what something is called in Danish, his favourite designation of the language is *lingua patria* "(our) paternal tongue" (§§46, 48, 57, 60, 63, 65, 87, 90, 92, 99, 110, 113, 127, 130, 142) or *ideoma patrium* "the paternal idiom" (§131). Mother is not quite forgotten, though, for *lingua materna* and *materna lingua* "(our) maternal tongue" also occur (§§ 26, 33), as does *natale ydioma* "(our) language of birth" (§33). *Uulgare nostrum* "our popular (language)" is used on four occasions (§§ 37, 38, 44, 52), and the bare *uulgare* once (§65); the corresponding adverb *uulgariter* "popularly" occurs once alone (§33) and once in the pleonastic expression *maternā linguā uulgariter* "in the maternal tongue popularly" (§26). That the variation is intentional is very clear in §33, where three Danish terms are introduced, each in its own way: the first with *que uulgariter appellatur* "which is popularly called", the second with *quos natale nominat ydioma* "which our language of birth names" and the last with *quod lingua materna nominat* "which our maternal tongue names" – notice here also the change from *appellatur* "is called" in the first instance to *nominat* "names" in the two remaining ones.

When Andrew uses circumlocutions, they tend to lift the language to a higher stylistic level than one would expect in a law. The already cited *natale ydioma* is an instance in case. The same stylistic elevation is effected when someone's father's house becomes his *sacra paterna* "paternal sanctuary" (§§3, 24).

§5 contains rules about a wife's rights if her husband sells property of hers. She is not to complain while he is alive, but if he dies she may raise a claim. The Danish version of the law simply says *Dør bondæn* "If her husband dies". The Latin text also covers the case of divorce and uses the ornate formulation *sed ab eo si iure diuino, vel ab eius herede quamuis communi filio, si dire mortis imperio soluta fuerit* "but if she has been separated from him by divine law or from his heir, be he even their common son, by orders of fearful death". *Dirus* is among Virgil's, Ovid's and Statius' favourite words. It makes ten appearances in Andrew's *Hexaemeron*.

A similar phrasing is used in § 22 *maternum affectum mortis imperio mariti consorcio viduatum* "motherly affection widowed, by orders of death, of the company of her husband". The motherly affection is a circumlocution for the mother, and the rest is a circumlocution for "if her husband dies".

3.2 Morphology and syntax

3.2.1 Compared to classical Latin

Differences in spelling apart, the morphology is that of classical Latin. A single medieval peculiarity may be noted: the periphastic perfect passive subjunctive is consistently formed by adding *fuerit* instead of *sit* to the participle, thus *si repertus fuerit* (§87).

The syntax is also basically that of classical Latin, although some rules of Ciceronian Latin are not obeyed. Thus Andrew happily writes *ad inuadendum possessiones alicuius iniuste et diripiendum bona ipsius* (§63) "to unlawfully invade someone's possessions and plunder his goods", using *ad + gerund + object noun*, which is the standard construction in Medieval Latin, instead of *ad + object noun + gerundive (ad inuadendas possessiones et bona ipsius diripienda)*.

Similarly, we find the object of a *verbum dicendi* expressed by means of a *quod*-clause, as in the following case:

> §34 per iusiurandi religionem *affirmantes, quod* nec alicuius odii causa nec fauoris gracia confingant aliquam [. . .] negociis falsitatem, *et quod* credunt esse verum quod asserunt, *et quod* idem ex relatu suorum antecessorum et prvdentium didicerunt antiquorum
>
> "affirming under oath that they are not by reason of enmity of favour fabricating some falsity, and that they believe what they say to be true, and that they have been told the same by their predecessors and reliable people of old".

Once again, this is standard Medieval Latin. What is somewhat surprising is how sparingly Andrew uses the *quod* construction compared to the classical accusative + infinitive. In fact, there is only one other instance of *affirmare quod* (§92), whereas there are eight instances of *affirmare + accusative w. infinitive*. There is not a single instance of an object clause introduced by *quia*, which is only used ten times in all, and always in the sense of "because". Similarly, there are no instances of *sic* or *ita quod* "so that", but only of *sic/ita ut*. Final clauses are regularly introduced by an *ut*, as in classical Latin, with *quatenus*, which was otherwise very popular in the Middle Ages, occuring just twice.

3.2.2 Period building

Andrew's periods are often longish and contain several subordinate predications and other syntagms, like the following one in §4, which consists of one super-ordinate sentence (main clause) with an embedded relative clause, followed by two subordinated, but mutually paratactic, *nisi* clauses, the first of which has two subordinate clauses of the ablative absolute type.

The detailed structure of the period is shown next. Parentheses and similar signs enclose syntactic units, words enclosed in backslash + slash-mark, like \uocet/, are such as break up a syntactic unit, creating a hyperbaton. The main verb ***comitantur*** is printed in bold and underlined, the verbs of the two subordinate *nisi* clauses, **uocet** and **protrahat**, in bold without underlining and the verb of the relative clause embedded in the main clause, *accessit*, as well as the participles *aspirante* and *vendicante* in the two ablative absolute clauses in bold italics.

{(⌐Alia predia¬ ⌐nouaque heredita [que <post contractas nupcias> <alteri *accessit*/ coniugum>¬]) (suos \semper/ dominos) (***comitantur***)}
{*nisi* (patrem) (ad [⌐bonorum omnium – tam mobilium quam immobilium –¬ **uocet**/ consorcium \superstes procreata soboles/ maternorum])

- (matre) tamen (ad [⌐paternorum bonorum¬ participium]) ([nullatenus] ***aspirante***) –
- sed (solo patre) (propter [⌐laboriose prouisionis¬ onera]) (istud \sibi/ priuilegium) ***vendicante*** – }

{*et nisi* ([hereditatem ⌐licet vberiorem¬ vel hereditates] [exceptis immobilibus]) ([primo obiecta] hereditas [haut ⌐tribus marcis¬ exilior]) (ad [particionis **protrahat**/ rationem])}.

3.2.3 Embellishment: hyperbaton and other figures

In the period analyzed earlier, there are no fewer than six hyperbata:

1   *alteri* accessit *coniugum*
2   *suos* semper *dominos*
3–4   nisi patrem ad *bonorum omnium – tam mobilium quam immobilium –* uocet *consorcium* superstes procreata soboles *maternorum*
5   *istud* sibi *priuilegium*
6   ad *particionis* protrahat *rationem*

The double hyperbaton in (3–4) is remarkable. The insertion of the verb *uocet* between the *bonorum &c.* and the noun (*consorcium*) governing the genitive is of the same harmless sort as (6), but by reserving *maternorum*, the final qualification of *bonorum*, for the end, Andrew has made the syntax rather tortuous.

§4 is by no means extraordinary by exhibiting cases of hyperbaton. Andrew demonstrates the same fondness for the figure throughout the text.

A few examples (without translation, as the hyperbata connot be reproduced in English):

§13 cum *duodeno* deferri debet defensio *sacramento*
§13 *omnem* eis amputent super diuisione facienda *materiam* litigandi
§14 *conferendi* habet monasteriis siue extraneis, quibus voluerit, *facultatem*
§58 comites rex Kanutus *sua* dignum duxit persequi *constitucione*

Repetition with *polyptoton* (same word in different grammatical forms) also occurs:

§24 *Diuersis* temporibus a *diuersis* regibus *diuersa* sunt iura prodita super concubinarum filiis "At various times various kings have issued various laws concerning the sons of concubines".

The same polyptoton occurs in the following grandiloquent period:

§43 Instigante humani generis inimico, quia proni semper fuerunt homines in nostris partibus ad homicidium perpetrandum, pacem angelicam deserentes et sedicionem dyabolicam amplexantes, *diuersis temporibus diuersa sunt iura prodita* super tanti reatus per multam pecuniariam castigacionem, quatenus et tantus excessus aliquatenus refrenari et amissionis dampnum quoquo modo posset satisfaccionis pecuniarie tristi solacio compensari.

"Because, at the instigation of The Enemy of the Human Race, people in our part of the world have always been prone to leave angelic peace in favour of diabolic strife and commit homicide, at various times various laws have been issued about punishing this enormous offence with a money fine, in order that such enormous excess might be somewhat restrained and that the damage of loss be in some way compensated by the sad comfort of a pecuniary indemnification."

This is the archbishop speaking! In fact, the elaborate period is the beginning of a preamble of his own invention introducing the paragraphs of the law concerning manslaughter. The preamble has no warrant whatsoever in the vernacular text. *Humani generis inimicus* was a stock circumlocution of *Satan*, and the brief version *inimicus* occurs in *Hexaemeron* 5989. Notice also the use of isocolon in the antithesis *pacem angelicam deserentes – sedicionem dyabolicam amplexantes*.

Andrew again feels inspired to use some elevated ecclesiastical language in a comment he adds on the law that a woman accused of adultery is to be thrown out of her husband's house and bed if she fails to pass an ordeal by fire:

§127 Verum in parte constat huic humane legi, velud famule obsequenti, velud pedisseque sequenti domine sue vestigia, per diuine legis preminenciam

171

derogari, que matrimonia iubet non fori, sed poli, non curie secularis, sed ecclesie spiritualis examini atque regimini subiacere, nec permittit eciam separacionem thori per igniti ferri iudicium celebrari.

It is, however, a fact that this human law, being in the position of an obedient maidservant or handmaid who follows in the footsteps of her mistress, is partly overruled by the preeminence of divine law, which bids that marriage be subject not to examination and rule by the *Thing*, but by heaven, not by a secular court, but by the spiritual church, and which also forbids a separation of bed to be determined by ordeal by fire.

Here we have the time-honoured comparison of the relation between secular and divine law or philosophical and theological knowledge to that of a maid to her mistress, and further an isocolic antithesis *non fori – sed poli*, involving the poetic *polus* for *celum*, followed by another isocolic antithesis *non curie secularis – sed ecclesie spiritualis*. Interestingly, there is a similar passage about the relationship between canon and civil law in *Hexaemeron* 2980–87:

Quamuis adueniat pactum, stipulatio fiat
de persoluendis usuris, faenore dando,
canonico iure repetuntur praestita, quamuis
non soleant repeti ciuili iure; sed aequum est
maiori dominae famulam parere minorem,
canonicae legi ciuilem cedere legem:
inde sequi tamquam dominae uestigia sacrae
legis canonicae non dedignatur honorans
lex humana, minor ancilla, pedissequa supplex.

Even when there is an agreement and a stipulation that interest should be paid, the money paid may be demanded back according to canon law, even though this is usually not the case according to civil law. But it is fair that the maidservant should obey her superior mistress and civil law give way to canon law; hence human law, the inferior maidservant and humble handmaid, does not object to honouring her mistress, holy canon law, by following in her footsteps, as it were.

When defending the pre-eminence of canon over secular law, Andrew could wax very eloquent!

Notes

1 I gratefully recognize my debt to Mr Tue E. Søvsø, MA, who not only produced a concordance of the Latin text for me, but also gave me access to his own notes about the law's vocabulary and style. Several of his observations have been tacitly incorporated in my essay.

2 Andrew's birthdate is unknown. Some time in the 1160s seems indicated. He can hardly have arrived in Paris much later than 1180. By the mid-1190s he was chancellor to the king of Denmark. The main sources for his early life are gathered and discussed in the introduction of Anders Sunesen, *Andreae Sunonis Filii Hexaemeron, Post M. Cl. Gertz*, ed. Sten Ebbesen and Laurentius Boethius Mortensen, Corpus Philosophorum Danicorum Medii Aevi, vols. 1–2, 11–11.2 (Copenhagen: Det Danske Sprog- og Litteratur Selskab, Gad, 1985–1988).

3 See Lars Boje Mortensen, "The Sources of Andrew Sunesen's Hexaemeron," *Cahiers de l'Institut du Moyen-Age grec et latin* 50 (1985), 111–216.

4 For the orthographical habits of the scribe of the *Hexaemeron* manuscript, see §5.3 of the introduction to vol. I of Sunesen, *Andreae Sunonis Filii Hexaemeron* (see note 2, earlier).

5 As Tue Søvsø reminds me, *bundo/bondo* also occurs in two slightly earlier texts produced in Denmark, viz. the anonymous *Chronicon Roskildense* and Sven Aggesen's *Brevis historia regum Dacie*. See the index in vol. II of Martin Clarentius, ed., *Scriptores minores historiæ Danicæ medii ævi. Ex codicibus denuo recensuit*, vols. 1–2, (Copenhagen: Selskabet for Udgivelse af Kilder til dansk Historie (1917–1922)). The texts can be found in vol. I of this series.

6 *Dig.* 37.5.8.pr.

7 *Pandectae (Appendix ad libros de nuptiis* c.2, art. I). This passage is not included in modern editions of the Pandects, but occurs in older editions. See e.g. Robert-Joseph Pothier, *Pandectæ Justinianeæ in novum ordinem digestæ*, 4th ed., vol. 2 (Paris: Belin-Leprieur, 1821), 165.

BIBLIOGRAPHY
Vocabulary

Blatt, Franz, Bente Friis Johansen, Peter Terkelsen, Steen Otto Due, and Aarhus Universitet, Institut for Oldtids- Og Middelalderforskning. *Lexicon Mediae Latinitatis Danicae,
Ordbog over Dansk Middelalderlatin.* 1. Edition, edited. Aarhus: Aarhus Universitetsforlag, 2014.

Gertz, Martin Cl. ed., *Scriptores minores historiæ Danicæ medii ævi. Ex codicibus denuo
recensuit*, vols. 1–2. Publ. by Selskabet for Udgivelse af Kilder til dansk Historie. Copenhagen: G.E.C. Gad, 1917–1922.

Heumann, Hermann Gottlieb. *Handlexikon Zu Den Quellen Des Römischen Rechts.* 9. Aufl.
Edited by Emil Seckel. Jena: Verlag von Gustav Fischer, 1914.

Kulturhistorisk leksikon for nordisk middelalder, Edited by Johannes Brønsted et al.
København: Rosenkilde og Bagger, 1956–1978.

Mortensen, Lars Boje. "The Sources of Andrew Sunesen's Hexaemeron." *Cahiers de
l'Institut du Moyen-Age grec et latin* 50 (1985). 111–216.

Pothier, Robert-Joseph, *Pandectæ Justinianeæ in novum ordinem digestæ*, 4th ed., vol. 2,
Paris: Belin-Leprieur, 1821.

Short, Charles and Charlton T. Lewis, ed., *A Latin Dictionary, Founded on Andrews' Edition of Freund's Latin Dictionary.* Revised, Enlarged and in Great Part Rewritten by
Charlton T. Lewis and Charles Short. Oxford: Clarendon Press, 1879.

Sunesen, Anders. *Andreae Sunonis Filii Hexaemeron, Post M. Cl. Gertz.* Edited by Sten
Ebbesen and Laurentius Boethius Mortensen. Corpus Philosophorum Danicorum Medii
Aevi, vols. 1–2, 11–11.2. Copenhagen: Det Danske Sprog- og Litteratur Selskab, Gad,
1985–1988.

GLOSSARY LATIN – ENGLISH

Merike Ristikivi and Tue Søvsø

Words included

Anders Sunesen's Latin version of the Law of Scania is a complex text to interpret. The text is an attempt to describe the legal norms of thirteenth-century Scania, and therefore knowledge of this society is necessary in order to understand the text. At the same time this description is carried out in the language of the Roman and contemporary law which Anders Sunesen was obviously well acquainted with. This glossary aims to make the peculiar Latin expressions used to describe the workings of Scanian society more readily understandable to the reader. The reader looking for a more thorough treatment of the vocabulary (and with some knowledge of Danish and German) is referred to the *Lexicon Mediae Latinitatis Danicae, Kulturhistorisk leksikon for nordisk middelalder* and *Heumanns Handlexikon zu den Quellen des römischen Rechts*

The glossary is made to be used in combination with Lewis and Short, *A Latin Dictionary*. Therefore, it mostly includes words and expressions that have a specific meaning in this text. Latin words in their standard meaning should be found in Lewis and Short. Apart from the word or expression itself and translation, we have included the word class (*subst.*, *v.*, etc.) and the references to its occurrences in the text. These references are written in parentheses and refer to the chapters of the text. Nouns are listed in a Latin nominative form and verbs in the present tense, first person singular.

Latin orthography

The Latin text included in this book is based on a late fifteenth-century manuscript and reflects the spelling of this manuscript. Considerable variation in orthographical practice is therefore present, and we especially wish to direct the reader's attention to the following features:

- t is in some cases replaced by c, most importantly in the suffix -tio(n)
- diphtongs (ae and oe) are reduced to e

Abbreviations

abl: **ablativus**	*impers*: **impersonale**
acc: **accusativus**	*inf*: **infinitivus**
adi: **adjectivus**	*part*: **participium**
adv: **adverbium**	*pass*: **passivum**
c: **cum**	*praep*: **praepositio**
dat: **dativus**	*subst*: **substantivus**
gen: **genitivus**	*v*: **verbum**

Glossary

ac si – as if (2, 11)

accusacio simplex – simple accusation (128)

accuso, *v.* – I. accuse: + *inf.* (48: accusetur aliquis spoliasse); + *aliquem alicuius rei* (94: si quis in iure coram communi audiencia furti quemquam accusauerit); or with *praep.*: + *super aliqua re* (49: accusatus super homicidio); + *de aliqua re* (92: si de furto accusatus); + *pro aliqua re* (135a: si dominus eius eum pro furto accusauerit); + *supra aliqua re* (116: accusatus supra dampno a suis apibus irrogato); II. find fault with: + *acc.* (19: qui empcionem accusat)

actor, *subst.* – plaintiff (37, 41, 68, 85, 86, 89, 90, 91, 92, 93, 97, 98, 99, 140)

actor regius – the king's official (95)

ad ius citatus – summoned to the assembly (6)

ad minus – at least (57, 70, 92, 97, 108, 110, 114)

adiudicacio, *subst.* – adjudgement, decision; *i.e.* the permission given by the assembly to seek execution of a claim (131, 137)

ago, *v.* – I. to do (111: quod illud non egerit; 126: penitenciam agat); II. to claim (68: ad restitucionem estimacionis agere dampni dati); III. agitur de aliquo – it is a matter of (16, 37, 41, 63, 78, 89, 131, 137)

agnatus, *subst.* – paternal kin, kinsman (21, 45, 47, 75, 76, 129); see also *cognatus*

alieno, *v.* – alienate, sell, to make something the property of another (5, 18, 20, 35, 90, 96)

alienacio (alienatio), *subst.* – alienation, sale (5, 18, 42, 96)

allegacio, *subst.* – allegation, claim (33, 65, 78)

anathematizo, *v.* – excommunicate (48)

anima, *subst.* – soul (46, 114)

animus, *subst.* – I. mind, mood (66: uel irato animo ad terram trahatur; 116); II. intention (70: ex iniuriandi animo et contempto; 150)

antistes, *subst.* – bishop, archbishop (29, 30, 33, 40, 56, 57, 67, 109)

apostolicus, *subst.* – pope (48)

appono, *v.* – pay out (38, 51, 69, 109)

arma, *subst.* – weapons (48, 60, 66, 68, 90)

assero, *v.* – assert, maintain (1, 20, 33, 35, 37, 42, 48, 67, 78, 87, 135a, 137, 144)

assistentes, *subst.* – people present, attending witnesses (16, 38); only used in the context of scotation, see also *scotatio*

astruo, *v.* – add, demonstrate, provide (35, 51)

auctor, *subst.* – builder (27); perpetrator (45, 57, 58, 61, 67, 69, 71); vendor (37, 85); seller (88)

auctoritas, *subst.* – authority (45, 49, 73, 131, 134, 137)

audiencia, *subst.* – assembly (109)

audiencia communis – common assembly (24, 57, 87, 94)

audiencia iuridicorum – hearing (111)

auxilium, *subst.* – help (34: petat auxilium uenditoris); remedy (87: hoc solum ei supererit auxilium); assistance (101: nullatenus obligato ad auxilium exactoris regii declinare)

beneficium, *subst.* – benefit (27, 35, 37, 45, 67, 73, 78, 102)

beneplacitum supra sue uoluntatis – beyond his own free will (10)

bondo, *subst.* – householder (5, 8, 24, 29, 37)

bona, *subst.* – property (3, 4, 5, 10, 11, 13, 15, 17, 18, 21, 22, 23, 24, 32, 45, 62, 63, 83, 87, 90, 102, 103, 119, 127, 131, 134, 137, 142, 146, 149); see also *dominium*

brutus, *adi.* – brute (64, 65, 70, 72)

calco, *v.* – walk upon (57, 99)

calumpnia, *subst.* – accusation, claim, calumny (88, 135a)

campus, *subst.* – countryside, field (59)

candens, *part.* – hot, burning (24, 25, 57, 58, 60, 65, 87, 90, 91, 92, 97, 99, 110, 113, 127, 132, 135a)

capio, *v.* – **I.** take, seize (68, 85, 87, 115, 129); **II.** capture (84, 95, 112)

capitalis portio – capital lot, a lot corresponding to the number of partners (87, 132)

castigacio, *subst.* – punishment (21, 43)

casualiter, *adv.* – by accident (67)

casus, *subst.* – **I.** case, legal matter (1); **II.** accident (52, 108)

catetus, *subst.* – perpendicular line (131)

cautela, *subst.* – surety (23)

caucio, *subst.* – oath of surety (46, 51, 86, 87)

caucio fidei – surety of good faith (80)

caueo, *v.* – give surety (67, 85)

cedo, *v.* – lack (14)

censura, *subst.* – legal rule (18, 24, 111, 119)

citacio, *subst.* – summons (7, 34, 41, 93)

cito, *v.* – summon (57)

ciuis, *subst.* – citizen, native, villager (93, 111)

ciuitas, *subst.* – town (29)

claritas, *subst.* – distinction (of the family) (22, 63)

claua, *subst.* – club (66)

cognosco, *v.* – examine judicially (35, 80)

cognatus, *subst.* – kin, kinsman (both paternal and maternal) (10, 17, 45, 52, 75, 76); see also *agnatus*

cogo (ad), *v.* – coerce into (20); constrain to (32)

collacio, *subst.* – bringing together (4, 24)

collatis possessionibus – collected property (16)

colligo, *v.* – bind (85, 95)

colonus, *subst.* – tenant (143, 144, 145, 146, 147, 148, 149, 150)

comes, *subst.* – companion (58, 59, 60)

comitatus, *subst.* – company (58)

commodum, *subst.* – benefit (2, 15, 33, 34, 37, 62, 125)

communio, *subst.* – partnership (4, 11, 13, 23, 135b)

communia bona – common property (11, 15, 32, 87, 134)

communis, *adi.* – common (5, 9, 10, 11, 13, 17, 24, 39)

communis consortio – partnership (9)

communis substancia – common property (3)

commuto, *v.* – exchange (18, 19, 34, 96)

comparacio, *subst.* – settlement, arrangement (101)

compareo, *v.* – appear, to be found (41, 85, 89, 90, 92, 101)

comparato precio – acquired for a price (1, 4)

comparo, *v.* – buy (19, 20, 65, 96)

compenso, *v.* – balanced with each other (4, 5, 43, 69)

competens, *adi.* – sufficient, suitable (114, 118)

competo, *v.* – qualified for (80)

compono, *v.* – compose (45)

composicio, *subst.* – composition, agreement (43, 45)

compre(he)ndo, *v.* – take (107, 108, 110, 111); seize, apprehend (114); comprise (69: *ualorem omnem comprehendat*); must be understood (37: *debet comprehendi*)

concedo, *v.* – concede (66); grant (115)

conciuis, *subst.* – a man from the same village (108, 110)

condemnatio, *subst.* – sentence (7, 93, 95)

condemno, *v.* – sentenced to pay (7, 11, 27, 29, 34, 41, 45, 131)

condicio, *subst.* – term, condicion (6, 23, 24, 73, 142)

condico, *v.* – legally claim back (89, 99)

conduco, *v.* – hire (139)

coniunccio sanguinis – shared blood (21, 45)

conniuencia, *subst.* – consent (115)

consanguineus, *subst.* – kinsman, kin (45, 74, 77)

consequor, *v.* – obtain (2, 14, 78, 82, 108, 109, 131, 137)

consors, *subst.* – partner (3, 32: consortes bonorum communium); consort, *i.e.* spouse (4, 22)

constat, *impers.* – it is known, established, evident (5, 33, 88, 107, 108, 127, 145)

constitucio, *subst.* – statute, enactment (45, 58, 65, 107)

constitutus, *part.* – decided (84, 102, 107)

consulo, *v.* – take care of (87)

consumacio, *subst.* – completion (37)

consumo, *v.* – exhaust (68)

contemno, *v.* – disdain to (7, 34, 41)

contendo, *v.* – allege (40, 135)

contingo, *v.* – belong (1, 3, 4, 9, 10, 15, 87, 93, 99); take hold of (someone's hand to swear an oath) (91); happen, turn out (37, 68, 72, 92)

contradico, *v.* – oppose (27)

contrecto, *v.* – steal, take unlawfully (95, 135)

contumacia, *subst.* – obstinacy (131, 134)

conuencio, *subst.* – agreement (17)

conueniencia in iure – right in law (109, 115)

conuenio, *v.* – agree upon, agree (17, 132); come together (85, 88); be suitable to (97, 99); *pass.* be judicially summoned (45, 52, 63, 97)

conuentus, *subst.* – gathering (40, 73, 131, 137); summoned (40, 117)

conuersacio, *subst.* – society (55)

conuerto, *v.* – resort to (15, 33); turn into (32)

conuolo, *v.* – fly to (22, 37)

coram, *praep.* – before, in the presence of (10, 17, 24, 40)

coram omnibus in iure – in the presence of everyone in the assembly (61)

corona, *subst.* – rim (131)

corroboro, *v.* – strengthen, corroborate (58, 78)

crimen, *subst.* – crime (48, 57, 62, 67, 85, 87, 92, 93, 94, 99, 127, 128, 135a)

curator, *subst.* – caretaker (45)

curia, *subst.* – courtyard, court (95, 107)

custodia, *subst.* – protection, restraint, care (104, 105, 107, 113, 131)

custos, *subst.* – guard; overseer (22, 48)

cyroteca, *subst.* – gloves (115)

dampnum, *subst.* – loss, damage (17, 43, 69, 70, 71, 72, 87, 103, 105, 107, 108, 109, 110, 111, 113, 114, 115, 116, 117, 118, 125, 131)

dampnum datum – loss inflicted (68, 70, 71, 108, 109, 111, 112)

dampni occasionem prestitam – opportunity for harm that has been manifested (118)

de cetero – thereafter (10, 15, 32, 45, 46, 67, 112)

declino, *v.* – resort to (101)

defensio, *subst.* – defence, protection (10, 16, 18, 36, 37, 42, 60, 64, 65, 92, 102, 114, 117, 118, 130, 132, 133)

defensio prescripcionis – the defence of prescription (37)

defensionis sacramentum – sacred oath of defence (33)

ius defensionis – right of defence (41)

defero, *v.* – **I.** grant (an inheritance) (8, 10, 14); grant to (10, 13: defensio deferatur, 36, 41, 42); **II.** accuse (16, 36, 57, 63, 90: deferat furti reum, 127, 137); **III.** bring, take (17, 109, 111: deferat queremoniam . . . ad iuridicorum audienciam)

deficio, *v.* – be wanting in (112)

de iure – by law (106)

delictum, *subst.* – offence (21, 37, 45, 46, 49, 129)

delinquens, *subst.* – transgressor (45, 62)

denarius, *subst.* – penny (45, 56, 65, 95, 97, 106)

depositio, *subst.* – deposit (134)

depositum, *subst.* – deposit (141)

deprehendo, *v.* – catch, discover, observe (17, 23, 76, 85, 88, 97, 114)

deputo, *v.* – allot (45, 105, 113)

deterioracio, *subst.* – destruction (139)

detestacio, *subst.* – hate, the detesting something (86, 97, 99)

dico, *v.* – claim, allege (114, 140)

dies iuridicus – fixed day, the day on which assembly is hold (57, 88, 90, 91, 92, 150)

differo, *v.* – defer (34)

diffinicio, *subst.* – definition, agreement (3, 143)

diffinitus, *adi.* – defined, determined (3, 36, 37, 45)

dyocesis, *subst.* – bishopric (45, 61)

distraho, *v.* – alienated, sold, taken away, given away (5)

distribucio, *subst.* – distribution, partition (47)

diuisio, *subst.* – division (4, 6)

dominium, *subst.* – ownership (26, 37, 38, 76, 81, 88, 101, 116, 118, 121, 135b)

domus, *subst.* – home, house (48, 59, 60, 61, 85, 86, 87, 116, 131, 132, 144)

duco, *v.* – consider (24, 58)

duodeno iuramento – with oath of twelve (49, 58, 132)

e contra – on the other hand (5)

elido, *v.* – counter (19, 66)

elongo, *v.* – withdraw, take away, depart (45)

emancipo, *v.* – give freedom, free; emancipate (10, 11)

emendo, *v.* – compensate, pay (10, 21, 48, 53, 58, 59, 65, 70, 72, 102, 107, 115)

emendacio, *subst.* – compensation (37, 43, 45, 46, 48, 49, 50, 52, 65, 66, 68, 108, 115, 117)

Epyphania, *subst.* – Epiphany (January 6) (99)

eque, *adv.* – equally (21)

equalitas, *subst.* – equality (46, 51)

equitas, *subst.* – equity (14, 21, 116, 119, 122, 145)

estimacio, *subst.* – assessed value (23, 65, 69, 70, 71, 90, 97, 107, 108, 109, 112, 115, 117); assessment (72)

euinco, *v.* – recover one's property (89)

exactor regis – king's official (45, 67, 76, 95, 100, 101, 109)

exceptio, *subst.* – exception, counterclaim (19, 136)

excessus, *subst.* – offence (10, 17, 45); excess (21, 43)

excipio, *v.* – make an exception (19)

exerceo, *v.* – make use of (99)

exhibeo, *v.* – provide (1, 25, 46, 51, 66, 69, 85, 88, 93, 97, 110, 111, 131, 137)

exigencia, *subst.* – necessities, what is needed (27, 87)
exigo, *v.* – require (24, 65, 68, 114, 115, 131)
expers, *adi.* – deprived of (peace) (87, 90)
facinus, *subst.* – act, crime (55, 126)
facta fide – having sworn (126)
factum, *subst.* – deed (60, 86, 115)
facultas, *subst.* – legal power, right (15, 18, 32, 57)
feria, *subst.* – day (99); used together with ordinal numbers to name the days of the
    week after Sunday, *i.e. secunda feria* = Monday, *tertia feria* = Tuesday
fideiussor, *subst.* – guarantor (85, 89, 114)
fideiussio, *subst.* – surety (85, 86, 88)
fides, *subst.* – credence, pledge, trust (8, 22, 81)
filia naturalis – daughter born out of wedlock (129)
filius familias – son of the house (3, 11)
fundus, *subst.* – house grounds (27, 105)
fungor, *v.* – perform (6)
funiculus, *subst.* – rope (20, 26, 27, 35, 63)
fustis, *subst.* – things which deliver blows (65, 66)
genus, *subst.* – family (22, 63, 73)
gradus, *subst.* – degree (14, 22)
primus gradus – first degree (of kinship) (3, 14)
priores in gradu – those of the first degree (14)
habeo, *v.* – be able to (do something) (15); have (18, 68, 69, 73, 81, 114); *pass.*
    held to be, accounted to be (90)
hasta, *subst.* – lance (66)
hereditas, *subst.* – inheritance (2, 4, 8, 14, 20, 24); estate (1, 12)
hoc nomine – on this account (54)
homicida, *subst.* – killer (45, 48, 49, 58)
homicidium, *subst.* – homicide (10, 43, 45, 48, 49, 50, 52, 53, 57, 58, 59, 61, 65,
    66, 68, 70, 73, 74)
hora, *subst.* – ounces (7, 8, 39, 41, 69, 70, 102, 108, 110, 114, 120, 125, 130, 131)
immobilia, *subst.* – immovable goods or property (1, 4, 12, 13, 23, 24)
impono, *v.* – impute to (58, 62, 87, 92, 94, 97, 135a)
impugnatio, *subst.* – accusation (137)
incisor, *subst.* – person who cuts a tree (53)
incumbo, *v.* – be incumbent (1, 37, 45)
indago, *subst.* – game park (117)
induco, *v.* – *pass.* be forced (45, 63); induce (48)
induciae, *subst.* – grace period, respite (87, 91, 132)
infero, *v.* – cause damage (55, 65, 99, 103)
infans, *subst.* – small child (in Roman law: under the age of 7) (21, 22)
infra, *praep.* – within, less than (45, 72, 101, 120)
iniquus, *adi.* – unjust, injurious (12, 23, 63)
in iure prouinciali – before the district assembly (85, 90, 131)

iniuria, *subst.* – injurious or unlawful act, breach, offence; injury, harm (46, 61, 64, 65, 68, 85, 99, 113, 114, 125, 127, 128, 129, 134, 143)

in ius procedere – procede, go to the assembly (90, 96)

in presenciarum – at the present moment, at the time in question (108)

in priuatis – in private (matters) (127)

in(m)pubes, *subst.* – child (in Roman law: a child under the age of discretion, which is 14 for boys) (18, 21, 45)

in pupillari – in wardship, belonging to a ward (23)

instanter, *adv.* – immediately, pressingly (45, 112)

instituo, *v.* – institute (45)

insultus facere – make an assault (66)

intersum, *v.* – be present at (10, 93, 134); *impers.* make a difference (21, 67: interest)

interfectio, *subst.* – killing (69, 110)

intuitu *c. gen.* – in consideration of (15, 37: intuitu ipsius)

irrefragabiliter, *adv.* – without exception (142)

irrito, *v.* – make void (39)

ita tamen ut – provided, however, that (68, 72, 91, 116)

iudicium, *subst.* – **I.** assembly (25, 39: communi iudicio, 93, 95); **II.** judgment, trial, sentence (20, 34, 65, 80: iudicio subtrahatur, 88, 90, 114)

iudicium ferri candentis – ordeal by hot iron, trial of iron (24, 25, 58, 60, 65, 87, 90, 91, 92, 99, 110, 113, 127, 132, 135a)

iuramentalis, *subst.* – oath giver (24, 28, 48, 49, 58, 70, 72, 78, 81, 86, 87, 88, 89, 91, 92, 93, 97, 101, 116, 117, 118, 129, 131, 132, 135a, 135b, 138, 139, 148)

iuramentum, *subst.* – oath (1, 16, 71, 99)

iuramentum equitatis – levelling oath (46, 66)

iuridicus, *subst.* – man of the assembly (41, 48, 57, 62, 88, 90, 91, 92, 95, 98, 102, 106, 111, 112, 125, 126, 131, 134, 137, 149, 150)

iurisiurandi religio – oath (1, 33, 92, 110, 115)

iuro, *v.* – swear (33, 46, 69, 92)

ius, *subst.* – **I.** law (14, 43, 70, 85: in iuris exequcione); right (42: iure perpetua, 92); lawfully (87); legal position (90); complaint in law (131); **II.** assembly (10, 11, 17, 18, 45: in generali iure, 85, 86, 87, 88, 93, 106, 112); **III.** royal or episcopal right of receiving penalty (45: tribus marcis iuri regio condempnari; 65: ad episcopale ius uel regium, 67, 87, 90)

iustus, *adi.* – legitimate (41, 60)

iusticia, *subst.* – justice (13, 25, 34, 45: iusticiam offerente, 85, 86, 111, 114, 134)

iuxta, *praep.* – according to (48, 69 70, 71, 72, 98, 99, 114, 143)

iuxta quantitatem – as to the amount (116)

latro, *subst.* – robber (45, 99)

ledo, *v.* – harm (64, 70, 71, 72)

lesio, *subst.* – injury (70)

legitime, *adv.* – legally (7, 17, 37, 99)

lex, *subst.* – law (18)

liberalitas, *subst.* – liberality, generosity (115, 136)

libero, *v.* – free, be freed (8, 10, 71, 93, 110, 135a, 137, 141, 144, 150)

licentia, *subst.* – authority (106, 137); right (126)

licite, *adv.* – legally, lawfully (110, 115, 117, 132)

ligor, *v.* – bound (106)

lingua, *subst.* – language (46, 48, 57, 60, 63, 65, 87, 90, 92, 99, 110, 113, 127, 130, 142)

lingua materna – mother tongue (26, 33)

liquet, *impers.* – it is evident (44)

locum habere – be applicable (37, 45, 46, 48, 65, 70, 117)

lucrum, *subst.* – gain, profit (17, 45, 73, 92)

maleficium, *subst.* – crime (45, 76)

maligno, *v.* – do evil (45)

mancipatus, *subst.* – under the power of (78, 116)

mancipium, *subst.* – slave (49, 51, 69, 72, 73, 83, 96); in Roman law *mancipium* comprised slaves, cattle and land used for agriculture

mancipo, *v.* – carry out (22, 39)

manipulus, *subst.* – bundles of hay (105, 106)

mansio, *subst.* – home, farm, dwelling (3, 49, 76, 109, 133)

mansus, *subst.* – bool, homestead (dwelling with arable land attached) (26, 34)

manus, *subst.* – hand, power (20, 39, 41 48, 56, 66, 69, 70, 110, 115, 131)

manus duodecime iuramento – with an oath of twelve hands (66)

marc(h)a, *subst.* – marks of silver (43, 48, 65, 68, 72, 129)

marcae nummorum – marks in money or pennies (50, 51, 53, 55, 56, 65, 72, 82, 87, 97, 100, 107, 108, 109, 110, 111, 116, 126, 127, 129)

materia, *subst.* – opportunity, reason, basis (13, 23)

mercenarius, *subst.* – factor (96)

minor, *subst.* – a minor, a person under age (45, 48)

minus legitime – not legally (7)

mobilia, *subst.* – movable property (1, 4, 6, 12, 23, 24, 62, 81, 139)

moueo, *v.* – *pass.* set in motion (17, 18, 20, 34)

multa, *subst.* – a fine (43, 134)

multum refert – much depends upon (91, 108)

mutuis intricatarum contactibus manuum – the mutual contacts of their entangled hands, holding someone's hands (41)

natale ydioma – native idiom (33)

naturalis, *adi.* – natural (119, 129, 145)

nemus, *subst.* – wood (114, 115, 116)

nomen, *subst.* – name (41, 87, 92, 95, 97, 114, 116: nomine satisfaccione)

nostris partibus – in our region (43)

nouus, *adi.* – later (4, 17, 24, 45, 65: nouo iure); most recent (62: nouissime)

noxa, *subst.* – noxal liability, punishment (50, 71); in Roman law one could be freed from responsibility by giving over the slave or animal causing damage

nullo, *adv.* – in no way (112)

nullo modo (nullomodo) – in no way (18, 37); by no means (81)

nutricium, *subst.* – food allowance (22)

obicio, *v.* – counter, present a counter-claim; (4, 63, 111, 114, 116)

obligo, *v.* – bound (45, 55, 60, 66, 89, 94, 97, 101, 102, 114, 128, 136)

obtempero, *v.* – obey, give obedience to (125)

occisor, *subst.* – killer (45, 46, 48, 51, 55, 74, 110)

occurro, *v.* – counter, meet (1, 4, 43); attempted to cure (45); appear (98, 114, 125)

officium, *subst.* – duty, office (63, 133); task, activity (122)

operor, *v.* – be effected (112)

oppressor, *subst.* – rapist (129)

opprimo, *v.* – crush, rape (53, 130, 134, 143)

opus, *subst.* – action (68, 69); labour (72)

ordo, *subst.* – order (45, 69, 85, 87, 90)

orthogonaliter, *adv.* – in a right angle (131)

parentela, *subst.* – kinsmen (13)

parcialis, *adi.* – parted (47)

parrochianus, *subst.* – parrochian (30, 40, 73, 93)

pars, *subst.* – part, share (1, 8, 11, 27, 34, 43, 44, 48, 91)

pars neutra – neither side (6)

paterfamilias, *subst.* – head of the household (4, 49, 87, 96)

patrimonialis, *adi.* – patrimonial, paternal (6, 13)

pax, *subst.* – peace (87)

pena, *subst.* – penalty, punishment (31, 34, 45, 67, 107, 135a)

penalis, *adi.* – punishable (68)

pensio, *subst.* – rent (35, 143, 147, 148, 149, 150)

percipio, *v.* – take possession of (73)

perimo, *v.* – void (68, 74); kill (110); annul, annihilate (136)

pertinente, *adv.* – belonging to (15)

pertineo, *v.* – be applicable to (54)

peruenio, *v.* – come into the possession of (8, 13); reach (45); bring to (102)

pes, *subst.* – leg, foot (65, 68, 69, 85, 99, 100, 116)

peticio, *subst.* – claim (8, 19, 48, 49, 93, 97, 136)

petitor, *subst.* – claimant, plaintiff (37, 41, 88, 131)

peto, *v.* – sue for, lay claim to (136); ask for (147); *pass.* is claimed (81)

peiero, *v.* – perjure (37)

pietas, *subst.* – familial devotion (22, 24)

plenarie, *adv.* – fully, completely (49)

pollix, *subst.* – thumb (65, 131)

pontifex, *subst.* – bishop, archbishop (21, 48, 67, 79, 133)

possessio, *subst.* – possession (1, 16, 18, 33, 36, 37, 41, 63, 85, 88)

possessio libertatis – condition of freedom (81)

possessio seruitutis – condition of servitude (78, 80)

possideo, *v.* – possess (5, 15, 20, 24, 41)

possido, *v.* – take possession of (20, 37)

postliminium, *subst.* – (law of) homecoming (84); in Roman law it is the term for the right of someone who has been captured in warfare to get his belongings back when he returns home

potestas, *subst.* – power (10, 11, 15, 17, 45, 80, 95, 97, 138)

prece uel precio – by prayer or price, *i.e.* unpaid or paid (101)

precium, *subst.* – value; price (4, 65, 70, 72, 75, 89, 109, 111, 136)

predium, *subst.* – land (1, 3, 4, 5, 6, 18, 19, 26, 35, 40)

prefero, *v.* – prefer (37, 114); *pass.* take precedence over (4, 14, 21)

prefigo, *v.* – appoint (17, 32, 41, 48, 88, 89, 90, 92, 102, 131, 134, 143, 144, 147, 150)

prefinicio, *subst.* – restriction, limit (121)

preiudicium, *subst.* – prejudgment, disadvantageous precedent (33, 84)

premitto, *v.* – offer in advance (113)

prescripcio, *subst.* – prescription (16, 36, 84)

presento (se), *v.* – show oneself, to appear (7, 34, 48, 88)

presto, *v.* – pay, provide (13, 18, 23, 39, 65, 66, 71, 72, 75, 112, 115, 117, 118, 120)

presumo, *v.* – dare (to claim) (116)

presumptio, *subst.* – affront (107, 113)

preuideo, *v.* – look after, foresee (1, 67)

preuigna, *subst.* – stepdaughter (4, 11)

preuignus, *subst.* – stepson (4, 11)

priuilegiatus, *adi.* – privileged (33)

probacio, *subst.* – proof (1, 16, 98, 112, 140)

probans, *part.* – defendant (1)

probo, *v.* – confirm (5, 10, 86)

procuratio, *subst.* – legal representative (35, 45, 128)

pro indiuiso – in common, undivided (23, 32)

proiure regio – with respect what is due to the king (67)

pro libito – according to his will (5)

promissio, *subst.* – promise (39)

propono, *v.* – offer (67, 97)

propria, *subst.* – private property (26)

prosequor, *v.* – pursue, prosecute (85, 93)

presul, *subst.* – bishop (109)

protestacio, *subst.* – affirmation (17, 73, 114)

protestor, *v.* – affirm (10, 40, 73, 111, 112)

prouincia, *subst.* – district (17, 33, 90, 131)

prouisio, *subst.* – providence (22)

prouisor, *subst.* – guardian, provider (4, 18, 21, 129, 146)

purgator, *subst.* – oath giver (87)

puta – as for instance, that is (62, 63)

rabie (uentorum) – savagery (of the winds) (101); toppling trees (117)

racio (ratio), *subst.* – reason, regard (20, 22, 24, 32, 34, 116)

racione – in the case that (117)

rapina, *subst.* – rapine (45, 106, 134, 137)
reatus, *subst.* – crime (10, 45, 60, 62, 66, 106)
recedo, *v.* – withdraw (116)
recompenso, *v.* – compensate (5)
redigo, *v.* – call in (23, 32)
refundo, *v.* – to give back, restore, refund (18, 96, 136)
refugium, *subst.* – recourse (127)
religio, *subst.* – religious life, life in a monastery (15)
remitto, *v.* – release a person (from an obligation) (136)
renuntio, *v.* – refuse, reject (73, 92, 145)
repeto, *v.* – take back (99)
rerum gestarum ordo – the way the case has proceeded (70, 85, 87, 90, 112)
res, *subst.* – property, belongings, thing (101)
respondeo, *v.* – be answerable (10)
responsalis, *adi.* – responsible (25)
restitucio, *subst.* – restitution (33, 108, 114)
reus, *subst.* – defendant, person accused (11, 41, 45, 46, 57, 60, 63, 86, 90, 92, 99, 113, 114, 116, 127)
reuera, *adv.* – indeed (72)
reuoco, *v.* – call back, recover (18, 19, 41, 84, 96)
roboro, *v.* – confirm, protect (5, 19, 39, 102)
robur, *subst.* – strength (8)
sacer, *adi.* – holy (3, 46, 91)
sacramentum, *subst.* – oath (29, 33, 36, 37, 40, 41)
sacramentum iuratorie cautionis – oath of surety (46)
sapienter, *adv.* – judiciously (23)
satisfaccio, *subst.* – compensation (17, 31, 37, 39, 43, 45, 48, 75, 108, 109, 113, 114, 116, 117, 118, 120)
Scania, *subst.* – Scania (45, 150)
scotacio, *subst.* – scotation, act of conveying land (16, 24, 37, 38, 39, 42)
seculum, *subst.* – the world (15, 127)
sella, *subst.* – saddle (59)
sentencia, *subst.* – judicial pronouncement, judgment, allowance (19, 90, 93, 95, 102, 111, 131)
sepes, *subst.* – fence (31); fish trap (123)
septuagesima, *subst.* – Septuagesima Sunday, the ninth Sunday before Easter (99)
seruitus, *subst.* – servitude (75, 76, 77)
seruus, *subst.* – slave (69, 72, 97, 98)
socius, *subst.* – companion (108, 110, 131)
solem(p)nitas, *subst.* – solemnity (24, 38, 39, 42)
soluo, *v.* – release (5, 95, 136); pay (89, 90)
solucio, *subst.* – payment (8, 54, 65)
soluta, *subst.* – a woman who is not a virgin (128, 129)
specialitas, *subst.* – particularity (135b)

spondeo, *v.* – vow, promise (73)
sto, *v.* – stand (5, 37)
sturgio, *subst.* – sturgeon (100)
subduplacio, *subst.* – a doubling of compensation (65)
subeo, *v.* – submit to (21, 23, 77)
subfero, *v.* – take away (99, 116)
subicio, *v.* – submit, subject (97)
substancia, *subst.* – property (3, 24)
subtractio, *subst.* – removal (48, 102, 114, 135, 149)
subtraho, *v.* – take away (65, 80, 131, 137)
Suechia, *subst.* – Sweden (88)
sui iuris – legally responsible for oneself, autonomous (17); a person who is not
   within a power of a householder
suscito, *v.* – produce, born (5, 12, 48)
tantummodo, *adv.* – only (11, 34, 116)
teneo, *v.* – *pass.* be held liable, be obliged (19, 21, 31, 45, 48, 52, 53, 55, 57, 58,
   66, 71, 93, 112, 118, 131)
terra, *subst.* – province (82, 85, 88)
testimonium, *subst.* – testimony (1, 38, 86, 135a)
titulus, *subst.* – title (20, 37)
tollo, *v.* – abolish (12)
translacio dominii – transfer of ownership (38)
transuersalis, *adi.* – transversal, collateral (14, 131)
tueor, *v.* – protect (35, 87, 89, 103, 116, 132, 135a)
tutela, *subst.* – guardianship (21, 22, 23)
uaginatus, *adi.* sheathed (66, 89)
ubicumque, *adv.* – wherever, whenever (50, 62, 65, 79, 128, 131)
uendico, *v.* – claim (4, 13, 35, 37, 68, 86, 101, 116)
uendicio, *subst.* – sale (19, 37, 38, 39, 40)
uexatio, *subst.* – harassment, vexation (20, 137)
uia, *subst.* – road (28, 29, 31, 48, 68)
uicium, *subst.* – vice (92, 108, 121, 137)
uilla, *subst.* – village (26, 28, 32, 33, 67, 70, 85, 102, 103, 108, 110, 111, 114)
uillicacio, *subst.* – bailiff (133, 134)
uillicus, *subst.* – bailiff (109, 131, 134, 135a, 146)
uincio, *v.* – bind (85, 106)
uindico, *v.* – revenge, avenge (45, 46, 61, 126)
uirilis porcio – capital lot (3, 14, 24)
unusquisque, *pron.* – each one (47, 65, 107, 131)
uoco, *v.* – call (4, 24, 34, 41, 45, 101)
uoluntarius, *adi.* – voluntary, intentional, willfully (24, 67)
uoluntas, *subst.* – will (10, 67, 70, 77, 85, 108, 114, 116, 117)
usus, *subst.* – use, usage; practice, custom (4, 5. 26, 44, 89, 99, 100, 122, 125, 131)
utilitas, *subst.* – advantage, benefit, utility (18, 26, 35, 102, 107)

uulgari nostro – in our common language, mother tongue (37, 38, 44, 52, 65)
uulgariter, *adv.* – commonly (26, 33)
uulneracio, *subst.* – wounding (64, 68, 69)
uulnero, *v.* – wound (61, 65, 66, 67, 69, 71)
ydioma, *subst.* – language (33, 131)
ypoteca, *subst.* – pledge (42, 136)

INDEX

Names, places and titles

Absalon, archbishop of Lund 4–5, 159
Architrenius 160
Augustine 160

Bologna 4, 159–60
Book of Succession and Crime 17

Church Law of Scania 11, 16
Comestor, Petrus 160
Corpus iuris civilis 166

Danmarks gamle Landskabslove med Kirkelovene 16, 144n1
Digest/Pandects 4, 145n25, 145n27, 147n54, 147n62, 147n66, 166, 173nn6–7
Diplomatarium Danicum 7n4

Ebbesen, Sune 159
Erik's Law of Zealand 144n8

Gesta Danorum 4, 167
Glanville, Ranulph de 4, 12–13
Gratian's *Decretum* 4, 144nn12–15, 145n21, 146n48, 147n67, 148n77, 148n84

Hexaemeron 160–3, 166–7, 169, 171–2
Historia Scholastica 160
Huitfeld, Arild 16

Iuul, Stig 150

John of Hauville 160
Jørgensen, Poul Johs. 14
Justinian's *Code* 4, 145n19, 145n21, 147n59

Justinian's *Institutes* 4, 8–9, 12, 144nn6–7, 145n22, 145nn25–6, 145n29, 146n44, 146n46, 146n50, 147n51, 147nn58–60, 148n89

Knud VI, Danish king 61, 77, 81
Knud VI's Ordinance on Homicide 5, 7, 146n35, 146n38, 147n54
Kofod Ancher, Peder 14
Kolderup-Rosenvinge, J.L.A. 14

Langton, Stephen 159
Law of Jutland 13
Law of Normandy 12
Law of Scania 3–4, 6, 8–9, 12–14, 15n7, 17, 144n2, 144n14, 145n19, 145n22, 145n30, 146n37, 146n43, 146nn47–8, 147nn52–3, 147nn59–61, 147nn63–4, 147n66, 148n78, 150, 175
Liber Extra 144n15
Lombard laws of Liutprand 144n15
Longchamps, William 12
Lucan 160, 167
Lund 3–4, 6, 11

Magna Carta 159

Novellae 4

Ordinance on Compensation 7, 146n35, 146n45
Ordinance on Ordeal by Hot Iron 7, 16–17
Ovid 148n81, 160, 166–7, 169

Paris 4, 159
Practica legum et decretorum 12

Roskilde 4

Saxo Grammaticus 4, 159, 163, 167–8
Scania 3, 5–6, 12–13, 61, 155n8, 146n35,
   148n74
Schlegel, J.F.W. 14
Schlyter, C.J. 14, 16
Statius 160, 167, 169
Sunesen, Peder, bishop of Roskilde 4

*Treatise on the Laws and Customs of the
   Kingdom of England* 12–13

Valdemar II, Danish king 5, 16, 61, 71, 75,
   79, 146n35
Valdemar's Law of Zealand 16, 144n8
Viborg 13
Virgil's *Aeneid* 160, 167, 169
Vulgate 160

Zealand 4, 144n8

General

absence, sentenced in absence *see* sentence
accident/by accident 10, 73, 85, 113, 117,
   119, 146n48, 148n91
accusation 75, 77, 81, 85, 103, 107, 119,
   121, 123, 131, 133, 139; accusation of
   homicide 77;
   accusation of theft 107
acquired land *see* land
acre *see* land
act 29, 59, 65, 71, 73, 75, 77, 85, 87, 91,
   109, 123, 125, 133, 146n45, 147n69;
   injurious or unlawful act 45, 65, 85, 87,
   95, 121, 169
adultery 11, 131, 171
age see legal age
agreement 35, 127, 135, 149nn93–4,
   149n106, 172
alienation/sale/disposal 27, 33, 37, 39, 51,
   55, 57, 59, 95, 97, 101, 107, 144n15,
   145n17, 145n28
allegation *see* claim/allegation
animal 12, 59, 75, 81, 87, 89, 91, 99, 115,
   117, 119, 121, 123, 125, 127, 146n44,
   146n50, 147n51, 147n57
archbishop *see* bishop/archbishop
assembly 7, 9–12, 29, 31, 35, 37, 43,
   47, 49, 57, 59, 61, 63, 67, 69, 71, 73,
   75, 79, 91, 93, 95, 97, 99, 101, 103,
   105, 107, 109, 115, 119, 121, 129,
   131, 133, 135, 137, 139, 143, 149n99;

common assembly 29, 31, 35, 43;
   district assembly 13, 95, 97, 101, 133;
   provincial assembly 11, 97, 103
assessed value/assessment
   see value/price
attending witness at the conveyance of
   land or property see witness
authority 11, 16, 61, 91, 95, 137, 139

bailiff 119, 135, 137, 143, 146n93, 146n96
baptism 10, 25
belt-fine (lindabot) see fine
benefit 7, 25, 33, 37, 39, 47, 49, 51, 53, 55,
   61, 63, 65, 77, 79, 91, 93, 113, 129, 133,
   137, 144n6
bishop/archbishop 3–5, 11, 13, 39, 47, 57,
   67, 75, 77, 83, 85, 93, 119, 135, 146n41,
   149n93, 159, 168, 171
bishop/archbishop's due see due, king's or
   bishop/archbishop's due
bishop's official see official
bought/acquired land see land

canon law 4–6, 10–12, 146n48, 148n86,
   159–60, 172
capital/full lot see lot
casting lots see lot
child 10, 25, 27, 31, 33, 37, 39, 41, 43, 45,
   63, 91, 93, 144nn9–10, 145n18; child of
   a concubine 43;
   child under age/minor 39, 63, 67,
   144nn14–15, 145n18, 146n40;
   grandchild 25, 33, 35, 39
church 4–6, 11, 41, 47, 67, 91, 111, 131,
   166–7, 172
claim/allegation 29, 37, 39, 49, 53, 55, 69,
   83, 85, 93, 105, 109, 137, 139, 145n16,
   145n31, 149n95, 149n97
claimant see plaintiff /claimant
common assembly see assembly
common ownership see ownership
common partnership see partnership
common property see property
community 47, 67
companion 71, 77, 79, 117, 119, 133
compensation 5–6, 10, 13n4, 27, 35, 39,
   45, 55, 57, 59, 61, 63, 65, 67, 69, 71,
   73, 79, 81, 83, 85, 87, 89, 91, 93, 115,
   117, 119, 121, 123, 125, 129, 131, 133,
   135, 139, 143, 146n35, 146n45, 146n48,
   147n54, 147n71; double compensation
   17, 101, 103, 121, 147n71

consent 11, 37, 53, 67, 99, 103, 105, 117, 125, 129, 133, 137, 141
conveyance/scotation 43, 55, 57, 59, 145n30, 165, 168; conveyance of land or property/scotation 29, 35, 43, 55, 57, 59, 145n30, 165, 168
counterclaim 139, 149n95, 149n97
court 6, 10, 12–13, 131, 165, 172
crime 8–11, 13, 29, 53, 59, 61, 65, 69, 75, 79, 81, 85, 93, 95, 99, 105, 107, 109, 115, 117, 121, 131, 133, 137, 147nn53–4, 148n90, 148n92

damage 6, 10, 39, 87, 89, 91, 115, 117, 119, 121, 123, 125, 127, 133, 135, 147n50, 147n57, 148nn90–1, 149n100, 164, 171
deed 61, 75, 79, 123, 127, 131
defence 4, 25, 29, 51, 53, 55, 59, 79, 81, 101, 105, 127, 131, 133, 135, 137
degree of kinship/heir see kinship
deposit (halzfæ) 13n4, 141, 149n103
disposal see alienation/sale/disposal
distribution/partition 31, 45, 47, 49, 59, 65, 145n34
district 35, 47, 49, 101, 105, 111, 133, 148n75
district assembly see assembly
division 27, 29, 31, 33, 39, 47, 51, 59, 65, 137, 145n34, 149n93, 149n95
double compensation see compensation
due, king's or bishop/archbishop's due 11, 51, 83, 85, 97, 135, 137, 147n71
duty 11, 135, 145n32
dwelling see house

emancipation 29, 144n7, 144n10
equality, oath of equality/levelling oath (jafhnethe eth) see oath
equity 10, 33, 39, 41, 51, 125, 127, 129, 143
excommunication 67, 75
excuse see legitimate absence/excuse

family 11, 41, 43, 63, 73, 81, 91
farm see house
fence 113, 115, 117
field see land
fine 5, 47, 59, 75, 77, 97, 115, 127, 135, 137, 141, 148n90, 164, 171; belt-fine (lindabot) 13n4, 73, 146n47
fixed day, i.e. the day on which assembly is held 67, 69, 95, 101, 135, 137, 143

folk weapon (folcwapn) see weapon
Fourth Lateran Council 5, 15n7, 147n52
freeborn/free man 6, 71, 73, 81, 83, 85, 87, 89, 91, 93, 164
freedom 11, 73, 91, 93, 95, 135
full lot see lot

gain/profit 29, 35, 41, 61, 77, 91, 97, 105, 107, 133, 144n6, 144n10
gathering 53, 57, 91, 101, 103, 105, 135, 139
generosity 10, 43, 125, 139
goods, movable/immovable goods or property see property
gornithings werk 13n4, 121
grace period/respite 99, 103, 135
grandchild see child
guarantor 95, 101, 123
guardian/provider 25, 35, 37, 39, 41, 63, 67, 117, 123, 131, 133, 144n14, 145nn19–20, 145n22; guardianship 37, 39, 41, 145n20

heir 25, 27, 31, 35, 39, 45, 53, 61, 65, 67, 69, 73, 77, 85, 91, 103, 145n19, 169
heir, degree of kinship/heir see kinship
home see house
homestead (bool) see house
homicide 5–6, 8, 10–11, 29, 59, 61, 63, 69, 71, 73, 75, 77, 79, 83, 85, 87, 89, 91, 145n33, 171
homicide, accusation of homicide see accusation
homicide oath (asswerueth) see oath
house 25, 31, 43, 79, 93, 95, 97, 99, 101, 107, 115, 127, 131, 133, 135, 141, 143, 147n70, 147n72, 168, 171; dwelling 71, 141; farm 117, 165; home 67, 79, 95, 99, 103, 117, 133; homestead (bool) 13n4, 45, 165
household 25, 135, 144n7
householder 27, 29, 45, 47, 53, 55, 59, 71, 97, 107, 144n9

immovable goods or property see property
inheritance 10, 25, 27, 29, 33, 39, 43, 45, 145n19, 166
injury 59, 79, 81, 89, 91, 131, 133
iron, carry iron (scuziærn) see ordeal by hot iron/trial of iron
iron, trough-iron (truxiærn) see ordeal by hot iron/trial of iron

justice 13, 31, 63, 97, 137

killer 10, 61, 63, 65, 67, 69, 71, 75, 77, 87, 91, 119, 131, 146n35, 146n42, 146nn45–6
killing 13n4, 61, 69, 77, 87, 89, 91, 93, 119, 121, 131, 146n46, 168
king 4–6, 11, 16, 29, 31, 39, 43, 47, 49, 51, 57, 59, 61, 63, 67, 71, 75, 77, 79, 81, 83, 85, 87, 93, 97, 101, 103, 107, 113, 119, 135, 137, 146n35, 146n45, 147n71, 149n93, 160, 164–5, 171, 173n2
king's official see official
king's or bishop/archbishop's due see due
kin/kinsman 25, 29, 33, 35, 37, 39, 41, 61, 63, 65, 67, 69, 73, 75, 77, 79, 91, 93, 97, 103, 133, 146n35, 146n42
kinship 61, 63, 73; degree of kinship/heir 25, 33, 43, 63, 65, 145n19

land 10, 13n4, 25, 27, 29, 31, 35, 37, 45, 49, 51, 53, 55, 57, 59, 113, 115, 127, 129, 139, 141, 143, 145nn30–2, 149n98, 149n100, 149n105, 165; acre 51, 113, 115; bought/acquired land 25, 27, 29, 31, 37, 49, 51, 55, 57; field 10–11, 79, 113, 115, 117, 119, 123, 127; land apart (hornome) 13n4, 49; meadow 115, 117, 123; other land 25, 27, 51
landlord 10, 141, 143, 149n105
landowner 4
language, in our common language/native language/mother tongue 45, 49, 53, 57, 65, 69, 73, 77, 79, 81, 99, 101, 103, 105, 109, 111, 121, 123, 131, 133, 141
legal age 37, 144n14, 145n18
legitimate absence/excuse 6, 12, 59, 103
leveling, oath of equality/levelling oath (jafhnethe eth) see oath
lot 25, 31, 33, 39, 45, 47, 49, 144nn8–9, 166; capital/full lot 25, 45, 166; casting lots 39

mark see money
mark of silver see money
meadow see land
men of the assembly 59, 67, 69, 79, 99, 101, 103, 107, 109, 115, 121, 129, 131, 135, 137, 139, 143
men of the district 35, 47
minor see child

monastery see religious life/life in a monastery
money 29, 37, 61, 65, 71, 73, 75, 81, 83, 89, 91, 95, 99, 107, 109, 113, 115, 117, 119, 121, 123, 125, 131, 133, 139, 141, 164, 171–2; mark 6, 27, 29, 31, 35, 37, 41, 47, 49, 55, 57, 59, 61, 63, 69, 71, 73, 75, 77, 79, 81, 83, 85, 87, 89, 91, 93, 95, 97, 99, 101, 103, 105, 107, 109, 113, 115, 117, 119, 121, 123, 125, 127, 129, 131, 133, 135, 137, 139, 141, 144n5, 147n57, 148n91, 164; mark of silver 69, 83, 91, 131, 147n57; ounce 29, 49, 57, 59, 87, 89, 95, 109, 113, 115, 117, 119, 123, 125, 127, 129, 133, 135, 141, 143; penny 107, 115, 133, 135, 164, 166
mother tongue see language, in our common language/native language/mother tongue
movable goods or property see property

native language see language, in our common language/native language/mother tongue
nominated man or householder 5, 31, 35, 47, 55, 65, 85, 99, 105

oath 9–10, 13n4, 25, 27, 29, 31, 35, 37, 39, 43, 45, 47, 49, 51, 53, 55, 57, 59, 65, 69, 71, 73, 75, 77, 79, 81, 83, 85, 87, 89, 91, 93, 95, 97, 99, 101, 103, 105, 109, 113, 115, 117, 119, 121, 123, 125, 127, 129, 133, 135, 137, 139, 141, 143, 144n2, 144n5, 165, 169; homicide oath (asswerueth) 13n4, 77, 111; oath giver 9, 13n4, 69, 89, 91, 97, 99, 101, 103, 105, 109, 113, 121, 135, 137, 139; oath of equality/levelling oath (jafhnethe eth) 13n4, 65, 85; oath of surety (thryg) 13n4, 65, 71; oath of twelve 25, 27, 29, 31, 35, 37, 39, 43, 45, 47, 51, 53, 55, 57, 59, 69, 71, 73, 75, 77, 81, 85, 87, 89, 93, 95, 97, 105, 109, 113, 117, 119, 121, 123, 125, 135, 137, 139, 141, 143, 144n5
offence 6, 11, 35, 61, 71, 79, 131, 133, 147n54, 171
office 5, 81, 135
official 61, 85, 93, 107, 113, 119, 149n93; bishop's official 85, 119, 149n93; king's official 61, 85, 93, 95, 107, 113, 119, 149n93

ordeal by hot iron/trial of iron 5, 9, 11,
43, 45, 77, 79, 81, 99, 103, 105, 109,
111, 121, 123, 131, 135, 137, 165,
171–2; carry iron (scuziærn) 111, 131;
trough-iron (truxiærn) 13n4, 105, 109,
111, 135; walk upon ploughshares 77,
109, 111
other land see land
ounce see money
ownership 9, 11, 53, 55, 57, 93, 99, 113,
127, 129, 137, 143, 146n50, 149n93,
149n95; common ownership 127, 137,
143, 149n93, 149n95

partition see distribution/partition
partner 25, 33, 47, 147n71, 149n95
partnership 27, 29, 31, 41, 97, 131, 144n7,
144n9, 145n22, 147n71; common
partnership 29
pay, sentenced to pay see sentence
peace 53, 59, 63, 67, 77, 79, 99, 103, 111,
147n52, 171
penalty/punishment 39, 47, 49, 59, 61, 63,
85, 89, 91, 101, 107, 117, 123, 125, 133,
137
penny see money
perpetrator 63, 77, 79, 85, 87, 89, 146n36
pilgrimage 12, 59
plaintiff /claimant 53, 55, 59, 85, 95, 97,
99, 101, 103, 105, 109, 111, 135, 139
pledge 59, 117, 123, 139, 147n60,
149n98
ploughshares, walk upon ploughshares see
ordeal by hot iron/trial of iron
pope 4, 15n7, 67, 168
possession 3, 16, 25, 35, 37, 39, 49, 51,
53, 55, 59, 81, 95, 99, 145n25, 145n29,
147nn66–7, 149n98, 169
power 5, 29, 31, 35, 63, 107, 109, 139,
141, 144n7
by prayer or payment, i.e. unpaid or paid 113
precedent 33, 39
price see value/price
profit see gain/profit
proof 5–6, 31, 77, 109, 121, 139, 143,
145n23
property 6, 9–10, 25, 27, 29, 31, 33, 35,
37, 39, 41, 43, 45, 47, 49, 51, 53, 55, 59,
61, 73, 79, 81, 87, 95, 97, 99, 101, 107,
111, 113, 115, 123, 127, 131, 133, 135,
137, 139, 141, 144n9, 144n15, 145n22,
145n29, 145n31, 146n36, 149n99, 165,

168; common property 25, 31, 33, 47,
97, 137, 144n9; immovable goods or
property 25, 27, 31, 43, 45, 79, 95;
movable goods or property 25, 27, 29,
31, 41, 43, 45, 79, 139
protection 6, 11, 39, 41, 55, 113, 115, 117,
123
provider see guardian/provider
province 5, 7, 95, 97
provincial assembly see assembly
punishment see penalty/punishment

rape 11
rapine 61, 137, 139
religious life/life in a monastery 33
respite see grace period/respite
restitution 49, 87, 89, 107, 117, 123, 127
right of defence 25, 53
road 45, 47, 67
robber/robbery 61, 107, 111, 146n36
robbing from corpses (walruf) 13n4, 69
rope/roping 39, 45, 47, 49, 51

sale see alienation/sale/disposal
scotation see conveyance/scotation
sentence 29, 31, 45, 47, 49, 59, 61, 93, 95,
99, 101, 103, 107, 109, 121, 131, 133,
135; sentenced in absence 45; sentenced
to pay 29, 31, 47, 49, 59, 61, 135
servant 45, 71, 107, 172
servitude 91, 93, 95
silver, mark of silver see money
slave/slavery 6, 12, 13n4, 45, 71, 81, 87,
89, 91, 93, 95, 107, 109, 131, 133,
144n7, 146n44, 146n46, 147nn60–1,
148n85, 148n90
society 5, 107, 125, 175
solemnity 57, 59
statute 5, 61, 75, 77, 79, 81, 146n35
summoning/summoned person 6, 9, 11–12,
29, 57, 59, 61, 71, 73, 75, 77, 103, 109,
123, 127, 164
summons 12, 27, 29, 49, 59, 75, 105
surety, oath of surety (thryg) see oath

tenant 10, 141, 143, 149n100, 149n105,
149n107, 165
testimony 25, 47, 57, 67, 75, 97, 103, 105,
121, 137, 139, 143
theft, accusation of theft see accusation
thief/theft 8, 11–12, 61, 95, 97, 101, 103,
105, 107, 109, 111, 115, 117, 123, 125,

129, 137, 147n55, 147n69, 147nn70–1, 148n73, 166; vice of theft 105, 117, 129

undivided/held in common 25, 27, 41, 47, 127, 137

value/price 27, 37, 55, 71, 83, 87, 89, 91, 93, 101, 103, 107, 109, 117, 119, 121, 125, 127, 129, 131, 137, 139, 141, 145n28, 146n44, 146n46, 147n57, 164; assessed value/ assessment 87, 89, 91, 109, 117, 119, 125, 127

vice of theft see thief/theft

village 8, 45, 47, 49, 57, 73, 89, 95, 97, 105, 113, 115, 117, 119, 121, 123, 165

weapon 69, 79, 85, 147n53; folk weapon (folcwapn) 13n4, 79

witness 25, 29, 35, 43, 45, 47, 49, 55, 59, 67, 69, 73, 75, 77, 79, 81, 93, 95, 97, 99, 101, 105, 109, 111, 121, 125, 131, 137, 139, 143, 147n70; attending witness at the conveyance of land or property 35, 55, 57, 59

wood 6, 11, 47, 123, 125, 127, 129

wounding 81, 83, 87, 89

year and a day 83, 101, 103, 113, 129